Building America

Building America

The Life of Benjamin Henry Latrobe

JEAN H. BAKER

OXFORD
UNIVERSITY PRESS

OXFORD
UNIVERSITY PRESS

Oxford University Press is a department of the University of Oxford. It furthers
the University's objective of excellence in research, scholarship, and education
by publishing worldwide. Oxford is a registered trade mark of Oxford University
Press in the UK and certain other countries.

Published in the United States of America by Oxford University Press
198 Madison Avenue, New York, NY 10016, United States of America.

Library of Congress Cataloging-in-Publication Data
Names: Baker, Jean H., author.
Title: Building America : The Life of Benjamin Henry Latrobe / Jean H. Baker.
Description: New York : Oxford University Press, 2019. |
Includes bibliographical references and index.
Identifiers: LCCN 2019003618 (print) | LCCN 2019004888 (ebook) |
ISBN 9780190696467 (updf) | ISBN 9780190696474 (epub) |
ISBN 9780190696450 (hardcover : alk. paper)
Subjects: LCSH: Latrobe, Benjamin Henry, 1764–1820. | Architects—
United States—Biography. | Civil engineers—United States—Biography. |
United States—Social conditions—To 1865.
Classification: LCC NA737.L34 (ebook) | LCC NA737.L34 B35 2019 (print) |
DDC 720.92 [B]—dc23
LC record available at https://lccn.loc.gov/2019003618

1 3 5 7 9 8 6 4 2

Printed by Sheridan Books, Inc., United States of America

For my family
Maybe one day it will be cheering to remember these things.
—Virgil

Contents

Acknowledgments

EDITORS REMAIN THE unsung heroes of historical research and writing, and I am especially indebted to those involved with the Latrobe Papers project. Given the inattention to architectural history, Benjamin Henry Latrobe's vast, rich archive and paper trail might forever have languished in separate libraries and repositories. Instead, as a result of the superb editorial work of Edward Carter, John Van Horne, Lee Formwalt, Jeffrey Cohen, Charles Brownell, Darwin Stapleton, and their assistants, its contents are now accessible in meticulously edited volumes.

The project to publish the Latrobe papers began in the 1970s and was completed fifteen years later. Supported by the National Endowment for the Humanities, the National Historical Publications and Records Commission, the National Science Foundation, and the Andrew Mellon Foundation, the editors collected Latrobe's architectural and engineering drawings, offering informed commentary on his various projects. Additionally they published his surviving journals, more than half of his letters, and selections from his watercolors and sketches.

Many of the original sources for this collection remain in the Maryland Historical Society, which provided support services for the Latrobe Papers project. The society remains the essential repository of Latrobe material, and its collection includes three portraits of Latrobe, his watercolors, and additional family material. Many thanks to the society's dedicated personnel—Francis O'Neill of the Library, Dan Goodrich of the Imaging Department, and Micah Connor of the Archives—who so efficiently, enthusiastically, and professionally helped my research. I appreciate as well the leadership of Mark Letzer, the president and CEO of the Maryland Historical Society, who understands the mission of the society and implements its objectives.

In various ways, a number of colleagues and friends have helped: Richard Wagner instructed me on architectural matters, Tina Sheller read early chapters, Donald Ritchie provided a special tour of the US Capitol, the late Jim Dilts read and commented on the entire manuscript. Many thanks to the several anonymous reviewers whose insights and criticisms improved this book. I have benefited as well from my meetings with the Latrobe family, especially Kathy Latrobe and Charles Latrobe who allowed me to use their private collection of Latrobe materials. Frankie Earle helped with the illustrations and computer matters.

Finally, I am grateful to Susan Ferber, editor non pareil at Oxford University Press, whose comments and general oversight have significantly improved this manuscript. Susan combines criticism and encouragement in a package that has benefited many books on American history, including this one.

Building America

Introduction

AMERICA'S FIRST ARCHITECT and engineer—Benjamin Henry Latrobe (1764–1820)—intended, more than once, as he frequently wrote in his letters, to begin life anew. He often did so, first as a young man who rebelled against his Moravian heritage and his father's and older brother's expectations that he follow them into the ministry. Instead he recreated himself as an architect and engineer in London before emigrating to the United States, a nation that, like him, intended to fashion itself into a new entity—a republic among monarchies. Latrobe believed himself as exceptional as this new country where there were seemingly unlimited opportunities for both public and private building. He quickly established himself and gained a reputation as the nation's first professionally trained architect and engineer. In every sense he was a founder of the republic—not of political ideas but of the neoclassical buildings and substantial internal improvements that expressed those ideals.

Even as he reinvented himself in the United States, Latrobe's early years in England and Germany had lasting effects. His rigorous Moravian education underwrote the technical aspects of mathematics, physics, and chemistry necessary for engineers and architects. Additionally, his expansive schooling reinforced a natural curiosity that led to Latrobe's lifetime interest in everything from English novels to the place of the classics in education. Yet the suffocating environment of Moravianism had come with too high a cost for this young rebel. After defying his parents, Latrobe became a critic of organized religion. He emerged as a deist who soon discovered that his American friends, many in high places, held similar ideas.

The most influential figure in his youth was neither his father nor his mother but a German noble, Baron Karl von Schachmann, who lived in a nearby castle, Konigshain. From this association young Latrobe, a student in the Moravian school in Niesky, near present-day Dresden, Germany, created an enduring fantasy that he might live just as the baron did, as a gentleman of leisure, amid books, paintings, and music and surrounded by a garden full of natural history specimens. In a notable expression of these intentions Latrobe described himself as having an "itch [for] Botany, Chemistry, Mathematics, and general Literature."[1] But he would never have enough time for such gentlemanly pursuits during his busy years in America, and he resented his inability to enjoy the leisured life of European aristocrats.

After his migration, Latrobe's life was that of a new American finding his way in a nation that resisted both his efforts to establish architecture as a profession and his associated efforts to educate his fellow citizens in good taste. In attempting to create an American style, Latrobe turned to the past, basing his architecture on Greek temples and some European, especially English, precedents. His architecture borrowed and imitated, and yet in the process of assimilation he found an expression that was uniquely his. Besides this professional tension of making a new style from the old, his personal story is a tale of his inability in a land of opportunity to resist financial gambles. If America never quite understood him, he, on the other hand, never fathomed its economic culture.

Latrobe was not alone in his financial difficulties. His years in the United States coincided with a time of risk-taking unleashed by the Revolution. Americans had not only overthrown a political system; they had freed themselves from the constraints of British mercantilism. Latrobe lived in urban centers where talk of investment in everything from land to currency was constantly in the air. After his second marriage he became part of a mercantile family whose overseas trading had made them wealthy. Latrobe joined in their speculations and often lost money.

Thirty-two-year-old Latrobe arrived in Virginia in 1796 and within months was dining with President George Washington, whose Mount Vernon home he likened in size and distinction to no more than that of an English clerk's. But that was the point in a fledgling democracy where novel conceptions of political representation, shared power, and executive restraint had fired the American Revolution. This charming, handsome, six-foot-three newcomer moved easily among the officials and landowners of eastern Virginia. Soon he was engaged in designing and building his first public commission—Virginia's penitentiary—along with a few private homes and a church in Richmond. To his brother Christian Ignatius he acknowledged his rapid professional progress. But Latrobe also explained in a rare moment of self-deprecation that he had left England because he might never have gotten ahead in London, given its many talented architects. Perhaps not, but he had also left England because his beloved wife had died in childbirth and because his creditors had initiated bankruptcy proceedings against him.

Self-fashioning in a new nation based on the sovereignty of the people did not come easily, given Latrobe's erroneous but unshakeable belief in the family legend that he was an aristocrat descended from Count Bonneval of Limousin, France. He had further increased a sense of his distinction by excelling at the Moravian schools intended to prepare him for the ministry. He traded the ministry's anonymity for a fictitious claim to nobility.

Latrobe carried with him to America eclectic interests that ranged from natural history to music. Along with his professional commitment to building not just as an architect but as an engineer intent on improving transportation, he wrote stories in his journal, engaged in philosophical discourses, studied insects, and developed new solutions for mathematical conundrums. Ever a supporter of innovation, he used a polygraph that duplicated his letters, over 9,000 of which exist. Latrobe was the very definition of the modern polymath; he was as well the embodiment of the eighteenth-century philosophical movement called the Enlightenment that displaced older values with new ideas based on reason and evidence.

Yet even as Latrobe sought to begin anew as a widower far from his creditors, he retained convictions and personal traits that harnessed him to the past and collided with popular attitudes in the United States. Although Latrobe supported Jefferson's Democratic-Republican political party, he could never slough off—nor did he try to hide—his sense of superiority. He remained a snob in a land of idealized equality. It was one of several conflicts.

After four years in Virginia, Latrobe moved to America's political and commercial center, Philadelphia, at the time the capital of the United States. Here he again remade himself, marrying for a second time and establishing himself as a designer of impressive public buildings, most notably the Bank of Pennsylvania. In a nod to his engineering expertise he developed a city water system powered by the new invention of the time—steam engines. He sheltered this ugly machinery in a handsome, classically themed building with a dome and two massive columns in a park that became a popular visiting place for Philadelphians.

Latrobe had left Virginia because there were not enough commissions for his survival; he had high hopes for permanent residence in Philadelphia. Instead he found few private commissions and a good deal of aggravation. He was working in a field unknown to Americans who relied on carpenters and millwrights to build their homes. Architecture was an innovation in this society. Public projects were insufficiently funded, and when he did receive commissions, Latrobe disliked compromising on any features of his plans. In Philadelphia he encountered another of his conflicts, when clients interfered with his designs, refused to pay the European rates that he insisted on, and in several instances hired carpenters to complete his designs. But no matter where he lived, Latrobe persisted in his mission of establishing the professional sovereignty of architects.

There would never be enough Americans willing and able to pay for his expensive homes. In the eighteenth century, as now, architecture was an elite enterprise enjoyed by the wealthy. That distinction was one of the reasons it attracted Latrobe, though it assured his financial turmoil. He never persuaded Americans that architecture and engineering were transactions among gentlemen. Perhaps it was to be expected that he earned a reputation for extravagance. Despising the use of wood, his structures, notable for their stone and masonry, were intended to be permanent. Soon the number of what Latrobe referred to as his unbuilt castles in the sky, that is, those buildings designed but never actually built, mounted.

In 1803 Latrobe wrote his acquaintance and soon-to-be-friend President Thomas Jefferson, asking for a badly needed job. Jefferson, one of a handful of Americans who appreciated Latrobe's genius, immediately appointed him to the public position of superintending the building of the nation's Capitol and the President's House. Washington, DC, was more primitive than the cities Latrobe had known in Europe, but it offered opportunities for the types of public buildings long before completed in London and Paris. Committed to the significance of such structures as representative of American values, Latrobe, among others, stamped the often modified US Capitol with a neoclassical vision appropriate for the governing principles of the United States. The building placed the nation's legislative bodies in two separate wings, joined, in a physical representation of its commitment to popular sovereignty, by a grand rotunda Latrobe labeled the People's Hall.

Latrobe chafed under the uncertain appropriations of Congress and the lack of appreciation for his dramatic development of the interior of the Capitol building, especially his spectacular meeting room for the House of Representatives. As he had been in Pennsylvania, he was never too busy as an architect to undertake the internal improvements that he considered essential to the future of the nation, especially a canal through Washington linking the Potomac and Anacostia Rivers. He surveyed the best routes for the roads he believed necessary to connect the nation's capital to other communities. He offered as well expert commentary on the best way to improve roads with the proper composition and arrangement of stones.

Ungraciously, Congress terminated his position after nine years. Lured by a get-rich scheme he moved his family to Pittsburgh, where he built a steamboat that he expected would make him a wealthy man. But amid a catastrophic misunderstanding with Robert Fulton, who had financed his operation, his sponsor ended his financial support. Latrobe became liable for debts that ultimately drove him into bankruptcy and to debtor's prison. After two years in Pittsburgh, he returned to Washington to rebuild the Capitol that had been destroyed by the British during the War of 1812. Unable to tolerate the interference with his plans by an ignorant supervisor, he soon resigned, shortly before he was fired. But again he had stamped the nation's most important building—its temple to liberty—with his genius.

A few months later Latrobe declared bankruptcy, moved to Baltimore, and began another journey in a life spent on the move. And when his commissions in Baltimore ended, he turned to another prospect for financial security—the New Orleans Waterworks. This ambitious civic improvement was nearly finished when Benjamin Latrobe died of yellow fever, his avenue for financial independence nearly achieved, his optimism undiminished, and his faith in the future undeterred. But his family was left penniless.

Occasionally subdued by migraine headaches, he was never immobilized by his financial and professional challenges. Some students of this complex man have concluded, incorrectly in my judgment, that Latrobe was a man constantly thwarted, and therefore depressed, by challenges in a nation little disposed to the kind of enduring, expensive projects he promoted. In such an interpretation his crippling migraines have been mistaken for episodes of depression.

In my view, Latrobe absorbed the American characteristics of optimism and resiliency, which reinforced aspects of his personality. However disappointed and gloomy, he never despaired, though he frequently complained. There were always, as he wrote his son Henry, "white pebble days," a reference to the happy days his favorite poet Horace always marked with a white pebble.[2] If he could not design private homes and public buildings, then he would support himself as an engineer, building steamboats and municipal waterworks. Or, again in his capacity as an engineer, he could improve transportation in this period of muddy roads when it was often easier and faster to travel by river and ocean than by rib-cracking stage coach rides.

During his quarter century in the United States, Latrobe engaged in almost every form of nation-building, designing the US Capitol, a national university, a marine hospital, a naval station, water systems for two cities, commemorative monuments, lighthouses, libraries, courthouses, jails, an army arsenal, a theater, a Catholic cathedral and several Protestant churches, banks, and possibly the only barn in the United States with a classical portico supported by Ionic columns. He designed the major spaces for public life in early America. Given his prodigious output along with the excellence of his designs, he stamped his architectural vision on the nation. To the extent that Winston Churchill's familiar aphorism "We create buildings and then they create us" is true, Latrobe shaped American habits and beliefs.

Although many of his designs were never built, Latrobe's income, though it varied, was more than that of most American men and well above that of artisans and clerks. Despite his impressive output, his unsuccessful speculations, again so very American, led to chronic financial difficulties. Speculators are by nature optimists, and often Latrobe invested in his own projects. A man of self-described natural cheerfulness and buoyancy of mind, he bought shares in risky ventures, purchased real estate that never reached its potential, signed the notes of friends that made him liable for their debts, and invested thousands of dollars of his own money in unpaid engineering projects that, if completed, would support his family and his anticipated life of leisure. As his debts mounted, he engaged in wishful thinking that provided some equanimity. He blamed his past for his chronic financial embarrassments: how could he have learned about finance in communal Moravian schools where all necessities were provided? Ultimately Latrobe gambled on a future of leisure and lost. But throughout his life he looked to the future, retaining his innovative instincts and hopefulness in the face of many seemingly insoluble dilemmas.

Latrobe took immense pleasure in his family, and certainly the contributions of his sons to their communities, especially to Baltimore, are part of his legacy. He was absorbed by a family that became a sanctuary from the harsh professional environment he inhabited. But such delight came with a barb: his profession demanded that he travel. In his letters and journals, he often lamented his absences from his wife and children, promising that in the future they would be together.

Living in six different cities during his quarter century in the United States, Latrobe, a perceptive observer of human life, saw as much of the country as anyone in the early republic. Given his broad interests, his observations provide insight into late eighteenth- and early nineteenth-century Atlantic history and the process of international exchange that took place in architectural ideas, fine arts, and technology. Throughout, Latrobe remained a pungent critic of American society in his journal, watercolors, and letters, even as he shared and promoted the nation's basic values.

As observation points, the cities where he lived, including London, appear in this biography as individual places whose culture is important for understanding Latrobe's life. In each of these cities, he confronted different reactions to his intended revival of the glory days of ancient Greece. Despite the constant turmoil of his life, Latrobe maintained his keen sense of what historians have described as an important aspect of this generation's republican virtue—a commitment to the public life of the community. He never charged churches and educational institutions more than his expenses. He believed that the public good emerged from a coherent set of values, and in both his engineering and his architecture he installed his vision of American ideals. Like his fellow Philadelphian Benjamin Rush, he considered every man public property whose talents belonged to the nation.

This biography is neither an architectural evaluation nor an engineering study of Latrobe's work, which already exist. Today Benjamin Henry Latrobe is remembered for a few buildings, among them the US Capitol, Baltimore's Catholic Basilica and a handful of private homes that have survived our destructive impulses. Scholarly interest in his life and work has waned, in part because architecture, unlike literature and art, has never been incorporated into social history. There has been no biography of Latrobe since 1955. Among contemporary architects whose contact with the history of their profession is limited, only Latrobe's name is known; little or nothing is remembered of his work. Yet in the 1970s, Latrobe was the beneficiary of an extensive historical editing project funded by the National Endowment for the Humanities (NEH) that laboriously gathered and handsomely published not just his architectural designs and engineering projects but his watercolors, journals, and nearly 6,000 (of the 9,000) letters he wrote to over 1,200 correspondents.

Largely based on the direct contact with him afforded by his letters and journals, *Building America: The Life of Benjamin Henry Latrobe* is the story of the intersection of his life and work with the early republic of the United States. It is a tangled personal story of an innovative architect trying to create a profession, an engineer determined to translate into the United States what he had learned in Europe even as he sought an American style, a speculator so certain of his success that he denied he took risks, a friend of presidents who went to jail for his debts, and finally a loving husband and father who left his family bereft. Latrobe often quoted from the classics and was fond of Homer's *Odyssey*. Certainly his own life's journey took the form of its first verses: "Sing to me of the man/the man of twists and turns/ Driven time and again off course," but who persisted throughout his journeys in the attainment of his ideals.

I

Itching Ears

Proclaim the message; be persistent whether the time is favorable or unfavorable; convince, rebuke and encourage with the utmost patience in teaching. For the time is coming when people will not put up with sound doctrine but having itching ears, they will accumulate for themselves teachers to suit their own desires, and will turn away from listening to the truth and wander away to myths.

—2 Timothy 3:14–15

IN 1776, A year of prodigious worldwide change and turmoil, Benjamin Henry Latrobe began the first of the many journeys that would transform his life. Twelve years old at the time, he had been chosen, along with three other boys, to leave the Fulneck Moravian community in Yorkshire, England, and travel to Niesky, the more advanced Moravian Paedogogium in eastern Saxony, near the Polish border. In the company of two adults, the boys left on foot, walking first the nine miles to Leeds and then traveling by stage coach to Hull for the trip down the Humber River into the North Sea. After they landed at Hamburg, Germany, they journeyed by foot, horseback, and boat to the town of Niesky. There these special boys, considered "clever" by their teachers, were expected to immerse themselves in an intense curriculum preparing them for their final program at the prestigious Moravian seminary in nearby Barby.

Benjamin was acquainted through hearsay with both centers of learning, since his older brother Christian Ignatius had set the expected course for his younger brothers—from Fulneck, England, to Niesky, then to Barby and finally to missionary service in one of the many Moravian stations that by the 1780s stretched around the globe. Full of a convert's zeal, their father, the elder Benjamin Henry Latrobe, intended that just as he had risen through the ranks of the faithful and found an enchanted life of piety among the brethren, so his sons would thrive by serving the Moravian faith.

Until his departure, young Benjamin Henry Latrobe had lived his entire life within the boundaries of the Fulneck community.[1] He was born there on May 1, 1764, during a period in his parents' lives when they were both active, public figures in the church—his father as head supervisor, though soon to leave for a permanent post as Provincial Helper in London, his mother as a teacher in the girls' division before she joined her husband. Born in Pennsylvania into a prominent Moravian family, fifteen-year-old Anna Margaretta Antes had been sent by her father to complete her education in a Moravian school in London. She never returned to the United States after marrying Benjamin Henry Latrobe, an emerging leader of that community.

As an infant, Benjamin lived briefly with his mother in the married quarters until he was weaned. Then at three years and a month he moved to the infants-in-arms choir, where maternal surrogates called single sisters tended the youngest children.[2] Parental contact was discouraged, since the elders believed that mothers especially spoiled children whose souls and bodies were not theirs to nurture but rather belonged to Jesus. Accordingly, it was necessary to replace the natural ties of biological families with the spiritual bonds enacted by a community of God's believers.

Moravians intended that members dwell in Christ and through a consciousness of faith imparted by their community, Christ in them. Their unique expression of Protestantism employed communal living to instill the bonds of this spiritual brotherhood, at the same time that their educated leaders served as evangelical messengers spreading the Moravian version of Christianity throughout the world.

Moravians took their name from the region in central Europe where in the fifteenth century their founders sheltered a handful of early believers. Given its emphasis on conduct over doctrine and established religions as corrupt, the Moravian Church was hardly an accepted faith. Both state officials and the Catholic Church treated them as heretics, and they barely survived the Thirty Years' War that raged in Europe from 1618 to 1638. In 1720, a small surviving band of the United Brethren, as they called themselves, crossed into Saxony and settled on Count Zinzendorf's estate, where they built what remains their headquarters. They named it Herrnhut, a German word that means "under the care of the Lord." As a small Christian community with an evangelical outlook, they spread to Ireland and England. In 1749, the British Parliament dispensed its sanction, recognizing them as a Protestant Episcopal Church. In such a tolerant environment the English Moravians in London and Fulneck developed restrictive, all-encompassing institutions that promoted their version of Christianity.

Children, it was thought, best discovered the spirit of God through a love of Jesus imparted by a society of spiritual believers, not through the private aspirations of their parents and certainly not through contact with outsiders. Few parents ever monitored their offspring as closely as did the brothers and sisters of the Fulneck choirs. When one father sent his son a copy of John Milton's *Paradise Lost*, a teacher tore out pages thought unsuitable for the young brethren. An older student hoped the staff would not find him reading a banned copy of Goethe's *The Sorrows of Werther*, another of the books judged by the supervisors to be "unprofitable and hateful."[3] Accounts of the brothers' courageous missionary endeavors in North America and the Caribbean replaced such forbidden materials.

When Benjamin was five, he moved to the little boys' choir, an age- and gender- segregated group. For six years, in a crowded dormitory divided into three large rooms, he slept and ate, studied and played with fifty-five other boys under the supervision of older Moravians. School regulations prohibited "backbiting, scoffing, idle words and gossip," permitted only quiet conversation during meals, and encouraged hours of study.[4] John Comenius, whose treatise on education informed the brothers' approach to schooling, offered the wisdom that Moravians instilled: "Let boys like ants be continually occupied in doing something. . . . Inactivity is injurious to mind and body."[5] Comenius also decried any course of study that neglected the natural world, including astronomy. There was much to learn from the Heavens and Earth, he believed, an understanding that the elders at Fulneck incorporated into educational programs predicated on the importance of having a general knowledge of all that is known.

When Benjamin was ten, his younger sister Justina, who had earlier been placed in the care of a wet nurse after her mother returned to London, died.[6] A service marked her death not as an occasion for private sorrow but as a celebration of her blessed opportunity to be united with Jesus. It was followed by her interment in God's Acre, the burial ground on the north side of Fulneck where she was entombed with other infants who had succumbed to the untreatable diseases of this generation's childhood—diphtheria, scarlet fever, whooping cough, pneumonia, and dysentery. In keeping with Moravian practice, the death of a sibling was a communal, not a familial loss, and Justina faded from her older brothers' memories.

A year later, in an elaborate celebration called an agape enriched by the music of the settlement's new organ from Switzerland, Benjamin, attired in the clothes of the "great boys," prostrated himself on the floor, received the kiss of peace to signal his union with Christ, and joined older students for his final year at Fulneck. He had lived these twelve years in terraced, plain brick buildings notable for their simplicity and avoidance of either the fussy rococo design or the grand Georgian architecture of the period. The physical presence of Fulneck reflected the Moravian mission.

The interiors of the buildings were divided by doors and individual entrances to the special rooms of the choirs; all living spaces were connected to the featured place of worship. Here, in keeping with the Moravian views on hierarchy, there was no pulpit, only chairs arranged in an imposing central space called "Grace Hall." The sexes remained rigidly segregated before marriages approved by the elders took place, the fervent, sometimes erotic celebration of Jesus's bloody side wounds on the cross a substitute for sex.[7] Moravians accepted women as spiritual equals and offered positions of leadership in the female choirs, though women held no administrative authority among the male elders.

There was an expectation that children would become, according to a diary written by a member of the Fulneck congregation, "sincerely concerned

FIG. 1.1 Fulneck. This photograph shows the north side of the buildings of the Moravian community in Fulneck, England, near Leeds, where Benjamin Henry Latrobe was born and lived from 1764 to 1776. The section of Grace Hall between the bell tower and the boys' school is the place where he was born to Moravian parents who espoused the communal arrangements of their faith. Fulneck Archives, the Reverend Hilary Smith.

in [their] hearts, acquainted with our Savior, and be His with soul and body and through His grace be made conformable to His mind."[8] Worship insistently emphasized Christ's role as the sole conveyor of God's grace. Moravians achieved true faith not through creed or priestly intervention but through a pietistic inner union with Christ, a sense of dwelling in Christ as Christ dwelled in them. The intended result that had brought so much peace and grace to Benjamin's father was membership in a self-acknowledged brotherhood of the redeemed, a community of regenerated men and women united to one another by the same spirit that celebrated their individual spirituality.[9] While not all Moravians lived in these utopian religious communities, those who did enjoyed life in cloistered, exclusive theocratic havens dedicated to the mission of Christ and the spiritual development of members who saw themselves as a small, elite flock.

In these surroundings Benjamin absorbed one of the most comprehensive educations available in the Western world. While the Moravians promoted simplicity, humility, and practical learning for the pious brethren, their aristocratic leaders, many of whom were university trained, cared about the arts and music as well as the languages essential for the faith's international missions. At six, Benjamin was learning German, the critical language for Moravians whose roots lay in central Europe. By eight he was studying ancient Greek, translating Hebrew, and memorizing a Bible verse every day before breakfast. As a result of his Moravian education, throughout his life he maintained various levels of fluency in French, German, and Italian, along with a store of memorized aphorisms from the classics.

There was time for the serious study of music and art as well as the geology, botany, and horticulture recommended by Comenius. Benjamin's older brother Christian was already a talented violinist and pianist who had begun composing the hymns that were a central part of Moravian worship with their didactic verses serving as short homilies. Christian had written the texts his younger brother sang, especially the popular "How great the bliss to be a sheep of Jesus" and "See Jesus seated midst his own."

Benjamin also studied secular subjects that differed little from those of other English schoolboys in academies, though he never met any children other than Moravian boys. Even sledding with the local boys from the nearby town of Pudsey was forbidden. "I remember," Benjamin recalled in a nod to his own sense of agency and intelligence, "that getting hold of a few plain instructions at 8 years of age, I made myself a tolerable geometrician about that period; and at 12 I was almost the master of *Mathesis pura* [a reference to a standard applied, as opposed to theoretical, mathematical text of the period], having studied it from an irresistible propensity and with very little help."[10] Years later as a father he acknowledged the excellence of his own schooling in geometry and trigonometry, which placed him far beyond his son's training in mathematics at a similar age.[11]

In the afternoons Benjamin and his classmates harvested the flax necessary for the textile production that created the broadcloth, gloves, and worsted cloth sold to the local community to support Fulneck's financially troubled utopia. "Like every boy in the School," he later wrote, "I was at 10 Years old acquainted with the whole process of weaving."[12] And there were occasional tramps through the wild moors and hills around Leeds, once to the canal locks at Bingley nine miles away, and several times to the ruins of Kirkstall Abbey which Benjamin sketched with the delicate artistry that forever marked his watercolors. He excelled at drawing in art classes that included the study of buildings. Years later his son John Hazlehurst Boneval Latrobe described his father as always with a pencil in hand, a habit begun as a boy.[13] There were as well festivals and Love Feasts (Singstuden), where special food accompanied the services, for the Moravians were by no means somber Calvinists. Every year on his May 1 birthday, schoolmates awakened him with a rousing fanfare of French horns and trumpets.

Because life and worship were intertwined, religion permeated every aspect of his schooling—from the services every morning and evening and three times a day on Sunday to the preparations on Saturdays before monthly communion. Moravians considered Holy Communion the pinnacle of sacraments, with the restriction that the cup of wine and bread of salvation, symbolic of Christ's blood and body, be given only to those exhibiting proper piety. The sacrament of communion was the exquisite fruit of a proper relationship with Jesus, not a means, as in some other denominations, of finding God, but rather an end in itself. Accordingly, all partakers were first subject to "a speaking"—that is, an interrogation by a supervisor monitoring the students' spiritual state, the degree to which they had bonded with Christ, and whether they had subordinated themselves to the community.

Given these beliefs, the brothers calculated that the worst punishment to be endured was to be denied communion and prevented from attending the frequent prayer services. Insubordination was corrected by removal from the central mission, though such a prohibition might best fulfill the intention of some miscreants. Corporeal punishment, the canings familiar to most English schoolboys of this period, was seldom necessary in this enclosed environment where disobedience rarely occurred. Instead, surveillance ruled, as members were encouraged to report rule-breaking and nonconformity.[14]

Benjamin spent five years in Niesky, the small Moravian community of 600 in Saxony. Niesky was a planned settlement like Fulneck in England but was intended for the training of future ministers and the children of those who served overseas. His class schedule for his third year at Niesky reveals a rigorous program of nineteen hours of languages a week, four of mathematics, four of music, two of history, and one of drawing; in all he was in class thirty hours every week, along with an unspecified number of hours devoted to religious instruction.[15] Even for older boys the principles of the United Brethren discouraged free time. And whenever he left the premises, one of the older brethren accompanied him. Meanwhile his brother Christian Ignatius served as his piano teacher, and at Niesky these two brothers created a lifelong bond of familial affection nurtured by lengthy affectionate letters. Benjamin's attachments to his two surviving sisters, Anna Louisa and Mary Agnes, and his younger brother John Frederick, all of whom were raised in the Fulneck settlement, were never as strong.

At first, Benjamin reveled in the resources at Niesky, especially the drawing courses. While at school, he observed the construction of several additions to the Moravian campus. Most important, he became the favored pupil of Baron Karl von Schachmann, whose nearby castle contained not just an extensive library, along with a print, painting, and coin collection, but extensive grounds where the baron instructed Benjamin in horticulture and natural history. Later Latrobe credited the baron, "an admirable draughtsman," not his teachers at Niesky, with the stimulation of "my young unbroken mind . . . its feelings fresh and vigorous, with every mental organ keenly alive to sensation and enjoyment."[16]

As an adult, Latrobe acknowledged that von Schachmann's comfortable existence depended on his serfs, "inherited bondsmen" over whom the baron held "unlimited power." Still these serfs lived "on enchanted Ground." The system, as orchestrated by the baron, had banished poverty and created happiness; the faces of the serfs were alight with "joy and delight." [17] The baron's leisured existence amid books, paintings, nature, and serfs became Latrobe's fantasy for his future.

As Benjamin Latrobe matured, he began to rebel against the ways of the pious brethren, becoming a heretic with "the itching ears" of Saint Timothy's biblical warning. He was not the only apostate, but given his father's status, he was the most notable. The elders removed him from Niesky, citing inappropriate behavior that his family vaguely described as "youthful indiscretion."[18] Sensitive to his father's prominence, in an unusual arrangement the authorities sent him to Gnadenfrey, another Moravian community in Silesia (now Pilawa Gorna in Poland). There, for about a year, Benjamin investigated the workshops of the community's noted craftsmen and artisans. In what became a lifelong pattern he also found a patron, later acknowledging the benefits of his association with Heinrich August Riedel, an expert in hydraulic engineering.

Meanwhile, his father, violating the Moravian rejection of parental authority, petitioned the elders to overlook his namesake's indiscretions and admit him to Barby, the next step in the progression to the ministry. And so, in 1781, seventeen-year-old Benjamin Latrobe arrived at the intellectual headquarters of the Moravians where, along with twenty-seven other students, he was expected to prepare for his future as a leader of the United Brethren. Besides the traditional classes six days a week he studied astronomy in a local count's observatory. He applied his physics training, using the new teaching tool of a "Pneumaticam" that measured the properties of air. During his early months at Barby, he may have joined some of the older boys who had organized a secret philosophical society and were reading banned materials such as Oliver Goldsmith's worldly novels and plays, David Hume's secular moralism, and Immanuel Kant's heretical views on God. He did well in his classes; it was in matters of spirituality that Benjamin Latrobe was deficient.

During a special "speaking" with the dean of Moravian theologians, Bishop August Gottlieb Spangenberg, young Latrobe was unable to manifest the proper spirit of blessedness. His soul lay dormant; he could not, as Moravians counseled, be still and wait for God to come. He was unable to surrender his autonomy and follow the motto of Unitas Fratrum: "Our Lamb has conquered, Let us follow."[19] As Bishop Spangenberg explained in his report, "Doubt and disbelief concerning the truth of evangelical teaching is expressed by a number of students. . . . [O]nly one or at most two find pleasure in persevering in this state. This is particularly true with Benjamin Latrobe whose continued stay here at the seminary seems very questionable and would cause a great deal of damage."

By July 1783, Benjamin had raised further suspicions: "He is confused and confesses his sins, but still has no comfort and has not taken hold of the Savior."[20] His failures had reached the dangerous level of a "seducer," guilty of luring his peers into his own sin of disbelief. As he had been taught, "If any member falls into sin and gives offence to the world of his brethren, he will be excluded from our fellowship."[21] Given his itching ears of a heretic, he had to leave the community. He was no longer a Moravian brother; he could no longer follow the course set by his father and older brother Christian.

Latrobe's rebellion was against the church and his proposed future as a minister. Still, as his father sadly acknowledged in a letter to a friend, he had previously observed the distress parents have for their "unhappy" children but never entirely grasped this anguish until he faced it with his own son.[22] Meanwhile, this son, who understood with growing certainty that he did not want to be a Moravian minister or even a Moravian, declared himself an "indifferentist," thereby continuing a family heritage of religious dissent. In the sixteenth century, his French Huguenot ancestors had challenged the Catholic Church, joining the Baptists in their new homeland of Ireland. His grandfather had left that communion for the Moravians. Benjamin's rebellion was against his surrogate parent—the Moravian Church—not the parents whom he barely knew.

Near the end of his life Benjamin Latrobe acknowledged that he had found good and bad men among Lutherans, Calvinists, Catholics, and Moravians, and "violent zealots among them all." Encouraged by his wife, he occasionally worshipped in the Protestant Episcopal Church, acceptable to him only because of "its liberality of practice." But he retained his suspicion of all organized religion, which he expanded into a toleration of different denominations: "every reasonable and benevolent man must be an Indifferentist, as to believe that sincerity is of more importance in religion, than a perfect knowledge of polemics and a preference of a decided creed."[23]

He shared his deistic beliefs about God as a universal force with the founders of the American republic, but in his case his early experience with the Moravian rejection of dogma had made him suspicious of all worship, especially that dependent on ritual and creed. Decrying religions in whose name so much blood had been shed, he sought instead "a temple in my own heart unprofaned by external dictation." He irreverently declared that "the Sabbath is made for man, not the reverse."[24]

By no means intimidated by his expulsion, brash young Benjamin informed the astonished elders that he wanted to go to Vienna and study military engineering, a further challenge to a community of pacifists who declined any involvement in politics.[25] Instead, he returned to London where through his father's contacts he was employed as a comptroller's clerk in the Stamp Office before beginning his professional career. He rarely acknowledged the beneficial influence of his Moravian background, only its failings. Yet the positive legacy of these early years seems apparent in his discipline and commitment to hard intellectual work; his excellent education; his exposure to natural history, music, and art; and his understanding, from a group that cherished its own singularity, that he had a special talent, not in his case to be a gift to God, but rather intended as a service to the new republic where he eventually made his home.

Later, Benjamin Latrobe went further, concluding that his early religious association had been harmful. Certainly his contact with Moravianism became the vehicle for a lifetime of self-deception. On the one hand, Latrobe insisted that he had limited contact with the society; "independently of having been when a boy, for some years at a Moravian School, I have never had any connexion with that society."[26] On the other hand, he complained that Moravianism had made him unable to deal with the world, especially in financial matters. Dismissing his early education as "erroneous," in a letter to his son Henry in 1814, he described the denomination's failings: he had never been taught that life beyond the confines of the Moravian settlements required money and that "neither love, friendship, sentiment of any kind, not even the enthusiasm of the arts, or of religion" could bring happiness unless one had "an adequacy of some sort" to keep out of debt.

And for this misunderstanding and his chronic status as a debtor, he blamed his Moravian training:

> How could a Man, whom his short stay at a Moravian school taught to consider wealth and honor as vanity, and to trust to providence for daily food, and whose constant association with German Noblemen till his 20th year gave him the persuasion founded on an habitual mode of thinking, (a thousand times more operative on conduct than rational conviction), that to support yourself by your own industry, was disgraceful; how could such a Man deprived of an independent fortune expect to go thro' the world otherwise than I have done?[27]

In 1783, a few months after the British government signed the Treaty of Paris, surrendering its vast colonial possessions in America and recognizing the independence of the United States, Benjamin Latrobe arrived in the war-weary city of London. It was a moment of national humiliation as British subjects decried the decline of their imperial power and lamented their future prospects. But after twelve years in Fulneck and seven years in cloistered communities in Germany, nineteen-year-old Latrobe found in London an exciting laboratory, available for testing his professional and personal possibilities.

He was not alone. There was "nowhere on earth where a man may live more according to his own mind or even his whims," concluded a traveling

German priest. Biographer James Boswell declared the city a place of self-fashioning in which "we may to some degree be what we choose."[28] For a young man freeing himself from a repressive culture, London offered the opportunity to recreate himself.

America might be lost and war with France threatening, but during George III's long reign London celebrated itself as the largest, noisiest, richest, most exhilarating place in the Western world. With a population of nearly a million, the city was twice as large as its closest European rival, Paris. Given that deplorable sanitary conditions annually killed more Londoners, especially children, than were born, the steady increase in population during the eighteenth century was the result of new arrivals like Benjamin Latrobe. Londoners of the late eighteenth century gathered to hear about and discuss local and international politics in the city's coffee houses. Latrobe was among them.

As the national capital and the center of British politics, the city introduced Latrobe to secular issues disdained by Moravians. Crowds gathered in Hyde Park shouting the slogan "Wilkes and Liberty" to honor John Wilkes, the radical member from Middlesex, twice expelled from Parliament and once jailed for sedition against King George. Latrobe was living in the city when anti-Catholic mobs protesting any loosening of the civic discriminations against Catholics took to the streets shouting "Down with Popery." In March 1789 the city celebrated George III's supposed return to sanity, an occasion when Latrobe intended "to be one of the Mob and have some fun."[29]

Besides its politics, London provided unparalleled cultural and social opportunities. The city had become a center for such musicians as George Frideric Handel, Franz Josef Haydn, and Johann Christian Bach, among others, who made pilgrimages there for royal patronage and popular support. Latrobe's father knew them all. There were print shops along St. Martin's Lane selling elegant watercolors in the popular style of Richard Wilson. There were book shops with material forbidden to Moravians. It was never hard to find scatological cartoons, lampooning the sexual peccadillos of the royals. A print by Thomas Hood ridiculing a missionary society, possibly the Moravians, showed an ugly minister who resembled a pig ranting at a sour-looking audience, with a picture on the wall depicting "savages" in the tropics.[30]

William Hogarth's ribald paintings and engravings portrayed Londoners of all ranks whom the writer Daniel Defoe arranged into seven classes: "the great who live profusely, the rich who live plentifully, the middle sort who live well, the working trades who labour hard but feel no want, the country people who fare indifferently, the poor who fare hard and the miserable, that really pinch and suffer want."[31] Latrobe saw them all and recorded his observations in lively journal entries. At the time, keeping a journal was part of Europe's Enlightenment culture of self-discovery. A gifted storyteller, Latrobe recounted tales of the nasty landlord who left his pregnant wife without food or money for a week, the poetry contest about a tame bear sent from America, and the foolishness of Arthur Young's wife who turned the cattle into a clover field and then called Latrobe to extricate the animals.

As this inquisitive new resident ambled through a walking city—it took only a couple of hours to walk across the city from east to west and no more than an hour to travel from its northern to its southern perimeter—he observed the eighteenth-century bridges that bound the two banks of the Thames River together: the new Westminster Bridge completed in 1750, the widened London Bridge finished in 1760, and Blackfriars Bridge that had opened in 1769. Later Latrobe praised the application of new technology in the iron supports of bridges, along with the nearby canals and the cast-iron water pipes that Londoners were installing to replace wooden ones.

Most important for his future, Latrobe observed a physical setting that had arisen from the ashes of the Great Fire of 1666—the massive public buildings, the private palaces of conspicuous consumption, and the terraced narrow houses of a growing middle-class population. A wooden city had burned and a more permanent one of marble, stone, and brick replaced it. Immense civic structures of exquisite proportions captured the eye. In one of the most fertile architectural periods in English history, there were lessons everywhere for a young man. "It has been an additional advantage to me to have seen and studied most of the great works executed on the continent and in England up to the years 1793, and to have compared them with those executed 100–300 Years ago," he later wrote a friend.[32]

The city emerged as a visual exposition of multiple styles of architecture. Sir Christopher Wren, the astronomer turned architect, had created the city's most famous building, St. Paul's Cathedral. For Latrobe its great dome offered evidence of daring design and complex stone vaulting. The school of Sir William Chambers gathered its inspiration mainly from the Italian renaissance, especially from the sixteenth-century Andrea Palladio, whose distinctive windows became the most notable feature of the Venetian's widely copied designs. As a clerk in the Stamp Office, Latrobe spent his days in the vast, recently completed Somerset House, the greatest government project of the time, designed by Chambers. While Latrobe admired the scale of the building's arcade along the Thames River, he disliked what he considered its fussy Palladian features, especially the arched windows braced by two narrower sections.

Latrobe studied as well the vivid buildings of the famous Adam brothers from Scotland, whose work was inspired by Roman temples and whose exquisitely designed interiors gave rise to the generic term "Adam style." The most sought-after architects in the city, the brothers brought oval rooms and modified Roman orders and columns to English country homes, and their talent at large-scale design was apparent in the impressive middle-class Adelphi Terrace development.

Additionally, as part of Latrobe's visual education, there were the designs of the explosively popular neoclassical movement, best represented in the work of Sir John Soane who had published an explanatory text *Design in Architecture* and who lectured audiences on the superior qualities of Greek architecture: "The Greeks," concluded the dean of English architects, "cultivated architecture so successfully that they left to succeeding ages only the humble task of imitating their works."[33] On a more practical level, Soane insisted on the crucial point that architects who drew up plans and designed buildings must have authority over carpenters, joiners, and stonecutters. In a new age of growing specialization, architecture must no longer be considered a trade but rather must become a learned profession, rising in social status to join the law and medicine. In his 1755 *Dictionary*, Ben Johnson had used surveyor, builder, and engineer as synonyms for architect; by the end of the century he could not have done so.[34]

The meticulous drawings of Greek ruins published by James "The Athenian" Stuart and Nicholas Revett in *The Antiquities of Greece* stimulated Latrobe and others to envision the exact proportions of the ruins of a much-admired era. Some young architects, even those who had studied in Italy as increasing numbers did, took their inspiration from Greek, as opposed to Roman sources, their lodestar, according to architectural historian Talbot Hamlin, "the simplicity, geometry, and rationalism" apparent in Soane's masterwork, the Bank of England.[35]

For the first time in his life, Benjamin Latrobe lived as a member of a conventional family with his parents at the Moravian center on Fetters Lane in central London. He was still surrounded by the physical presence of the community he had rejected. There were choir houses at both ends of Fetters Lane and community houses on either side of the chapel. Given this setting, Benjamin's introduction into a nuclear family took time: "Not being used to a family when I was a boy, I always hated it. They seemed to me only as so many wasps, for one told me I was too silent, another wished I would not speak so much & all of them find some fault or other. But now that I am come home to live & am constrained to be with them I enjoy it very much."[36] Reconciliation with his parents came more easily because he had rebelled against the church, not them.

No matter how ashamed, his father never disowned this defiant son. At the time one of the leaders in the Moravian movement and a public figure in the city's intellectual, musical, and religious circles, Benjamin Henry Latrobe Sr. had used his many contacts to obtain a job for his rebellious namesake. The position in the Stamp Office paid sixty pounds a year, a little more than the standard clerical salary, and young Latrobe retained the position for nearly ten years, despite its routinized tasks of checking ale licenses, birth records, and other documents for their necessary tax stamps and collating the results. His father also introduced him to influential figures such as Sir Charles Middleton, later the First Lord of the Admiralty, a connection that led to a useful education in the Royal Naval Yards.[37] That help was accompanied by paternal versions of the detested Moravian speakings, as father made son aware of his failings especially his "insatiable thirst for every sort of knowledge, which, when younger, was my 'besetting sin,' to the neglect of more profitable pursuits."[38]

Perhaps the lack of any earlier attachment to this impertinent child and the need, in his old age, to establish some intimacy with his son explained his father's interventions. Perhaps his mother eased his entrance into a conventional family, though Latrobe hardly knew her either. During a brief period with her son in London before her husband's death and her move to Yorkshire as a widow, Anna Antes Latrobe shared stories of her pioneer ancestors in Pennsylvania—how her father Henry Antes, a prominent landowner, had organized the Moravian settlement in Bethlehem and how her brother Frederick had served the country as a colonel in the American Revolution.

Anna Latrobe also educated her son about American leaders including Thomas Jefferson; her son's classical education had held no room for contemporary politics. More practically she left him an inheritance of land in Pennsylvania. To his maternal uncle Henry, Latrobe, a young man who craved a family, expressed his interest in becoming part of the Antes clan in Pennsylvania: "I am interested in becoming acquainted with a branch of my family, the only one now remaining. . . . I hope you will believe that the affection which my mother taught me to bear to you by her frequent and affectionate mention of you remains undiminished and can only be increased by a personal acquaintance of your character." Latrobe closed by sending his "best love to my aunt and my cousins and all my relations," signing his letter "your affectionate nephew, Benjamin Henry Latrobe."[39]

He knew less about his paternal family, perhaps because his father's fervent devotion to the "body and blood of Jesus" held precedence over actual blood relationships with any ancestors. Much of what Latrobe did absorb was fictitious: throughout his life he believed himself the descendant of the storied Count de Bonneval, an eighteenth-century adventurer and French aristocrat. He also believed the entirely fictitious story that his grandfather James Latrobe had visited the United States, thus establishing two essential claims: his high status and his American roots. He created as well another myth: that his father had been so supportive of the American Revolution that he had removed all of his children from England after it began.

In fact, on his paternal side Latrobe was descended from a family who lived along the Tarn River near Montauban in the Languedoc region of southern France. The surname of its earliest patriarchs came from the anglicization of the designation given medieval troubadours—la trobe. While hardly aristocrats, as Latrobe imagined, they were prosperous millers and weavers. By the sixteenth century they were also Protestants, that is, Huguenots, in an intolerant Catholic France. Although it was illegal to leave France under the repressive regime of Louis XIV, one Latrobe—Jean Henri (1670–1760)— escaped to Holland and there joined William of Orange's international army of Dutch, French, Germans, and Swiss when it crossed the English Channel to claim the English throne for William. Jean Henri Latrobe fought at the legendary battle of the Boyne south of Dublin after William's army chased James II across the Irish Sea.

There, after recovering from his wounds, Jean Henri Latrobe remained. He made his living as a prosperous merchant in the textile trade, as did his second son James, who in keeping with the family tradition became a religious dissenter—first a Baptist and then, influenced by his son, a Moravian. For this eldest son, Benjamin Henry (1728–1786), James Latrobe chose the name Benjamin, honoring the last born of the biblical Jacob's twelve sons and the eventual progenitor of an Israelite tribe. The name Henry honored the French king who had briefly protected Protestants in the Edict of Nantes. James also made sure that his talented son received the best education possible in Dublin's private academy for boys and later in the theology department of the University of Glasgow in Scotland.[40]

In a contemplative moment, Latrobe pondered the impact of ancestors. Assessing the mutual influence of nature and nurture, he came to believe that nature—that is, "the habit of the organs of sense inherited from parents"—prevailed. He used the mechanical ability inherited from the Antes side of his family to make the point. Many of his maternal relatives had special talents, especially his mother who was "ingenious" and his sister Anna Louisa who could have been a watchmaker. He took pride in his own "immense store of knowledge chiefly mechanical and mathematical and that I have only to resort to in difficulty and am never disappointed." Even the way humans behaved—their dispositions and personalities—were hereditary, the gifts of nature, not the nurture he had come to despise as a dissenter from Moravianism.[41]

Keeping his emotional distance from his father, he once told a friend of his dissatisfaction that he had enjoyed no family life as a child and was, by Moravian practice and his father's choice of that denomination, separated from his parents.[42] In what became the important task of self-creation, he informed correspondents to direct their letters to "Mr. Benjamin *Henry* Latrobe, Stamp Office, London which will distinguish me from my father in whose house I live."[43] Throughout his life he signed his letters B. H. Latrobe, B. Henry Latrobe, and occasionally B. Henry Latrobe B., the second B. for Bonneval.

Still, Latrobe admired his father's "most winning address, his enchanting eloquence, his penetration, and intimate knowledge of the human heart, and above all his whole soul devoted to the service of mankind."[44] But only a rebellious son would then complain that despite "his astonishing talents and conspicuous virtues, and the very extensive *fashionable* connexions he had, added some celebrity to that very quiet silent set of Christians, but he was not at their head. However he was the most learned and accomplished Gentleman of their Society, and was distinguished from them, and their rather morose address . . . by his elegant and winning manners. His Children did not follow his example [as Moravians] excepting one of my brothers."[45] This last statement, while technically true, elided the point, for besides Christian Ignatius there was only one other brother, John Frederick, who became a physician. But the faith did permeate the family: one of his two surviving sisters married a Moravian minister, and nieces and nephews remained faithful Moravians.

In an age when impending death was an occasion for the gathering of relatives, Latrobe faulted his father as a family man. He recalled that only he and Christian had been at their father's deathbed in 1786. And his father had not even been home during his illness, instead spending his final months at a friend's manor house.[46] In this oblique criticism Latrobe drew attention to Moravian practices that had destroyed kinship bonds, though his father's funeral in London was a well-attended public affair, measured by the fifty-eight coaches escorting the mourners. It was the lack of family mourners that distressed Latrobe.

Throughout his life Latrobe overlooked the role his father played in his inherited friendships and even in securing his position at the Stamp Office. He advised Christian that fathers should use their influence "with persons in power in favor of your children and not like our most disinterested father, make the fortunes of others and leave your children to scramble for themselves."[47] In his letters Latrobe never commented on what his own defection from the family commitment to the Moravians must have meant to his parents.

After his father's death, he and his brother Christian shared rented rooms in Greater Titchfield Street in the heart of London. Benjamin later acknowledged these years as among the best of his life. He had received "all the pleasure, happiness, and instruction which the goodness of his [brother's] heart, and the brilliancy of his genius render inseparable from his society & conversation. The winter of 1788, during which we lived together will ever be memorable to me as almost the happiest of my life." This admirable obedient brother was what he could not be. As he punned, "So wonderful a Christian is not easy to be found."[48]

Full of witty conversation, the handsome, curly haired Benjamin Henry Latrobe was welcomed into the drawing room of the famous musicologist Dr. Charles Burney, calling on his married daughter Charlotte Burney Francis and playing the clarinet during the informal Sunday concerts held in the Burney home. Christian played the violin, at least until the elders told him to work harder on Moravian affairs and "mute his violin."[49] As the writer Frances Burney described a year after Latrobe's arrival, "One of the Moravians was here again the other evening and was really entertaining enough by the singular simplicity of his conversation."[50] Meanwhile, observing the rapid worldly transformation in the brother he called Benny, Christian worried that his brother's "connexion with the brothers [the Moravians] will dwindle into nothing. Poor Lad, I often tremble for him."[51]

More than once Benjamin exhibited the kind of behavior that had led to his expulsion from Barby. Charlotte Burney recounted how during one evening's entertainment, Latrobe had interrupted "an execrable composition.... At the end of one of the tunes Benjamin La Trobe ... though it was in the middle of the overture set up a violent clap and [shouted] encore," thereby ending the performance and embarrassing the musician who had written the piece.[52] It was an example of the eagerness of temper that his father often complained of.

This same fault was on display in a self-reported incident. In 1785 at a dinner party Latrobe, a skilled impersonator, mimicked a rough Scots dialect, not realizing that the most prominent guest, the Lord of the Admiralty Sir Charles Middleton, was a Scot, until informed by Middleton's son-in-law. "Now was I horror struck! I almost fainted. I was only 21 at the time. So horrible were my feelings that I fell back in the Sofa on which I was sitting, got up as soon as I could, staggered to the door and ran off." An example of his lifelong sensitivity, when Latrobe later met Middleton, he described himself as "almost hysterical," scarcely able to refrain from tears and thus giving "up one of my best connexions." Twenty years later Latrobe was still bothered by this "silly thing."[53]

He found time for all aspects of life in London: poetry contests with the Burneys, his intervention when a friend ran away with an abusive coachman employed by the family and later ran away with another groom, his visits to bookstores, and his trips with Christian to the village towns surrounding London to look at English country villas and once to investigate the new prison building in Clerkenwell designed by Sir John Soane. Latrobe also cultivated his acquaintance with the controversial Whig politician Charles James Fox who had broken with the Pitt government and supported the early phase of the French Revolution, as did Latrobe. Fox, it appears, recognized Latrobe on a London street after an initial meeting and took him to a coffee house. Later he sought out the young architect's advice when considering his position on a proposed parliamentary tax on bricks.[54]

During his years in the capital, Latrobe was always busy, a lifetime legacy of his Moravian background and his own temperament. His sinecure at the Stamp Office, just the kind of position that angry Americans opposed as exemplifying corrupt royal patronage, took little of his time and attention, and he filled the hours by writing personal letters and reading while in his office. Something of an autodidact, he organized a full curriculum of studies, frequently focusing on architectural texts. He studied the pattern books of the profession and traced the details of the ancient Greek orders. In a small leather notebook that has survived—one of the few existing sources from his London years—he examined the chemical composition of various synthetic building materials.[55]

At some point Latrobe managed the obligatory trip to Italy where he studied the ruins, listened to the conversation in the drawing room of Sir William Hamilton, the English consul in Naples and his mistress, Emma Hart, and like the other young men who flocked to the Hamiltons' gatherings, admired the couple's renowned collection of erotic vases.[56]

A man of Enlightenment instincts, Latrobe adopted liberal principles of toleration and reason, in part as a personal reaction to the authori-
tarian practices of the Moravians, in part because he was exposed to them
in London. He supported religious tolerance, freedom of thought, political
liberty, and the superiority of human reason over superstition. Such cosmopolitan ideas circulated around him: Thomas Paine published *The Rights of Man*
in 1791; Mary Wollstonecraft, who lived nearby, published her *Vindication of
the Rights of Woman* in 1790. The latter no doubt influenced Latrobe's observation that while he heard talk of the rights of man, discussion of the rights
of woman was nonexistent. Such interests in worldly matters continued to
worry Christian Latrobe, who feared, correctly, that his younger brother had
joined that most secular of associations, the Freemasons.[57]

During these years, Latrobe edited three manuscripts, most likely while he
was immobilized by a broken leg. Two—*Characteristic Anecdotes to Illustrate
the Character of Frederick the Great* and *Authentic Elucidation of the History
of Counts Struensee and Brandt*—were translations from German and French
material to which Latrobe added impressive introductions. The third, initiated
through an Antes uncle, was James Bruce's *Travels to Abyssinia*. Of the last, he
claimed that the first volume along with the drawings was published from his
manuscript, but because of a disagreement over his pay, for which he sought
legal counsel, Latrobe received no acknowledgment in any of the published
editions of this popular work.[58] But his books on Frederick the Great and
Count Struensee received favorable reviews.

Latrobe's political ideas, along with his sophisticated understanding
of history, were displayed in the introductions to his translations. No one-
dimensional tyrant, Latrobe's Frederick the Great was a complex figure who
mixed despotism with generosity and personal bravery. Latrobe had appar-
ently witnessed one of Frederick's tyrannical acts in Silberberg in 1781 when
the emperor ordered the arrest of a local official who had failed to complete
the nearly impossible task of constructing a moat around his castle. Despite
Frederick's failings, Latrobe admired his effectiveness, which he considered
necessary for the governance of Prussia, though intolerable in England.[59]

In a second book translated from the French, Latrobe edited the gothic
tale of the Danish Revolution in 1772 and the emergence of the Rasputin-
like figure Count Struensee as an authentic, if temporary, reformer. The tale
of the drugged, possibly insane king and his advisor Count Struensee who
assumed political power in Denmark appealed to Latrobe, and he calculated
it would sell among English readers, especially when England's own George
III was suffering from some sort of mental illness. The appeal of the historical

event to Latrobe emerged in the tension between illegal power and its use for good works, a philosophical exercise in the ancient question of the relationship between ends and means. His introduction displayed the skepticism that led him to reject the givens of the Moravian church. In an analysis worthy of a modern relativist, he argued that the outlines of factual history could be "fixed," but "the causes and sources of events [are] always difficult and not infrequently impossible." Instead historians "placed facts in some particular light and were misled by patriotism, party or principle," distortions from which he admitted his own manuscript might not be exempt. Besides, myths and legends made great stories.[60]

In 1789, six years after his arrival in London, Benjamin Latrobe joined the office of the well-known London architect, Samuel Pepys Cockerell. The position, most likely, as architectural historians Michael Fazio and Patrick Snadon have written, was "as a low-paid draftsman or assistant, perhaps even an improver, an established eighteenth century category for one who worked in an architect's office to acquire practical skills and remedy deficiencies in specific areas of knowledge."[61] Latrobe brought to Cockerell his buoyant enthusiasm, some drafting and engineering experience, and his strong background in geometry and drawing. He had already completed a set of architectural drawings for a new Moravian community in Fairfield, England, a commission no doubt orchestrated by his father. Evidently, he also spent a year in Sir John Smeaton's engineering office studying canals, although he is not mentioned in Smeaton's papers. For this generation of civil engineers, most work involved locating the best route for canals and building bridges.

Later Latrobe claimed that he joined Cockerell's office only to learn the practical aspects of his chosen profession, not to absorb what seemed most appropriate—the scientific laws of construction and their relation to design. These he already knew from his innate ideas: "the immense store of knowledge chiefly mechanical and mathematical that I must have inherited." He recalled efforts to "load my memory with arbitrary rules of measuration, and workmanship with a new set of words." He remembered being sent "to measure work of which I knew nothing against an old surveyor," with the result that after an hour the young, brash novice could beat the older man "in celerity and method."[62]

Cockerell offered the self-assured Latrobe training in one of London's most active architectural practices. Largely overlooked today, Cockerell also held a number of those essential surveyorships that provided income during lean times and established status in an overcrowded field. As well, he had numerous private and public clients, including British admirals whose

Admiralty House he designed and Warren Hastings, the beleaguered, soon-to-be-impeached governor general of India. During Latrobe's brief tenure in the office, Cockerell had, write Michael Fazio and Patrick Snadon, "four church projects on the drawing boards or under construction and several commissions for town and country houses."[63] Yet Latrobe's name does not appear on any of the office's surviving plans, though he certainly absorbed the Cockerell approach to neoclassical design, that is, buildings that featured simple elevations, flat exterior walls, and eye-catching bays.

He also imbibed Cockerell's understanding of architecture as more than a skilled vocation for amateurs. Nor was it a simple construction project overseen by carpenters who moved backward from practice to theory rather than the reverse. Cockerell had been a founding member of the recently formed London Architect's Club, the profession's first organization in England. Later, perhaps exaggerating, Latrobe described himself as "conducting Mr. Cockerell's office and making many of his designs."[64] No matter what his specific contributions to the firm, the apprentice absorbed Cockerell's eclectic approach to both interior and exterior design and his attention to architectural drawings.

In 1789, while in Cockerell's office, Latrobe began courting Lydia Sellon, the daughter of the Reverend William Sellon, a longtime priest in the Clerkenwell parish, and his wealthy wife, Harriet Littlehales Sellon. The young lovers had met through Latrobe's ever-widening circle of London acquaintances, perhaps through Sir Charles Middleton, perhaps through Christian, who knew most of London's clergy. It was an affair of the heart. The charming Lydia was three years older than Benjamin, a little "unformed," according to the catty Frances Burney, but optimistic, affectionate, and from a distinguished family, "mostly men of rank or country squires," according to Latrobe.[65]

But he, however attractive and whatever his pretensions to French nobility, was a nobody in a society measured by rank and family status. Consequently, it was not so easy to obtain the family's acceptance. Traveling to the Sellon's country home to ask the Reverend Sellon for Lydia's hand in marriage, Latrobe quickly gained his future father-in-law's assent with an affectionate squeeze of the latter's hand, but the family's acquiescence came grudgingly and in some cases not at all. Lydia's brothers and sisters had hoped for a richer, more distinguished relative. In Latrobe's account of an uncomfortable first meeting, there were "aunts, cousins, brothers, sisters, brothers-in-laws and sisters-in-laws to be consulted. . . . Mrs. Fraser the aunt looked *spiteful*, Patty seemed chagrined, and *Sophy* smiled archly at her sister. The eldest Son William gave me a distant welcome, Jack the barrister a hearty one, but Joe scowled his ill temper without reserve. . . . The tea began to be poured in silence."[66]

Reverend Sellon made Latrobe's acceptance in the family more difficult by settling a thousand pounds on his favorite daughter, angering her sisters who had received far less in their dowries. But love triumphed, and the two married in Reverend Sellon's church in Clerkenwell in February 1790. They spent two months in the country before returning to London and setting up housekeeping in central London as far away as possible from their Sellon relatives. The bridegroom took time to pose for a portrait by Carl Von Breda, a young Danish painter studying in London with John Turner. In this portrait, Latrobe, attired in elegant velvet coat and lace cuffs, stares ahead, ready to take on the world. He wears his hair in the pageboy style of London's young dandies, has an amused, cocky look on his face, and defines himself as a thinking man by the books and accoutrements on his desk.

A few months after their marriage, Lydia's father died, and as recounted by Latrobe in one of his hilarious journal entries, a fight broke out among the seven Sellon children over the will. One spoke what several others thought: "It was an odd whim of our father's to give Lydia that settlement and rob the rest of his Children." Another declared that she would starve with the pittance she had received; still another wondered who had drawn up the will. For Latrobe the controversies revealed the hypocrisy of human nature. What Latrobe believed to be his father-in-law's "most equitable" will divided a family who seemed on the surface so "proverbially affectionate."[67]

Denied the intimacy of a family of his own during his youth, Latrobe gloried in his marriage. To his dear Lydia, he wrote, "*You* smiled; *your* hand returned the pressure of mine, nor did your eyes refuse to look upon me and happiness was around us."[68] He was the most uxorious of men, forever unhappy when he was away from home, though absence was the habitual condition of his profession. Sometimes he took Lydia with him, noting when one of his clients paid special attention to her. A year after their marriage the couple had a daughter named for her mother, and in 1792 a son was born— Henry Sellon Boneval Latrobe, the Boneval supposedly honoring his father's deathbed request and extending the family's ancestral myth. In 1793, Lydia was pregnant again. Meanwhile, encouraged by both his wife's emotional support and her dowry, Benjamin Latrobe left Cockerell's firm and set up his own practice. But throughout he retained his sinecure in the Stamp Office and is listed, in official documents, as a comptrollers' clerk from 1784 to 1794.[69]

One day Benjamin Latrobe was at home in the tiny house he and Lydia rented on Grafton Street, studying his architectural books when John

FIG. 1.2 Carl Von Breda Portrait of Benjamin Henry Latrobe. This is the first of four portraits of Benjamin Latrobe. Von Breda was a young Swedish painter who studied in London with Joshua Reynolds. Latrobe posed for Von Breda around the time of his marriage in 1790. Courtesy of the Maryland Historical Society, 1956.89.1.

Sperling, the Cambridge-educated son of a prominent Sussex County family, came calling. Finding Latrobe unengaged, Sperling commissioned him to design and build a mansion near East Grinstead to be called Hammerwood Lodge.[70] With wealth from an Irish brewery, Sperling and his Irish-born wife maintained a home in London. Like others among London's wealthy residents, they intended to build a villa in the country as a retreat from the increasingly grimy metropolis. Perhaps the Sperlings had met Latrobe socially and were impressed by this self-confident young man; perhaps they admired

Cockerell's domestic architecture but found the older architect too busy to accommodate them.

In any case, after a morning's conversation with Sperling, Latrobe had his first independent commission for a large home on what Christian described "as delicious a Spot as any in the Kingdom."[71] An earlier house existed: Latrobe's task was to expand that structure into a statement of his client's status, while retaining the sense of rustic simplicity in a home designated as a lodge. In his watercolor perspective he responded to these intentions, placing his client John Sperling with his gun and dog on the new portico he designed and Mrs. Sperling gracefully seated under a tree with the couple's three children.

As the plans developed, Latrobe fashioned a daring neoclassical exterior with a terrace in front, a stone villa with pavilions on either side of the main structure graced with porticoes and enhanced by a future characteristic feature of his architecture—his elegant simple treatment of the Greek orders. Overall, Hammerwood Lodge was an unorthodox structure with separate parts that nevertheless created a unified whole. "Economy of construction, a quest for simplicity, the search for origins, and the return to nature for physical and moral improvement, all became themes associated with the revival of the Greek Doric," write Michael Fazio and Patrick Snadon in their fifty-two-page analysis of a home that established Latrobe's reputation and earned him another commission.[72]

Trayton and Anne Fuller were members of a Sussex family connected to a local iron foundry. After an inheritance, they purchased a tract of land three miles from Hammerwood Lodge and no doubt observed its construction. In 1792, they hired Latrobe, who merged the priorities of his clients with his own intentions. He designed a handsome structure that was not overwhelmed by features of its Greek heritage such as columns, fancy orders, and proportions more suitable to public buildings, but that contained functional spaces for family living as well as large rooms for entertaining. The exterior featured cut sandstone with portico columns made of white limestone and, on the interior, rooms that were not organized in the traditional axial fashion. The rigidity that sometimes marred buildings of the neoclassical style was softened by floor length windows and simple Ionic capitals.

The outstanding feature of the Fullers' Ashdown—for like Hammerwood Lodge all houses of the gentry had names—was the entrance temple that served as a portico, an entrance vestibule, and an interior room from which to observe the handsome grounds. In this arrangement Latrobe solved the challenge of integrating a classical domed temple into the façade of a traditional multistoried English house.[73] The portico was, marveled a contemporary observer, "not to be found elsewhere, excepting, perhaps, in Greece. I think, however, the thing is original, for its taste is to me original. The dome is made of Coade's artificial stone and is covered with Italian marble. . . . It seems to be of one piece but consists of more than one hundred stones, each is enriched with a sculptured panel of beautiful design."[74]

These were busy, successful years for Latrobe. He had arrived in London with little more than his father's reputation and his own ambitious brilliance. Less than a decade later he had achieved status in a profession that suited his abilities and interests and that offered a powerful, satisfying stage for his future. Along with his two commissions he had been appointed surveyor of London Police Offices and as such had designed one station and renovated several others. He had also taken on a complicated, politically entangled engineering project for a canal connecting the small town of Chelmsford with Malden on an estuary that flowed into the North Sea.

FIG. 1.3 Ashdown. This recent photograph shows the south façade of Ashdown, Latrobe's second private commission during his years in London. Located in Sussex and begun in 1792, this large stone villa displays Latrobe's innovative circular temple portico. The interior with its sequence of spaces and attention to internal scenery was unique in English country houses and was an elegant foreshadowing of a major architectural talent. Michael Freeman Photography, London, UK.

For Latrobe, buildings came to represent the permanence he had lacked earlier in life. Creating the designs for them engaged his intellectual capacities and utilized his facility in mathematics and drawing. Architecture, with its material forms, served as an antithesis to the Moravian spirit world. Of course he worked hard and would throughout his life: "I applied myself very industriously to my profession in which I succeeded with uncommon rapidity."[75] His brother agreed: "Benjamin seems to be succeeding in his Endeavors to get forward in the World," though Christian, still hopeful that "the Lord would somehow change his heart," feared his beloved Benny knew too little about the world "to plunge into it."[76]

Amid the successes there were disturbing signs of Latrobe's inability to manage his financial affairs. He had taken on too much work and paid little attention to establishing not just the amount of his fees, but a schedule as to their timing and the costs of the project. Nor did he insist on a retainer. He had even assumed some construction costs for his renovation of several police offices and had not been reimbursed by the government, something he dismissed as the naiveté of someone "young in business."[77] Serving as contractor as well as architect, as many architects still did, he had difficulty paying workers on his private projects. Given his use of elegant materials, costs often exceeded budgets, the result of his use of materials such as the expensive Coade stone in the portico of Ashdown. Both Hammerwood and Ashdown took longer to complete than he had anticipated, and he remained unpaid. A declining economy did not help. He had fewer commissions as English clients faced hard times during a recession in 1794.

Later his family explained his financial negligence as the result of his impractical enthusiasms, generous character, and inability to decline when asked to cosign a friend's debt or lend money. "He was prey to the worthless and improvident," his wife concluded.[78] Meanwhile Latrobe continually complained that his Moravian background had sheltered him from negotiating the realities of finance. To make these deficiencies worse, he had chosen architecture, a most uncertain and often cruel profession, as his life's work. In December of 1795, after several creditors petitioned, the Bankruptcy Court of England declared Benjamin Henry Latrobe bankrupt.[79]

A personal tragedy also unraveled Latrobe. His wife Lydia, pregnant with their third child, died in November 1793 along with a second son, "her pale cold boy,—my boy, for she was mine," he lamented. No doubt the cause of death was one of those many hazards that made childbirth such a dangerous affair—perhaps a hemorrhage, a traumatic event during the delivery or a postpartum bacterial infection that overwhelmed mother and child. Childbearing in this period was often lethal, and Lydia, during the forty-five months of her marriage, had been pregnant for twenty-seven of them.

A desolate Latrobe revealed his misery in a poetic remembrance titled "An Ode to Solitude." An example of his romantic temperament, its overheated rhetoric included compassionate words to the family he and Lydia had created—his now motherless "wretched babes." "O break my heart! For she is mine no more! She's gone, she's gone! Did ye not hear the knell? . . . To the dark vault they bore her lovely corpse." True to his spiritual beliefs, he hoped "the present God" could offer some comfort. And he inveighed his children—"those pledges of our spotless love"—to help his wounded heart and strengthen him "to act a father's part." Meanwhile, Christian worried as his brother lapsed into melancholy, informing their brother John Frederick: "The loss of his first wife quite deranged his affairs and almost his mind."[80]

Even the charms of London had disappeared. He had become disillusioned with the metropolis, complaining that it was "the sink and hiding place of every vice and misery," a place where now he saw "so many villains, fools, tormenting wives, Lords, pickpockets, beggarly rich men, false friends and conceived fools, who bear marks of having an affinity to one's self."[81]

Two years later, with his two young children living with relatives, a partially recovered Benjamin Latrobe fled his debtors as well as the city that had taught him so much. He left for all the private reasons that drive emigrants— in his case the personal tragedy of his wife's death, the impending bankruptcy and angry creditors who believed he had committed fraud, the competition with other architects in a deteriorating economic environment for building prospects, and his inappropriate sexual attraction to the children's nurse that might have caused a scandal. He had lost the emotional anchor of the English family that had secured him after he had abandoned his Moravian roots. Half-American through his mother, he was drawn to the United States by his inherited land in Pennsylvania. More important, he sought opportunities to participate in the shaping of a new republic.

2

This New American

I am already an American of the fourth Generation.
I am therefore a travelling Engineer only by having
travelled home.

BENJAMIN HENRY LATROBE TO THOMAS MOORE, January 20, 1811

IN NOVEMBER 1795, Benjamin Latrobe traveled to Gravesend, the morbid but accurate name for the town where the Thames River meets the North Sea. All burials from this point eastward were watery ones. There, with a sizable trunk that included his journal and writing and sketching supplies, as well as his pianoforte, he boarded the schooner *Eliza*, bound for Norfolk, Virginia, under the American flag. With his parents and wife dead, his business stagnant, his creditors threatening, and a new age of liberty dawning in the United States, he had resolved to leave "a country where everything reminded me of how happy I had been and how miserable I was."[1]

Sympathetic to the ideals, if not the practices, of the increasingly violent French Revolution, Latrobe described himself as "head and ears in love with *Man in a state of nature.*" He predicted "the dawn of the Golden age itself," more likely in the United States than in France and another reason to leave London.[2] Earlier Latrobe had sent ahead on an English packet ship his precious library of 1,500 books, along with his architectural instruments, pens, brushes, and an extra pair of eyeglasses. Only months later did he learn that all were lost after the ship was captured by a French corsair during the ongoing conflict between France and Great Britain.

Ready to leave his native land permanently, he joined twelve other passengers and sixteen members of the crew, along with assorted pigs, goats, chickens, and two horses for a voyage expected to last eight weeks. Instead the journey took fifteen increasingly miserable weeks on a ship that spent two weeks in English waters before managing to sail out of the English Channel southward toward the Azores. There the westerly trade winds, strongest in the winter, promised the *Eliza*'s progress across 3,000 miles of ocean toward America. Lacking a chronometer, the instrument to calculate longitude, the incompetent captain never knew the location of his ship. As the days dragged on, water was rationed. The flour turned wormy. The horse died of dehydration, and the baby goat was slaughtered. The few candles for reading at night, so essential to Latrobe's well-being, burned low.

When the *Eliza,* desperate for water and food, finally entered the maritime web of commercial Atlantic coast shipping off the United States, its weary passengers anticipated a calm entry into Norfolk, Virginia. Instead, a late winter gale battered the ship for a week. The *Eliza* finally landed in March 1796. Thirty-two-year-old Benjamin Latrobe joined a handful of English emigrants, more than a hundred French refugees from St. Domingue, and numerous African slaves arriving that year in Virginia's busiest port.

For all its hardship, anxiety, and boredom, Latrobe never faltered in his enthusiasm for his journey and especially the aquatic world he observed. The long voyage gave him the necessary time to distance himself from the two children he had left behind, his beloved brother Christian Ignatius, and his Moravian past. As he did intermittently throughout his life, he kept a journal and a sketchbook on this trip. Journal-keeping had been a recommendation of his father, who informed his son that "at the close of every year I extract all the generally useful facts and burn the remainder."[3] Latrobe found additional reasons for his wide-reaching observations: they served to record "facts in which my personal interests and actions were not immediately concerned." His journal also served as a form of relaxation. He kept it for his family as a remembrance of his life, rendering in Latin the expectation "Let us proceed to what, we hope, may be happy, favorable and successful to me and to my children, to whom these books are dedicated."[4]

In his account of the voyage, Latrobe recorded the behavior of whales, described dolphins as "peacocks of the sea," and dissected the seaweed in the Sargasso Sea. When repairs and uncooperative winds made it impossible to leave the English Channel, he studied the tides and provided the captain with an accurate measure of their variations. He chronicled the gales that lashed the *Eliza*, using his talent as a watercolorist to depict the ship roiling and rocking in gigantic waves. While his journal testified to an abiding zest for observations about the natural world, he congratulated fellow passenger "Brother Brewster" on his excellent library and read, not for the first time, Thomas Cooper's recently published *Some Information Respecting America* and the familiar works of Edward Gibbon and David Hume.

As intended, Latrobe's journal included little of his private emotions. He disdained the recording of his own feelings, which he reserved for his letters. But he had plenty to say about his fellow voyagers on the *Eliza*: "We are like actors of dramatic scenes who are so engaged with their own parts that they hardly ever study the performance of others." He planned to do otherwise.[5] In the adages popular in this generation, most notably generated in France by Montaigne and in the United States by Benjamin Franklin, he offered authoritative, sometimes satiric pronouncements about human behavior: "Nicknames are durable things"; "Ignorance and obstinacy go together"; "Human felicity is a precarious treasure"; "Those who have a redundance of curiosity have a great deficiency of prudence"; "When novelty ceases to keep [good humor] up, habit may throw a veil over that which now offends." Latrobe criticized his religious heritage in longer comments: "There is an order of men who if they can insure eternal life by the doctrines they are educated to teach might be permitted to render the present less pleasant to their disciples than it would be were they to remain ignorant and be damned."[6]

FIG. 2.1 "Dover as seen from the *Eliza*." Not much of Dover is seen from this watercolor by Benjamin Latrobe, despite the title he gave it. Instead, the drama of his fifteen-week voyage to the United States in 1795–96 aboard the schooner *Eliza* is apparent in the roiling of the vessel in the waters of the English Channel. Never without some drawing material, Latrobe first sketched the image and then completed a finished watercolor in his sketchbooks. Courtesy of the Maryland Historical Society, 1960.108.1.1.3.

Periodically Latrobe engaged in philosophical commentary that revealed his satiric tendencies and his occasional melancholy. A lengthy surveillance of the predatory relationship of spiders to flies elicited a discussion of the meaning of life: was it to be happy? If so, Latrobe wondered, "Why then is half our life at least spent in misery and a great part of the remainder in sleep and apathy? Is there a smile but what is brought with a tear? Is there a glory but what cost the wretchedness of thousands? A feast but what is enriched by the spoils of Death?"[7]

Finally on American soil, Latrobe spent three and a half years in Virginia, traveling throughout the state. After only a few months in Norfolk he moved to Richmond, the capital. There, a beneficiary of America's fluid society as well as his own charm, he became friends with Bushrod Washington, the president's nephew. A visit to the president was proposed, and so, only four months after his arrival in Norfolk, Latrobe enjoyed lunch, dinner, and an overnight stay at Mount Vernon, home of the president of the United States. George Washington was in the final years of his presidency and had left Philadelphia to spend the summer of 1796 on his beloved estate on the Potomac River. The two men discussed the merits of iron plows. Latrobe, with an appreciation of the importance of patronage, later sent Washington a new version of the Rotheram plow, promised to repair the president's broken one, and hoped to be of assistance "to your agricultural views."

Privately Latrobe judged Mount Vernon's architecture as "of no striking appearance . . . good and neat but by no means above what would be expected in a plain English Country Gentleman's house of 500–600 pounds a year."[8] And he was chagrined that dinner at the president's home was a silent affair without the lively conversational exchanges in which he excelled. Still, the fact that within months an unknown émigré, even one introduced by Washington's nephew, could dine with a national hero suggested an open society with promising opportunities for professional advancement and personal associations with the leading men of the republic.

Certainly Latrobe's Freemasonry credentials helped connect him to Washington, Monroe, and other leaders in the new republic. There were three Freemasonry lodges in Norfolk, and the group had established several in Richmond, where Latrobe was listed as a member, most likely after undergoing a process of reconfirmation. Earlier he had joined the brotherhood in London where it originated. His brother, now a rising star in the Moravian ministry, had expressed dismay at his attraction to a fraternity whose secular ideals threatened the established church. But in the United States, membership served as a letter of introduction for a young stranger to those Latrobe described as "the most respectable Men here."[9] Freemasonry also testified to the political views of this new American, who was attracted to the association's idealized vision of a country committed to virtue, education, and support of the arts. Socially, Latrobe's membership in the Freemasons, a group recognized as a collection of elite, genteel Americans, was a useful credential that set him above the common man.[10]

The connection helped business as well. A year after his arrival in Virginia, Latrobe was commissioned to design a grand lodge in Richmond, which was never built and for which he was never paid. In 1807, a Philadelphia Lodge of Freemasons hired Latrobe to design a "Lodge or Free Masons Hall with accommodation for a dancing assembly." For whatever reason, perhaps its estimated cost of $4,000, Latrobe's plan was not chosen, and typical of many American clients, the Freemasons refused to pay Latrobe for his plans after they chose another architect. Complaining that he had "employed my best talents," Latrobe wrote to the Philadelphia brother who had engaged him: "All I want is that reward to which I am entitled and which if the fraternity refuse to a brother Mason, will assuredly be awarded to me by the Federal Court to whom I have requested my Attorney to address himself in the next instance." But he neither collected the $150 nor went to court.[11]

Latrobe learned about Virginia society in Norfolk before moving to Richmond. Norfolk, the center of the tobacco trade with its deep, safe harbor on the confluence of the Elizabeth River and the Chesapeake Bay, had been largely destroyed during the American Revolution. Few communities had suffered as much. More than a decade after the war, Latrobe found it desolate and full of poverty, the ruins of old houses and streets *"irregular, unpaved, dusty or dirty* according to the weather."[12]

Immediately accepted by the local gentry and his fellow Freemasons, this attractive newcomer to a community of nearly 4,000, more than a third of whom were enslaved, supported himself by tuning pianos, consulting on the almost endless engineering projects in the tidewater region of Virginia, and, on one occasion, designing a staircase. He received his first American architectural commission soon after his arrival as the result of a "trifling wager" with the merchant Captain William Pennock. Every man in Virginia, Latrobe observed, attached some military rank to his name. Some were not just members of the local militia but had actually fought in the Revolution.

Pennock wagered that Latrobe could not design a house with a narrow forty-one-foot front, the front door in the center, three rooms, and a principal staircase and backstairs on the ground floor. It was Latrobe's introduction to the local gambling culture of betting on everything from horse races and billiards to the size of the annual tobacco crop.[13] It was also a prelude to his perpetual difficulties with American building practices.

Latrobe produced what became a hallmark of his domestic architecture: a simple symmetrical exterior (similar to his former home on Grafton Street in London) that accommodated an asymmetrical distribution of interior spaces. In the presentation drawing a spectacular staircase turned back toward the street and then swept up to the second floor. Latrobe won the wager, but having no idea that Pennock would actually execute the plans, only later learned that, under the direction of a carpenter, his design had been bastardized.

Local gossip had it that a Frenchman (Latrobe's surname lent itself to this frequent mistake) had made "the most preposterous design." Workmen were at a standstill and, when Latrobe returned to supervise, "the mischief had already been done." His plans had been dismissed as too plain for a wealthy merchant in post-revolutionary Norfolk. Even Latrobe's cornices were deemed boring, not "tasty and fine" enough. A plasterer had been hired to make the decoration fancier; a carpenter had executed the interior. Pennock's house was no longer Latrobe's creation. No one recognized a point that Latrobe would insist upon in his lifelong mission to educate Americans in good taste: the importance of hiring the designer of the building to supervise its execution.[14]

During his years in Virginia Latrobe traveled extensively—from Williamsburg to the Dismal Swamp, where, hired by the Dismal Swamp Company, he surveyed some of the 40,000 square acres of its bogs, marshland, and timber. Ever curious, he admired Lake Drummond in the swamp's interior as "a magnificent sheet of Water . . . as smooth as glass."[15] He walked and rode horseback from Fredericksburg to several farms in Cumberland County along the Appomattox River, including one appropriately named Hors Du Monde—Out of the World—which, in the view of this former resident of the most sophisticated, crowded city in the Western world, was the isolated condition of much of Virginia. Colonel Skipwith's house astonished Latrobe: like many similar estates, it was without "communication by letter or visit, but by riding half a dozen miles *into* the world."[16] In his capacity as an engineer, Latrobe offered solutions everywhere for clearing rocks and timber from Virginia's rivers and digging canals around impassable falls. From the beginning of his life in the United States, he intended to use his training in the engineering of English waterways to improve transportation in a country whose vast space made communication an existential requirement.

Latrobe preserved his view of America in his sketchbooks, noting that like many of its customs and names, the landscape near Richmond along the

FIG. 2.2 "View in Perspective of Mr. Pennock's Hall and Staircase." Latrobe designed a house in Norfolk, Virginia, for the wealthy merchant William Pennock. Latrobe proposed this elegant stair hall in his presentation drawing, though he had nothing to do with the actual construction of the house. Note the fancy classical dress of the humans and the recessed panel doors and window jambs. Latrobe's presentation drawings brought a new element of architectural planning to the United States. Library of Congress, LC-USZC4-24.

James River resembled that of the Thames River near Richmond, England. Virginia's colonial governor William Byrd had noticed the same thing, hence the name for what had grown from a tiny seventeenth-century settlement into a small city of 4,300 by 1800. Of course, there were differences: in the United States the setting was wilder and lacked the finish and neatness

Latrobe admired and chose for his buildings. In this new world nature was raw, mostly neither adorned nor sullied by any man-made structures. Latrobe observed the region's snakes, fish, and insects. Like all Virginians he suffered from mosquito bites, and in 1797 he sketched a humorous view of Colonel Blackburn's solution—"Colonel Blackburn's Specific against Muskitoe bites." The colonel had swathed himself in an impenetrable five yards of broadcloth, secured by twine at his knees and feet.[17]

In another memorable watercolor he sketched the alewife, an edible fish common in the rivers of Virginia. As always, Latrobe probed beyond simple description to analyze the extraordinary, in this case a "disgustingly corpulent" parasitic louse found in the mouth of alewives. In a paper later delivered to the American Philosophical Society he provided the first technical description of the alewife, naming it *Alosa Tyrannus*.[18] On another occasion, after catching a three-and-a-half-foot-long garfish in the York River, he sketched "this singular fish" with a unique snout similar to that of a dog's.[19]

Latrobe observed the people as well, sketching Virginians including George Washington. Unlike his precisely rendered landscapes, his sketches of

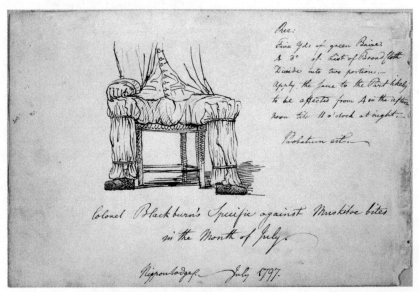

FIG. 2.3 "Colonel Blackburn's Specific against Muskitoe . . ." A student of nature, Latrobe sketched American insects and animals along with landscapes. During a visit to Colonel Thomas Blackburn, Latrobe drew the colonel's solution to mosquitoes, an insect unknown in England. He included a joking description of the material necessary to fend off the insects that would play a critical role in his life. Courtesy of the Maryland Historical Society, 1960.108.2.19.

humans, perhaps corroborating his skepticism about the goodness of human nature, lacked virtuosity. In fact, his humans all looked much the same—whether judges or tavern owners, plantation owners or the enslaved. Rather it was in scenes from nature that Latrobe excelled: "I believe I should have given the precedence to the representation of the Beauty of Nature and not to that of the actions of man."[20]

In his "Essay on Landscape Explained in Tinted Drawings" written in 1797–98 as an instruction manual for a friend, he declared himself "deficient" in talent but offered the observations of a skilled amateur on how to make watercolor drawings. His essay of over 12,000 words and thirty illustrations was intended for Susanna Spotswood of Orange County, Virginia. It contained a central theme of Latrobe's life: too much dependence on past theories and too little self-confidence stifled originality. "You must have patience with yourself," he wrote in words for her but warnings for himself. Yet "the Common disease of men of superior abilities is intolerance." For Susanna he advised: "Your own taste, your quick perception of effect and accurate observation of nature will guide your pencil." In recognition of the picturesque style in his chosen field of architecture, he emphasized that artists must attend to "the simplicity of nature" and forget "the folly of grandfathers who laid out gardens by the rules of heraldry."[21]

Latrobe told Spotswood that she should study nature directly and first sketch out the major themes, whether of trees or of a river. She should practice bold strokes that convey the essence of the subject; she must learn how to express the tree without detailing every leaf. After a first sketch, she must build up through layers of wash a picture rich in color, as his examples illustrated. With a little instruction, he assured his young friend, anyone could enjoy the medium. For him, landscape drawing was a diversion: "During a life of much vexation and disappointment I have derived such solid relief from it."

His final advice to this young Virginia woman spoke to the resolution of his own dilemmas and his choice of the building crafts of architecture and engineering:

> The exceeding variety of talents among men, has often excited observation. Every individual, who has any capacity at all, seems to come into the world with a predisposition to some peculiar mode of employment, and furnished with a talent peculiarly adapted to excellence in one appropriate species of activity. The ambition of men to conquer difficulties, indeed, makes many neglect that path, by which they would with little trouble have arrived at eminence and chuse another,

in which they have to fight their way through thorns and briars, without ever arriving at the end of their labor. [22]

Following the local passion for landowning and his own appreciation of nature, Latrobe spent some of his "moderate capital" on the purchase from Bushrod Washington of an eighty-acre island in the James River.[23] While it is not clear how much money Latrobe brought with him from England, he came with some resources besides the land left to him by his mother, which he later calculated as worth $15,000. He had protected his money by fending off his British creditors and migrating to the United States. Once in America, his purchase of an island, as well as a lot in Richmond, demonstrated his understanding that the ownership of land conveyed wealth and prestige in Virginia. But, having spent his financial resources, he had already begun borrowing money from friends and acquaintances.

Despite his confident assertion to his brother a year after his arrival in America that he "was in much business here," Latrobe experienced intermittent periods of melancholy that he attributed to his "morbid sensitivity."[24] He was not immediately at home among Virginians, despite their hospitality. Nor was he ever constitutionally or economically fortified to endure the professional battles required of an architect in a nation that recognized neither his profession nor, at times, his talents. While Latrobe recognized that "in our country indeed the profession of an Architect is in a great measure new," he was forever at odds with the carpenters and master builders who controlled building in the United States.[25] Latrobe saw architecture as a gentleman's craft, requiring training. To his mind, it must become an established, learned vocation like medicine, law, and religion, but such thinking contradicted the views of most Americans who could more cheaply hire a carpenter to supervise the building of their houses.

He was ill-equipped to deal with the periods of inactivity between commissions and, given his Moravian childhood when food, housing, and education were provided, he knew nothing about handling his financial affairs. Nor did he understand the building economy of America. It soon became clear that he could not apply his architectural and engineering genius to the economic realities of establishing a stable source of income.

Latrobe never acknowledged that leaving England required the wrenching loss of contact with his children, though he did lament the separation from Christian Ignatius whose birthday he marked every year with a letter. Only in his correspondence with his brother and with Giambattista Scandella, an Italian doctor he met in Richmond, did he reveal the pain of an émigré. To

Scandella he described his lifetime fantasy that he would shut "myself up in my island to devote my hours to litterature, agriculture, friendship and the education of my children. . . . I am here truly unhappy."[26] His recent rejection by a young woman, at a time in his life when a wife was a necessity if he was ever to bring his children to America, deepened his sadness: "Ingulph me, Earth! crush me, ye Skies,/ My quiv'ring soul is on the Rack/On John, she's turn'd her beauteous eyes/ On me -------her back!"[27]

He found no replacement for his beloved brother. Bushrod Washington, "my only friend," who could "feel" with him, was a lawyer, while the polymath Latrobe had "the itch of Botany, of Chemistry, of Mathematics, of general Literature strong upon me yet."[28] Who could talk to him of these things, except Scandella and a recent French visitor to Richmond, Count Constantine Volney, both of whom soon abandoned Richmond for Philadelphia? Who could discuss Hadley's Quadrant and the new way in which through his geometric calculations he believed distances could be measured? Meanwhile he was bored by the perpetual partisan discussions of what he considered trivia that raged between Jefferson's Democratic Republicans and Adams's Federalists. In America he found everyone a politician, their talk "cramped [and] local."[29]

Besides politics, much of the discussion in Virginia taverns and plantation homes involved foreign affairs, especially the new republic's proper alliances. For this generation of Americans, foreign affairs engulfed partisan issues. Norfolk's citizens, many in debt to British merchants, remembered the destruction of their city and supported the French in the latter's perpetual maritime wars against the English. The city also served as a haven for French refugees from St. Domingue. Some enthusiasts had formed a Democratic Society with their neighbors across the river in Portsmouth, despite President Washington's stern call for partisan neutrality.

In Richmond, where merchants depended on British markets for the export of tobacco and flour, Latrobe found opinion more divided, with Federalists supporting the controversial Jay's Treaty with its requirements that the English abandon their western forts and allow American ships access to the Caribbean markets. To his friend Scandella Latrobe described political storms and fanaticism—"petitions to Congress, remonstrances to the Executive . . . the politcomania has seized me even."[30]

Always a snob despite his republican instincts, Latrobe created a social circle in Virginia that consisted mostly of wealthy public figures whom he courted with obsequious letters. Of the eighty-four men and women mentioned in his letters and journal during this period, nearly all were landowning patricians.

Within a year of his arrival he was consorting with governors, visiting the homes of the gentry, and making the acquaintance of Virginia's famous families—the Randolphs of Tuckahoe, the Spotwoods of Orange County, and the nation's founders: Jefferson, Madison, and Washington.

An opponent of slavery, Latrobe did not discuss the subject with his acquaintances in a state where one-third of the population was enslaved. The post-revolutionary period in Virginia was a rare moment of limited slave emancipation, permitted by a legislative act in 1795. A few owners near Norfolk had manumitted their slaves, mostly for economic reasons as the returns from tobacco fields had dwindled. But the institution was hardly a subject for debate. And Latrobe was no abolitionist. Like his father and brother, both of whom compromised their ideals as they dealt with slave-holding planters in areas where Moravians established missions, he opposed slavery in theory. He promised his friend Scandella a treatise on the matter that has been lost or, more likely, was never written.

In several of his drawings Latrobe revealed his feelings, most obviously in his famous sketch of "An Overseer Doing his Duty," a cynical view of a white overseer lazily smoking a cigar while standing on a log watching two black women chop wood. The watercolor perfectly conveyed both the sexual and physical power of white men over enslaved black women.

Latrobe understood the historical and cultural relativity of vice and virtue, finding an example in the different reactions that made the English blush at sexual practices accepted by the Italians. Applied to slavery, it explained his disgust for the institution. "We are children of habit," he wrote in his journal, using slavery as an example. In Virginia, naked little black boys and girls ran about plantations, and whites paid no attention. Pubescent slave girls with bosoms uncovered attended their white owners. What would have been in-delicate for a white woman did not matter because "poor wretched Blacks" were "Outcasts of the moral as of the political world . . . your *loves* on a level with those of the dogs and cats, denied protection to your affections, and deemed incapable of that sentiment."[31]

Besides the immorality and oppression of slavery, Latrobe despised its violence. Weeks after his arrival, in a trip down the Elizabeth River, he commented on the "shocking remembrance of thousands of miserable negroes who had perished there with hunger and disease." Expecting a new life in England or Canada, they had gathered on the river's eastern shore after Lord Dunmore, Virginia's colonial governor, had promised them freedom during the American Revolution if they supported the British. But in the hasty evac-uation, the British navy abandoned them and most starved to death, "leaving

FIG. 2.4 "An Overseer Doing His Duty." Latrobe gave a sarcastic title to a scene that he witnessed near Fredericksburg, Virginia. The watercolor conveys the sexual and racial power of white men over black women. It is frequently used to illustrate slavery as it existed on Virginia plantations during the early republic. Courtesy of the Maryland Historical Society, 1960.108.1.3.21.

the bones of Men, women and Children, stripped of the flesh by Vultures and Hawks."[32] Years later in New Orleans, Latrobe was horrified by the ways in which "soft beauties handled the Cowskin," referring to white women who whipped their enslaved ferociously.[33]

And yet, in time, Latrobe's antislavery ideals gave way to the practicality of owning a slave. In 1804, Latrobe, living in Pennsylvania, acquired seven-year-old David Smith at a moment in that state's history when slavery was still legal. In the blurred distinction between contract indentured labor and slavery, the Pennsylvania legislature in 1780 had established a system of "freedom by degrees" whereby the male enslaved became free only when they reached twenty-eight years of age. By 1810 there were still 795 slaves in the state, and most likely David Smith's condition was more that of an indentured servant than a slave. But he was not a free man. For twelve years he served, in the euphemism of the day, as a "manservant," among other duties driving Latrobe's carriage and managing his horses.[34]

No matter what the failings of America, Latrobe intended to be a patriot. As an apostate from both his Moravian heritage and his English roots, he claimed no previous national identity before his arrival in the United States, and he insisted, inaccurately, that his father had so disliked Britain that he had sent his children out of the country during the American Revolution. Contrarily, Latrobe's international background heightened his nationalism. Declaring himself a man without a country until his arrival in the United States, he insisted that he was Irish American, though he had never lived in Ireland and had spent his formative years in England and Germany.

But he had made his choice. "I am already an American of the fourth Generation," he explained to a friend.[35] Encouraging his brother to move to the United States, Latrobe used the possessive pronouns "we, ours, and us" when referring to his new country. "We" Virginians were less cold-hearted and cautious than the English. "We" Americans were more welcoming of strangers, though when a lonely Latrobe dissected various forms of hospitality, he found little more than the "mutton and beef" meals of initial contact followed by no return invitations. Most Virginians failed to offer the "literary hospitality" he craved, but he denied his friend Scandella's assertion that Americans in general were rude and inhospitable.

There were many ways to demonstrate his national spirit in these early years before his buildings did so. He joined a company of the Richmond militia as an engineer officer; he wrote a detailed genealogy of the iconic Virginia couple Pocahontas and John Rolph. He attended court sessions, noting with satisfaction the wigless justices, and he was present at one partisan rally opposing the controversial Jay's Treaty, considered by Jefferson's Democratic Republicans to be too favorable to the British. Fervent in his respect for the founder of the country, he exhorted his fellow citizens to celebrate George Washington's birthday and emulate his patriotic contributions to the nation. In fact, Latrobe compared the nation's first hero to the Roman emperor Augustus, paraphrasing from his favorite source of epigrams, Horace's celebrated *Odes*: "The passion of the public never shakes the man who is just and firm from his settled purpose."[36]

After Washington's death in 1799, a special congressional committee, appointed to commemorate "the profound sorrow" of the nation, recommended a marble monument be erected in the nation's capital. A competition ensued to honor the esteemed father of the country. Latrobe felt a special bond with Washington and provided a sketch for "a Monument erected to the Memory of the Founder of American Liberty [to be] as durable as the Nation that erected it."[37] As on all matters of aesthetics, Latrobe had strong opinions about the form and material of any proper remembrance. Believing that marble was subject to injury and destruction, he cited the statue of the Virginia colonial governor, Lord Botetourt, which had been decapitated by William and Mary students during the American Revolution because it paid homage to English authority. On the other hand, employing bronze led to stiff, ugly, and expensive memorials.

As for the form of monuments he opposed statues and obelisks. But pyramids, embraced as symbols by Freemasons, endured for centuries, and that is what Latrobe designed—an imposing Egyptian-style pyramid, a mausoleum with an interior chamber to be erected on the bank of the Potomac River using local granite and white marble from Pennsylvania and Loudoun County, Virginia.[38] There were other proposals for Washington's monument, some for an equestrian statue, a few for an obelisk. Congress dallied, while the national fervor to honor the founding father diminished. Only years later in 1836 did Latrobe's student Robert Mills receive the commission for the obelisk that today honors Washington in the city that bears the first president's name.

In the winter of 1798, Latrobe, whose insomnia helps to explain his productivity, wrote a play in three days. Eager to participate in one of Richmond's popular entertainments, he completed a satire on Secretary of the Treasury Alexander Hamilton's much publicized extra-marital love affair with Mrs. Maria Reynolds, the script for which has disappeared. Although he proclaimed boredom with the incessant political conversations in Richmond, his play ridiculed the Federalists, and the reaction to it propelled Latrobe into the partisan battles of the late 1790s. Hamilton, he believed, was the kind of man who talked religion and order but went to church on Sunday from the bed of a friend's wife.[39]

Latrobe included a comic character, Skunk, easily recognizable as Peter Porcupine, the nom de plume of William Cobbett, the irascible editor of *Peter Porcupine's Gazette and United States Daily Advertiser*, a Federalist paper in Philadelphia that advocated war with France and an alliance with Great Britain. The actors in the play's only performance had not known their lines, nor could they pronounce some of the words. In the end they had slunk off the stage amid the audience's laughter and booing. An editorial battle in the Richmond newspapers ensued with Latrobe ridiculed as *"Mr. Thing'um Bob there with the one ey'd spectacle,"* referring to his use of a monocle after his glasses had broken during his travels.[40]

Familiar with such battles in London, Latrobe prepared an incendiary response. His friends cautioned against its publication. Within the week the theater mysteriously burned, and Latrobe, resilient and never so despondent as to surrender to inactivity, was hard at work designing a new theater, hotel, and ballroom to be financed by subscriptions, an ambitious multipurpose structure worthy of the great houses in Europe. But subscriptions faltered; eighteenth-century Richmond was not ready for such grandeur. The drawings became another example of Latrobe's "Castles in the Air," those designs that were never executed on the ground.

At the time, Latrobe was overseeing his first exercise in American civic architecture—the Virginia State Penitentiary. He had received the commission after winning the competition over several designs, including one sent from France by Thomas Jefferson. The design of Latrobe's prison incorporated the latest liberal views on humanitarian rehabilitation for prisoners who were to be kept in solitary cells at times, the better to encourage contemplation of their transgressions, but at other times to work and sleep in communal spaces. Extended solitary confinement was, for Latrobe, "as bad as the rack."[41]

The massive building had what Latrobe achieved in all his buildings: character—that is, the design from the exterior building material, in this case rough stone, to the interior spaces revealed its purpose. The huge half-circle of individual cells on three levels around a court, the location of the keeper's house that permitted surveillance, the workshops and dormitories, the arched windows and dramatic vaulting, the sinister power of enclosure along with the mitigating air and light testified to the cornerstone description that the building was "the Monument of that wisdom which would reform while it punishes the criminal." Latrobe intended the words to be engraved in Latin as well as English, but a frugal legislature declined the Latin version.[42]

The legislature also refused to pay what Latrobe considered a fair recompense for his work. In his arguments over the matter with Governor James Wood, Latrobe began his self-appointed task of teaching Americans universal (that is, European) practices relating to architects' remuneration as "in England confirmed by many decisions of the Courts." It was not just that the superintendent of buildings denied Latrobe's authority to direct the work, though this was galling enough; it was the insulting ignorance of the governor about the established custom of paying architects. "Our *enlightened* and *virtuous* Executive is playing a very ungenerous game with me. By keeping my claims against them *afloat,* they [con]trive to retain my services while they *delay,* if not *refuse,* to reward them."[43]

The proper payment, advised Latrobe, included a commission of 5 percent on the cost of the building, a certain sum for drawings "according to their difficulty number or beauty, and expenses," plus a per diem. Perhaps, he suggested with his habitual satiric edge, "The customs of old countries ought not to govern the practices of this State." But even if that were the case,

Latrobe provided comparisons to the pay of contemporary professional men in the United States, especially that of engineers.

While he had been given an initial $100 for his plans, payment lapsed in an environment in which there was no understanding of the financial relationship of the client to the architect. And in public projects the commitments of quixotic legislatures ruled, while Latrobe considered haggling beneath him. Anxious for some accounting, he offered a plan in which he would superintend all state public works, but the governor declined. Grudgingly Latrobe accepted an annual salary of $200 for his work on the penitentiary, though he promised that he would never "suffer my services to be to be underrated by way of beating down my reward."[44]

At the time he was already in debt, having borrowed from Henry Banks, a friendly merchant and lawyer in Richmond whom Latrobe promised to repay. To Banks, he laid out his future intentions: "Pay you, I will notwithstanding, and with my first monies, but I will neither go to jail nor will I ask any man to be my security, *while I live,* for a debt. I will borrow money but never accept bail."[45] Two years later he still owed Banks as well as some creditors in London.

In late December 1798, Latrobe left Virginia. He moved to Philadelphia, as he explained, "*to begin the world anew.*"[46] Before he left, he drew an elegant album, perhaps intended for Christian or as a first chapter in a future folio of his works. It was entitled "Designs of Buildings Erected or Proposed to be Built in Virginia from 1795–1799," by B. Henry Latrobe and in smaller letters he had added Bonneval to his name. The cover illustrated Latrobe's architectural work in Virginia. He sketched those structures actually completed, including Captain Pennock's house and that of Colonel Harvie whose modifications of the design he scorned as "garbled and disgraced and I disdain it."[47] In an explanatory paragraph he noted that "the Wings on Colonel Harvie's house" were never built and "are thus following the other buildings into the sky." In his watercolor he pictured in the clouds several structures that had not come to fruition, for Latrobe was an architect whose ratio of presentations to completed structures was always low. To the right hovered a winged angel in flight, representing the architect's imagination. And in her hand she carried a model of the bank that brought Latrobe to Philadelphia. "She is leaving the Rocks of Richmond and taking her flight to Philadelphia."[48]

In 1798, Latrobe waited until the Virginia penitentiary was nearly finished, explaining to an irritated Governor Wood, who had evidently been persuaded of the importance of architectural oversight and wanted Latrobe to remain in Virginia, that "highly advantageous circumstances" had encouraged his move.

At the time, he had lost out on a design for the Norfolk fortifications, passed over for "a millwright," he believed because his Jeffersonian, pro-French politics were not to be trusted.[49] He had waited as well until Philadelphia's annual scourge of yellow fever had passed. Then he left Virginia, developing in his mind the details of the state bank to be erected on Philadelphia's Second Street between Chestnut and Walnut. Latrobe would live in the Philadelphia-Wilmington area for eight years. As he created structures for others to live and work in, he never enjoyed a permanent residence or owned the kind of rational, practical home he was developing for his American clients.

When Benjamin Latrobe arrived in Philadelphia, the city of 61,000 dwarfed other American cities in size and importance, including its principal rival, New York. An inland port, its access to the Atlantic from its site on the Delaware River assured its primacy as a merchandising center, receiving agricultural products from the Middle Atlantic area and exporting wheat, flour, and lumber by ship to other parts of the United States, the Caribbean, and Europe. When the chronic wars between Great Britain and France did not disrupt trade, Philadelphia imported finished goods—glass from Germany, finished textiles from France, and iron tools from England.

The city's wharves bustled with people as well as produce. As many as a thousand emigrants from Ireland and Germany arrived annually, along with, before the 1808 constitutional prohibition, slaves from Africa to be trans-shipped to the tobacco plantations of the Chesapeake. Rarely was the city William Penn had located on nine blocks between the Schuylkill and Delaware Rivers without ships in its harbor, their masts like leafless trees, swaying with the tides that brought prosperity to the city.

Thanks in part to its most famous booster Benjamin Franklin, Philadelphia had the kind of civic associations that represented Latrobe's ideal of a civilized community—a library, Charles Willson Peale's museum of natural history with its extraordinary mastodons, and the voluntary associations that visitors from Europe considered so exceptional. There was a commitment in this temporary national capital to the importance of the public sphere. Within months of his arrival in the city, the American Philosophical Society had elected Latrobe to membership, and a year later, he delivered the first of several lectures to this august body of 400 members, which included Vice President Thomas Jefferson. There he met the native intellectuals who talked literature, science, and the arts, while émigrés from France and St. Domingue met at Moreau de Mery's nearby book store.

Latrobe soon purchased Peale's innovative polygraph, "this excellent little Machine," a two-penned contraption that made simultaneous copies of his correspondence. Now he could refer to his previous letters, as he saluted Peale's invention that "never betrays the confidence it receives, for though it *repeats* everything entrusted to it, never publishes a *hint* of its Masters secrets."[50] Thereafter, copies of the nearly 9,000 letters that Latrobe wrote from 1802 to 1817 survived, assuring his legacy.

Besides its intellectual advantages, Philadelphia was the political center of the new nation. Latrobe dubbed it "the national metropolis," the place where the American Revolution had been defined and organized. In 1790 it had become the capital of the United States, with Congress meeting in Independence Hall and George Washington exerting his limited executive powers but vast personal authority from his residence on Market Street. "You will consider," explained the merchant Robert Morris, "Philadelphia to be to the United States what the heart is to the body."[51]

Latrobe discovered that politics was even more in the air than had been the case in Virginia, especially after John Adams's controversial Alien and Sedition Acts and the arrest of Matthew Lyon of Vermont for his supposedly seditious criticism of the president. Federalists in the city were clamoring for more restrictive immigration and naturalization policies to disenfranchise the "wild Irishmen" who were hardly off the boat before they were voting for Jefferson's Democratic Republicans.[52] Temporarily, the nativists were successful; the year that Latrobe arrived in the city Congress passed a restrictive naturalization act. Latrobe claimed citizenship through his mother who had been born in Pennsylvania in 1728, though such status for those born outside of the United States did not adhere through the maternal line until the twentieth century. On his paternal side he believed the fanciful family tale that his grandfather James had, at some point in his life, emigrated to America before returning to Ireland. In any case, Latrobe reconsidered his legal status and filled out a Declaration of Intention to become a citizen, something he thought he already was.[53]

As he did wherever he lived, Latrobe took stock of the physical features of his new home. He admired the wide paved streets that intersected at right angles and the city's three public squares; he discovered a few handsome brick residences, along with one of the ugliest houses he had ever seen. The wealthy merchant Robert Morris had built "a complicated, unintelligible mass . . . a monster," with the columns so important to Latrobe's own architecture, "of the worst taste." In Virginia he had been told that the Morris house was the handsomest thing in America. Intent on improving the nation's aesthetic sensibilities, Latrobe questioned in his journal who was the "maddest—the architect or his employer," both of whom, he noted, soon went bankrupt.[54]

Some of his walking tours took him along the city's wharves, where the annual scourge of yellow fever was concentrated. Latrobe learned that only five
years before his arrival the city had lost 3,500 residents in a particularly severe
yellow fever season. He discovered these epidemics were annual visitations;
later they became a family curse.

Still, with all its challenges and shortcomings, Philadelphia was the logical
place for an aspiring American architect to establish his practice. Latrobe had
first spoken of moving there after an earlier visit to investigate the city's famed
Walnut Street Prison in preparation for his own work on the Virginia State
Penitentiary. Even before his visit, he had understood that this city offered
an opportunity for both public and private commissions, the latter among
the wealthy entrepreneurs and merchants whose homes clustered along the
Schuylkill River. He had determined that Philadelphia was "the only situation
in which I ought to reside."[55]

On his first visit, or so the family story goes, he had hastily drawn the
outline of a bank for Samuel Fox, a prominent Quaker merchant and head
of a group of wealthy entrepreneurs. Their intention was to establish a Bank
of Pennsylvania, a risky proposition, though they were well funded, since
the city already had two other banks, including the First Bank of the United
States. Latrobe, who never found much to admire in the work of others,
dismissed the architecture of the First Bank of the United States as a "copy of
a European building of indifferent taste and very defective in its execution."
Still, the fact that the building existed at all testified to what he admired about
Philadelphia—"the bold proof of the spirit of the citizens who erected it and
of the tendency of the community to force rather than to retard the advancement of the arts."[56]

Latrobe believed that what he called "a refined simplicity" was the highest
characteristic of taste not just in architecture but in rhetoric, dress, and manners. In Philadelphia he found a congenial home, especially among Quakers,
who embraced "simplicity in principles and the good taste in the arts established in your city and thence to pervade the United States."[57] As occurred
several times during his life, a design tossed off in a casual moment suited a
perceptive Quaker client who appreciated this innovative genius's talent.

In designing the bank, he called upon "an immense store of knowledge,
chiefly mechanical and mathematical that I must have inherited." He did not
need pattern books or even his library lost at sea. Buildings existed in his mind
before he sketched them on paper and then "arrangements, construction and
decoration are [arrived at] so simultaneously that I seldom materially change
the design first elaborated in my idea." Such a process explains the rapidity

with which he developed his buildings, sometimes two or three variations of a design in a week:

> So little study did the thing [designing the bank] cost me that except in the mechanical effort which demanded very laborious concentration, I do not recollect any fatigue of the mind or fingers. . . . It was a plaything to me and so in fact are all my designs. My designs come of themselves unasked in multitudes and I commonly welcome the first that comes and execute it with very little if any alteration. . . . In my greater works therefore I go on with a confidence, and almost nonchalance that frightens my employers. . . . Now the real truth is, and why should I write anything but truth, that this faculty may be called Genius.[58]

Latrobe believed that in England he had only studied architecture's practical elements, not "the scientific laws of construction . . . but the methods, the tricks, and the knacks of workmen with the technical vocabulary belonging to them." That is why he had entered Samuel Cockerell's office in London, specifically to "load my memory with arbitrary rules of measuration and workmanship with a new set of words." He did not need to study design. Today we are sensitive to such conceit. But in earlier centuries the concept was part of a general debate over innate ideas. In his self-description, Latrobe employed his generation's understanding of genius as an inherent gift, a supernatural force, a magical deliverance, unconscious, unwilled, unpremeditated, and, in his personal case, an indication of his exceptional talents.[59]

With sufficient funding and minimal interference from his clients, Latrobe's Bank of Pennsylvania was soon under way, its chaste white marble a contrast to its red brick neighbors on Second Street. Employing the exterior plan of an antique temple, capped by a stepped dome and cupola with vertical windows, Latrobe created two stunning Greek Ionic porticos of six columns for the bank's front and back. On the interior he developed the soaring vaulting that soon became a hallmark of his architecture. Using Pennsylvania stone, he fashioned a building with its character revealed by its strong shape and its rough square-hewn rocks called ashlar alternating with neat-sized panels. In an extension of the architect's contemporary role, he dictated the colors of the interior. They should be Greek style, he advised Samuel Fox and the painter John Holland: "The walls to be pale but warm Oker or straw color, . . . the margins of the dome pale blue, the mouldings white and the panels a pale yellow."[60]

Visitors walked through a dark passageway into the vast, open, well-lit space of the rotunda. The structure conveyed the essence of banking: the Bank of Pennsylvania was solid, dependable (though the skylights soon leaked), imperishable (though by the late twentieth century it had been replaced by a parking lot), an impenetrable fortress. In short, it was a temple of capitalism.

In this building Latrobe fulfilled his intentions of creating "a pure specimen of Grecian simplicity in design and Grecian permanence in execution." Later critics charged that he had simply copied a Greek temple. Latrobe protested: "The grossest ignorance alone could assert that the Bank of Pennsylvania is the copy of a Greek temple. . . . Even the Porticos vary in every part of their proportions of columns and entablature from every temple in existence."[61] Intending the creation of an American architecture, he did not mention its resemblance to John Soane's Bank of England. In any case, Latrobe had no difficulty collecting his $4,000 fee, and he had discovered in Philadelphia a pool of skilled artisans and marble-cutters who could accomplish his designs. The result—he always believed it one of his best works—was a masterpiece that would have "*cut a dash*," even in sophisticated London.[62]

Praise came as well from two visiting Frenchmen who observed the building in silence for a few moments. Then one turned to the other and exclaimed, "Si Beau! Et si simple!" William Birch featured the bank in his famous engravings of Philadelphia. A character in novelist Washington Irving's *Salmagundi* declared that "everybody has heard of the famous Bank of Pennsylvania which since the destruction of the tomb of Mausolus and the Colossus of Rhodes, may fairly be estimated as one of the wonders of the world."[63] Success led to an office on Mulberry Street; he accepted several students whom he called his "eleves." No longer unknown, Latrobe attracted imitators who used variations of his design for their own temples, mostly in the courthouses and state capitols proliferating throughout the United States.

The Bank of Pennsylvania was not Latrobe's only immediate success in Philadelphia. No sooner had he arrived than in his capacity as an engineer he had been asked to devise a plan for providing the city with pure water. In other American cities, efforts to provide wholesome water were under way, and Philadelphia was a good candidate for such an improvement. Its water supply came from wells subject to pollution from nearby privies, an especially serious threat magnified by the porousness of the soil. Local water pumps acted as funnels, bringing up not just water but the noxious gases that sickened city residents in the summer. There were rumors of citizens fatally stricken as they put their mouths to the pumps for water and breathed in the fatal effluvium.

FIG. 2.5 Bank of Pennsylvania. This bank, begun in 1798 and completed in 1800 in Philadelphia, established Latrobe's reputation as the most important architect in the United States. Universally admired, it advanced his neoclassical style. As the first Greek revival building in the United States, it became a landmark in the history of US architecture. Designed as a central square block lengthened by two wings with a portico at each end, the stone building had a shallow domed roof and a cupola. On the interior the bank was notable for its masonry. Courtesy of the Maryland Historical Society, 1897.1.5.

Contaminated the water might be, but there was not even enough of it to fight fires and clean streets. Like many citizens, including the city's famous physician Benjamin Rush, Latrobe believed that the city's annual curse of yellow fever festered in this miasma—the gas from the wastes in filthy streets. Offensive smells carried the disease, and those residents who did not flee the city during an epidemic covered their mouths with scarves treated with camphor. While some perceptive residents associated the increased numbers of pesky mosquitoes around the waterfront with the outbreaks, it would be years before anyone considered them the source of yellow fever.

Latrobe had been in the city only a few days when the Watering Committee, officially the Joint Committee on Supplying the City with Water, asked him to investigate a nearby spring north of the city for its suitability as a water source. With characteristic boldness he went far beyond his mandate, creating in a week a complicated plan for clean, abundant city water. His eleven-page report, "View of the Practicability and Means of Supplying the City of Philadelphia with Wholesome Water," detailed a project that he over-optimistically estimated could be completed in eighteen months. First water from the Schuylkill would be collected in a basin constructed in the

FIG. 2.6 Demolition of the Bank of Pennsylvania. In 1867 the Bank of Pennsylvania was demolished to make way for a parking lot. Here the process is photographed with the columns of the portico temporarily resisting the bulldozers. The Library Company of Philadelphia.

river; from there an engine powered by steam would pump it to street level, there to flow through a mile-long brick tunnel to a second steam engine that would raise it to an elevated reservoir inside the Centre Square Engine House. Finally, by means of gravity, six-inch wooden pipes would distribute it throughout the city. Latrobe intended the water to be free at the pumps, with a fee to those who installed water taps in their homes, and he promised a maximum daily supply of three million gallons. The cost, he underestimated, would be $75,000 for the pumps and $52,000 for the initial distribution system, the final cost including the engine house not to exceed $275,000.[64] With characteristic optimism he anticipated that residents would invest in an enterprise that in time would return a profit.

As work on the basin and brick conduit proceeded, Latrobe designed its end point—the Centre Square Engine House. In his view, the Engine House, in one of the city's central locations, must not simply be a utilitarian, functional structure. Instead he intended to hide the ugly machinery in a handsome but practical building. With the picturesque fountains and public bathhouses of Rome in mind, he envisioned embellishing the city with his urban architecture. And so he did, with an artistic success that became a showpiece for natives as well as visitors. He created an elegant neoclassical structure graced by a marble façade, with an attractive domed cylinder rising from a rectangular block, arched windows, and Greek Doric columns. The Centre Square Engine House displayed Latrobe's lifelong commitment to the importance of combining practicality with attractive public architecture that enhanced the community. Good design, even if more expensive, a point Latrobe forever denied, symbolized the power, prestige, and permanence of the community.

It was the steam engines that made the project expensive and controversial. Latrobe had worked with this new innovation in England, and to reassure the suspicious Watering Committee, he described its successful applications in both London and Paris. Less technologically advanced than Europeans, Americans of the early republic were either unfamiliar with them or thought them dangerous devices that exploded. Latrobe provided assurances in his written report: "Soon after the invention, steam engines were justly considered dangerous, man had not yet learned to controul the immense power of steam, and now and then they did a little mischief. A steam engine is, at present, as tame and innocent as a clock."[65]

To find such a machine, Latrobe visited one of the only companies in America that manufactured steam engines. In New Jersey he met Nicholas Roosevelt, entrepreneur and owner of the Soho Works, named after Isaac Watt's famous engine works in Birmingham, England. Latrobe and Roosevelt were kindred spirits, similar in their enthusiasm for new ideas and their taste for speculation. After consulting with Roosevelt, Latrobe promised the engines would be ready in the summer of 1799, and the Watering Committee signed a contract with Roosevelt whose workforce, Latrobe noted with approval, included European technicians.

In the meantime, there were aggravations. The Watering Committee, comprised of prudent businessmen and thrifty Quaker merchants, made Latrobe's payment contingent on the success of the project—a waterworks "of a permanent stability and good and perfect in kind" that lived up to its name and actually delivered water. At first the committee refused his demand of 5 percent of "whatever it may cost—or $6,350."[66] Eventually Latrobe prevailed, earning $7,000, but not before challenges to his professional integrity and a pamphlet war with competitors. While disagreements over money rankled, even more infuriating was the stipulation that the system must operate before he was paid. In an angry meeting with the committee, Latrobe compared his work to that of other professionals, such as doctors and lawyers who were paid for their expertise, not whether a patient was cured or a will uncontested. Coming from a family of ministers—the clergy representing the earliest trained professionals—Latrobe was particularly sensitive to the issue.

He complained that he was being treated like an artisan who must have "penalties to tie him to his duty." This was "the first instance in which the profession itself has been degraded below that of a Merchant, a Lawyer or a Physician; to whom property and life are intrusted without any restraint by deeds or other legal fetters." Like other professionals, he was an expert by virtue of his judgment and training as well as his status as a gentleman. He expected to be adequately compensated for his mental labor and his oversight of the project. It was a matter of honor among educated gentlemen. Latrobe chafed at what he considered the indignities of his life. It was, he believed, his great misfortune to be "born and educated a *Gentleman,* at least on this side of the Atlantic," forced to haggle with clients and committees about fees.[67]

Latrobe had promised a working water system by 1800, before the annual yellow fever crisis. But the delivery of the steam engines was delayed. Members of the Watering Committee began to question his expense and time estimates. A suspicious member of the committee, respected Quaker merchant Thomas Cope, traveled to the Soho Works to investigate and returned with the news that "the two scoundrels," that is, Roosevelt and Latrobe, had conspired to obtain the contract by deceiving the committee about when the pumps would be finished and how much they would cost. Cope already knew the project was over budget, perhaps, he insinuated, the result of padded payrolls. Latrobe was "a cunning, witful, dissimulating fellow, possessing more ingenuity than honesty," wrote Cope in his diary, as he pressed unsuccessfully for Latrobe's dismissal.[68] Only water in the city's pipes would end the carping over an under-subscribed project that eventually cost nearly $600,000 and forced the city to sell a public bridge and ferry to a private company to pay its costs.[69]

On a cold night in late January 1801 Latrobe, Roosevelt, and his friend Samuel Fox, along with several workmen, lit the coal fires under the boilers, first in the engine house on the Schuylkill and then in the center of town. Gradually, as this new technological powerhouse of steam pressure produced energy, the pumps began their incessant noisy work—thump-a-thump, thump-a-thump—of delivering water. A new day had dawned in Philadelphia as the city awoke to find water flowing through the streets from the hydrants that Latrobe, in a stroke of showmanship, had left open. Hailed as a genius for a successful city improvement, Latrobe found his reputation as an engineer assured. The city was guaranteed what he had promised—an adequate supply of wholesome water, though a motion to thank him was defeated by one vote in the Watering Committee. That summer fewer mosquitoes festered in the now unnecessary barrels of water, though some survived and others arrived on ships from Africa and the Caribbean. The city's annual yellow fever epidemics continued.

Meanwhile, Latrobe had invested in an irresistible new venture— Roosevelt's rolling mill that used the surplus power from the steam engine on the Schuylkill River to shape sheets of copper and iron into useful sizes. There were already customers, among them Thomas Jefferson who wanted sheet iron for his roof at Monticello. The firm had a profitable contract with the Navy Department for copper bolts as well. The possibilities for business seemed endless, and, violating an earlier resolution, Latrobe gave Roosevelt power of attorney over his shares in the rolling mill. He also signed Roosevelt's notes. Then as often happened to entrepreneurs of this generation whose buyers defaulted, the navy canceled its contract and the business failed. For the time being, the cost of using steam pressure as energy to process iron and copper proved too expensive and difficult in a nation full of cheap timber and powerful rivers.

By 1805, Latrobe owed $20,000 to a third party who had bought Roosevelt's notes. With characteristic good intentions, he had also made himself liable for a series of minor claims, in one instance endorsing the note of a friend traveling to Europe who defaulted. Meanwhile a new employer, the Chesapeake and Delaware Canal Company, no longer paid in cash. As often happened in these undercapitalized ventures, his payment came in the form of eventually worthless company stock. To ease his financial difficulties, Latrobe counted on the sale of Roosevelt's mill, but this too became a discounted asset.

He expected some relief from his dead wife's inheritance. But his English brothers-in-law, the Sellons, refused to fulfill their obligations and send the money left to his children from their grandfather's estate. Latrobe found the Sellons' conduct "unpardonable and dishonest" and asked his brother to make his claims. But the family refused to see Christian or answer his calls.[70] Now threatened with arrest when third parties who had purchased Roosevelt's notes demanded payment, Latrobe consulted a lawyer about the possibility of declaring bankruptcy. Eventually with help from relatives and the sale of the lot he had purchased in Richmond, a temporarily chastened Latrobe sold his "patrimony at great sacrifice, [but] I kept up my own credit." He calculated a loss of more than $15,000.[71]

For all his intentions to avoid debt, like many Americans of his generation, Latrobe found land speculation irresistible. Even in a year when he was being pressed by his creditors, he invested $675 in the purchase of a tract of land at the intersection of the proposed Chesapeake and Delaware Canal and a feeder canal. Using his knowledge as an insider to make a purchase that today would be considered unethical, he had "no doubt that this little speculation will turn out admirably." But when the Canal Company collapsed, his invest-ment became worthless.[72]

Later he held Nicholas Roosevelt responsible for his financial woes. Certainly Roosevelt had misused Latrobe's power of attorney, entangling the architect in a collateral bankruptcy. Latrobe wanted nothing more to do with his former partner: "I could fill many sheets with the detail of my miseries and deprivations on account of my connexion with Mr. Roosevelt's concerns. . . . I have never derived an advantage in a pecuniary point of view to the amount of one Cent from them. . . . While I have committed myself to him with a confidence that knew no bounds, he has observed a caution and suspicion in all his transactions which has kept him entirely out of my power."[73]

Meanwhile, despite his early success, his architectural commissions flagged. For some, such as Old West, a building at Dickinson College, and the plans for a grand cathedral in Baltimore, a long-term project, he charged only his expenses because he was committed to the lofty principle, as he believed all gentlemen should be, that it was the "duty of every citizen to promote . . . the education and *civilization* of which he and his children are to live."[74] He also charged only expenses for his alterations of Nassau Hall at the College of New Jersey. But after his plans were modified, he denied any connection to that project. Meanwhile, several designs were never built, and he was never paid for his work renovating Philadelphia's Chestnut Street Theater. Even America's largest city could not support him.

Latrobe did create a fanciful round house for the British consul, intended more for its possibilities than any reality. His work on a home in Maryland for the Stiers, an aristocratic family from Antwerp, ended in acrimony. In Latrobe's view, Baron Henri Joseph Stier and his son, wealthy émigrés from the French Revolution with an important art collection, were the kind of interfering amateurs who had no professional training. In their view, Latrobe, whom they hired in December 1800 and fired after two months, "was one of those who do not finish their work and who will not be suitable for us in the future."[75]

His design for a national military academy to accommodate seven professors and fifty students languished in Congress. After drawing an el-egant temple structure with a low saucer dome for a city hall in New York City, he complained that he had lost out to "a brick layer and a St. Domingo Frenchman" in one of the competitions he despised. His "best design" for the

New York City Hall had been rejected for "a vile heterogeneous composition in the style of Charles IX of France or Queen Elizabeth of England," the kind of building that Latrobe felt violated the republican simplicity installed by George Washington in politics and by his neoclassical buildings in architecture. Yet his design was considered too plain and lacked the kind of grandiosity that the judges found compelling. For Latrobe, "ornaments increase in proportion as art declines, or as ignorance abounds." It was "barbarians" who designed complicated structures like the New York City Hall. Complaining about this "extremely inconvenient and humiliating" competition process in which "*unprofessional* men" made judgments not based on merit, but on politics, he resisted entering contests but never succeeded, given their popularity.[76]

Sedgeley, a large estate along the Schuylkill River, was one design that was built. Yet it became another of Latrobe's orphans, disowned by the architect after a disagreement with his client and the powerful Philadelphia Carpenters Company. William Cramond, a rich second-generation merchant, wanted a showpiece along the river. Displaying his virtuosity, Latrobe designed a Gothic building with open arches and triple triangular windows, scalloped eaves, two-story corner pavilions, and a piazza with slim columns—architectural features that Latrobe's neoclassical instincts mostly disdained. And yet his only Gothic house, a trailblazer in its way, had the kind of proportions and picturesque features that, even as a precursor to American Gothic architectural styles popular later in the nineteenth century, still manifested classical proportions and symmetry.

Cramond proved a difficult client. He boasted that he was spending the enormous amount of $40,000 on his new home, thereby reinforcing Latrobe's local reputation for extravagance. Far worse, the carpenters installed expensive ugly window sashes and, when Latrobe tried to intervene, Cramond, according to Latrobe, took the side of the carpenters, dismissing the architect's authority as "out of my profession to judge of Carpenter's work." Refused oversight, like the father of a wayward child, Latrobe renounced any relationship: "I have never been nearer to the house than the Canal bank road." His relationship with Cramond led Latrobe to resolve that he would never again design a house for a private gentleman. It was a promise, like avoiding architectural competitions, that he never kept. To one client in 1807, he was still threatening "for the last time in my life . . . a design the way you want it. But I forewarn You, as I foresee myself, that we shall both *forever hereafter* repent our connexion on this business, on these terms."[77]

Such frankness, along with his reputation for costly projects that overran their budgets, limited Latrobe's residential commissions. Wealthy

Philadelphians continued to pay carpenters' companies who used pattern books for mundane designs and to hire untrained builders listed in the city directory. But during his early years in Philadelphia Latrobe did complete some houses. He called them his "professional children," and it was during the process of thinking about domestic life, as his own family circumstances changed, that he created a new American house—"the rational house," such as he would design for himself but never did.[78]

Given the customs and warmer climate of the United States, in Latrobe's view American houses must be different from those appropriate for the gentry in France where husbands and wives had separate bedrooms and in England where the central hall was "a kind of turnpike road through the house over which everyone must pass, . . . paying toll to curiosity," a space serving as "a common sewer to all Chambers and parlors." Principal rooms, given the heat and suffocating summer suns unknown in Europe, should be located in the north. Americans were pragmatic and simple, characteristics that jibed with his own preferences: "Nothing appears so clear from the general ascent of all ages, as that a graceful and refined simplicity is the highest achievement of taste and art. . . . [S]implicity gains daily more admirers."[79]

Latrobe's commitment to antiquity paralleled the new republic's adoption of ancient Greece and Rome as its political models, while in his domestic architecture his pristine, straightforward neoclassical approach matched the nation's habits. Even the furniture he created for a few clients reprised, but modified, traditional Greek styles. While it employed variations of the ancient colors of yellowish ochre, gold, and red, his furniture included practical features of more comfortable seating and durability.

To avoid what Latrobe called the frying pan of appendages, he located kitchens in the house. Convenient to the lady of the house, they should be light and airy and have masonry vaults to prevent fire. There should be a cellar below grade and a suite of rooms including the ladies' apartment on the first floor for a sick woman or one recovering from pregnancy. While such principles seem obvious, Latrobe's genius appeared in the ways that he created interior diagonals and picturesque views from such simplicity. According to architectural historians Michael Fazio and Patrick Snadon, "With his dense European education and his close study of American society and the American landscape and its environmental forces, Latrobe was able to make a unique contribution to American domestic design. . . . [He] was the first architect to consciously invent an 'American house.' "[80]

Soon after his arrival in Philadelphia, Benjamin Latrobe met Mary Elizabeth Hazlehurst, the daughter of a prosperous Philadelphia merchant.

Her father, Isaac Hazlehurst, had emigrated to the United States from Manchester, England, in 1742. Trained as a clerk in a counting house, he settled in Philadelphia, married into a prominent local family with Huguenot roots and established a profitable international import-export business on Philadelphia's Second Street. His business flourished until the American Revolution stifled trade. A member of the Episcopal Christ's Church, Hazlehurst was president of the St. George's Society, an association formed to give advice and assistance to Englishmen in distress.

Reestablishing his business in the late 1780s, Hazlehurst extended his operations, in part through his partnership with Philadelphia's most famous entrepreneur and second richest citizen, Robert Morris. Morris soon went bankrupt, but Hazlehurst, according to one of his granddaughters, had resisted most of Morris's schemes. "Had he not done so [Morris's business dealings] would soon have brought him to a jail," wrote Julia Latrobe. Instead, when his revived mercantile house failed again in 1808, Hazlehurst retired to Clover Hill, his country estate across the Delaware River in Mount Holly, New Jersey. His family crest featured a squirrel, the prudent animal of saving and storing. The family motto heralded "Nothing without work." Isaac Hazlehurst had failed to avoid bankruptcy, but he had been true to his family's values.[81]

Mary Elizabeth was the eldest of Isaac Hazlehurst's seven children and his only daughter. Her six younger brothers had all attended or graduated from the University of Pennsylvania. Educated in one of the city's academies for young ladies, she had learned the social graces from her mother and, as she often told her daughters, she had poured tea for the social luminaries of Philadelphia— Mrs. President Washington, Mrs. General Knox, and the Episcopal bishop's wife. In her specialness as an only daughter, Mary Hazlehurst absorbed the details of managing a large and lively household of younger brothers. Beloved of her parents who depended on her, at age twenty-nine, she was older than most women of her time and class, when she married thirty-six-year-old Benjamin Latrobe.

This time there were no disapproving relatives despising Latrobe for his social standing. This time there were no complex inheritance considerations. On May 1, 1800, the groom's birthday, with the Episcopal bishop the Reverend Dr. White officiating in Christ's Church, Mary Elizabeth Hazlehurst and Benjamin Henry Latrobe married. Latrobe had found what he needed most in his personal life: a wife whom he adored, a woman who treated her stepchildren as if they were hers, a physical and intellectual partner who created the kind of nurturing craved by a sensitive man who had never had the security of an intimate family. As he declared in sentiments that remained true throughout his marriage:

> When I think of you, my dearest love, my heart melts at first into ten-derness such as I never before knew; but it soon rests itself upon that superiority of mind, that soundness of reasoning, and that command of your feelings which I know you possess, and then I take my level on my shoulder, and march forth as strong as a lion to push forward to the end of my labor when your arms and your kisses, if I dared to think of them, shall reward all my fatigues. Oh my love! [82]

After a three-month honeymoon, some of which was spent with Mary's parents, Latrobe arranged for a friend to accompany nine-year-old Lydia and her younger brother eight-year-old, Henry Sellon Boneval Latrobe, across the Atlantic to Philadelphia. Mary Latrobe's approach to stepmothering, never an easy relationship even in a generation when early mortality made it a fa-miliar one, was a triumph. According to her husband, her own biological chil-dren did not "even suspect that the two others have a stepmother."[83]

Soon there were more Latrobes in a family that, as its patriarch recognized, enjoyed "the blessing of fertility," but also the pain of infant mortality. In the first eight years of their marriage six children were born to Benjamin Henry and Mary Latrobe. Three daughters died as infants; only two sons—John Hazlehurst Boneval Latrobe and Benjamin Henry Boneval Latrobe—and a daughter, Juliana Elizabeth Latrobe, survived. Constantly pregnant, often ill, and managing a household on slim, uncertain resources, Mary Latrobe earned a grateful husband's admiration.[84]

For all the turmoil with his professional children, twice Latrobe had been lucky in love. To his brother Christian he provided an explanation based on his own sexual discretion, having declined the advances of his children's very pretty nurse: "As to actual enjoyment of happiness, our shares in the world are rather proportioned to our *right or wrong* conduct than to any adventitious circumstances of more or less knowledge or even health."[85]

Sometime after his remarriage, Benjamin Latrobe sat for a portrait by his friend Charles Willson Peale. It was his second portrait, though he was suspi-cious of the merits of portrait painting in general and hardly had the funds to pay one of the most famous and prolific portrait painters in the early republic. Who did such paintings benefit, he wondered, except the vanity of the sub-ject? It was a trade, rather than an art, he insisted, though he admitted that Americans had produced several excellent portrait painters.[86] Still, for all his hesitations and complaints, Latrobe sat for four portraits during his lifetime. He had hoped for a fifth, but the renowned Gilbert Stuart insisted on his usual $1,000 fee, placing the portrait beyond Latrobe's means.[87]

In Charles Willson Peale's portrait Latrobe has moved far beyond his communal Moravian past and London foppery. He has grown in maturity and has a distinct personality. The full-faced Latrobe is an American, gazing with stern myopic eyes beyond the viewer into the future. "Look at me," he seems to say. His clothes are neat, elegant, and high-style, but not those of an English dandy. His cravat is tied in the kind of bow gentlemen of this era favored. Peale, a friend whom Latrobe called "the amiable and indefatigable Polygraphist," painted his subject with his trademark glasses in his hair, the ironic symbol of an architect who did not see well. There are none of the usual accoutrements used to identify the profession or interests of a subject. None were needed. Latrobe had already become a famous architect.[88]

FIG. 2.7 Charles Willson Peale Portrait of Benjamin Henry Latrobe. This is the second and most famous portrait of Benjamin Latrobe. Currently it hangs in the Map Room of the White House. Peale liked to reveal character in his portraits and here displays an earnest, trustworthy, upper-class American gentleman. © White House Historical Association.

Mary Latrobe furnished her husband with the large family and well-run household that Latrobe had lacked in his youth. He absorbed her family as his own, treating Mary's parents as "my dear father and mother" and becoming to them "your affectionate son." Her brothers became his, and he grieved with his wife when her brother Robert died in 1804. Latrobe insisted that whenever any Hazlehursts traveled to England they meet his brother Christian and sister Mary Agnes, as their families were knit together by marriage. And when he was separated from his in-laws, he acknowledged his attachment in long letters full of news: "We think of you and our Mother every day, with that interest and affection which we so much owe to You." [89] Isaac Hazlehurst, well known for his strictness with his own sons, adopted Latrobe as a member of his family but worried that this brilliant, mercurial son-in-law was not settling down. And settling down required the impossible—"a fixed and known residence."[90] In fact, Latrobe made his family into the itinerant that he was.

As a family man needing a steady income, Latrobe turned to his other profession—engineering. For several years before coming to the United States, he had apprenticed in the office of John Smeaton, a premier English engineer, and had worked with Smeaton's assistant William Jessup. Assigned to canal projects, he learned the essential aspects of canal building including scouring, the practice essential in the United States of preventing silting in tidal channels and rivers. Shortly before Latrobe left for America, he had overseen the construction of a bridge and received his first independent commission to improve the channel of a river in Essex County, an expensive local project. Full of imaginative ideas, he had suggested that the cost of the improvement be reduced by selling the rocks that had been removed by deepening the river, and he had testified before Parliament on the need for government funding. But Latrobe emigrated before the matter was settled and before he was paid for his survey.[91]

Meanwhile in Philadelphia, the city fathers had discovered that their city's economic future rested with the Susquehanna River. While the river sliced through the rich interior farmlands of Pennsylvania, its natural course into the Chesapeake Bay gave a rival city an advantage. Grain, whiskey, and iron went to Baltimore, and from there they were exported throughout the world. Even before the American Revolution, Philadelphians had understood the necessity of establishing control over the Susquehanna River commerce. In an age of river transportation, the wise men of the American Philosophical Society as well as the state's legislators debated the question of how to connect the Susquehanna and the upper Chesapeake Bay to the Delaware by means of a canal.

All agreed that more information was needed; a joint public-private company was chartered to survey the river. Latrobe's uncle, his mother's younger brother Frederick Antes, was hired as chief engineer and he in turn hired his nephew as an assistant. After Antes's death, Latrobe was put in charge and spent six months surveying forty miles of what he called "this savage but beautiful river." The result, completed in early 1802, was an extraordinary map with all the hallmarks of its author's brilliance. Setting a high standard for such engineering surveys, Latrobe's exquisitely detailed, artistically drawn, doggedly accurate map displayed not just his drawing ability but also his appreciation for the geology of the lower Susquehanna. Later he successfully lobbied the governor for $2,000 of state funds to complete river improvements that mainly involved removing boulders and debris in the river channel. Remembering royal patronage, Latrobe often complained about the failure of American public entities to support private ventures, but his experience, in this case, shows otherwise.

A private enterprise, the Chesapeake and Delaware Canal Company, founded in 1799 and chartered in 1802, had begun the process of raising money through a stock subscription. The directors intended to finance a canal that would connect the Delaware River, Philadelphia's window onto Middle Atlantic trade, to the Susquehanna and Chesapeake Bay. The company opened their subscription books for 2,500 shares, each costing $200, and for a time the stock was a popular investment. Today we remember the Erie Canal as the prime example of this era of canal transportation, but in the early years of the nineteenth century, the proposed Chesapeake and Delaware was the largest canal project of its time.

Initially the board hired Latrobe as an engineer for eight dollars a day, and he undertook the first surveys. By 1804, he had become the chief engineer of the project with a salary of $3,500, paid mostly in stock and company notes, all the "plotting mapping and calculation done in my office." The first task in what he assured directors was the "principal business of my life" was to locate the best line. Then he had to survey and create a feeder line providing sufficient water to the main canal during the summer months.[92] The complications were many and included building an aqueduct with a forty-foot span over a rapid creek, digging through stony ground, hiring and keeping workers who lived in the field, organizing a quarry to provide stone for the canal's masonry work, persuading landowners to give the company easements through their property, and not least, dealing with a board that too often treated him without the respect he believed his status as a professional engineer warranted.

By the fall, Latrobe had nearly completed the feeder line from the Elk River and was forging ahead when the company faced a financial crisis. Many investors had not paid their promised subscriptions. Latrobe, already familiar with undercapitalized American improvements from his experiences in Virginia, sent a petition to the Pennsylvania state legislature. He argued, as he would repeatedly, that public works required government support, that the canal was of importance as a source of national unity, and that in wartime it would give Americans a military advantage. But the legislature declined any additional financial aid and Latrobe knew better than to lobby the notably fervent advocate (but occasional abuser) of states' rights, now-president Thomas Jefferson. By the fall of 1805, nearly two years after he had first joined the company, Latrobe reported to a friend: "The Canal Co. are *aground* and all that are embarked with them, except the Officers, and they may stay by the wreck and starve if they chuse."[93]

Besides its financial disappointment, Latrobe's involvement with the Canal Company brought other challenges. By this time Latrobe was familiar with the requirements of a profession "ill-suited to the regularity and quiet of domestic comfort." But as a husband and father, his situation rankled. He was never home more than several days at a time when he was surveying. Absent for weeks, at other times he saw his wife and children only on weekends. Full of complaints, he compared himself to a day laborer. Yet as he contemplated in a letter to his wife, happiness was in their reach. But "the necessary circumstances of our lives, refuse to permit to us the enjoyment of *all* that we can paint to ourselves as *possible*." In the same letter he acknowledged Mary's tranquilizing effect: "But after writing the first words of my letter, after calling you, my dearest Mary, my dearest wife, my beloved wife, the whole world vanishes from my imagination, and I see none but you. I seem to stretch my arms from the rocky Walls of the Susquehannah in vain towards you."[94] Never in robust health, the lonely Latrobe suffered from headaches, fevers, and the kidney stones he considered an inherited condition, along with an occasional "melancholy depression of spirits."[95]

At first Latrobe refused to be separated from Mary and his children and moved them to a rented house in New Castle, Delaware, "the Gravesend of Philadelphia," thirty miles south of the city. Here at the urging of the local commissioners, he provided a comprehensive town plan for $500. He compared the community to little country towns all over the world with grandiose ambitions. The result was classic Latrobe: a meticulous and ambitious proposal to drain street water into gutters, fill in nearby marshes, create a town square, and add more land to the wharves that would become the engine of New Castle's growth.[96] Like so many of his ideas, only parts of these plans were carried out.

In the summer of 1805 Latrobe moved his family again—this time to fifty acres he had recently purchased on the Delaware River, a site that would be a critical point on any future canal and therefore a good investment. There on Iron Hill, in a spectacular setting 300 feet above the river where on a clear day four states were visible, the Latrobes—pregnant Mary, two-year-old John, one-year-old Julia, Henry, Lydia, and occasionally his students—spent the summer. He declared it one of the happiest times of his life, as he lived a modest version of his fantasy. With his habitual enthusiasm, Latrobe intended to improve the log cabin for permanent occupation, until his father-in-law objected.

No one, not even Mary Latrobe, could persuade Isaac Hazlehurst of the merits of this plan. Hazlehurst wanted his daughter to live properly, in a residence in the city. "[My father-in-law] persisted in pleading the necessity of my living in a situation and style to call for the respect from the public which is always paid to apparent or real independence as to property."[97] At the time, Latrobe had only the property at Iron Hill and the worthless stock certificates of the Chesapeake and Delaware Canal Company. After demanding that the Latrobes abandon the cabin, Isaac Hazlehurst offered a substantial temporary home in Wilmington rent free, an offer that could not be refused.

Again Latrobe had to find employment. Again he had to move, this time away from Philadelphia, the city where he had expected to live permanently, to Wilmington, with its nonexistent opportunities for an architect. To a friend he wrote that he expected to "do well *in time.* But my affairs are like the Countryman's road which had a good bottom but it has a d--d long way to it."[98] In fact, his next position in Washington afforded unique opportunities for a man who had arrived in the United States only seven years earlier. From the new capital of the United States, this new American would be able to shape the public architecture of the republic and simultaneously ensure his own reputation.

3

Capital Projects

I shall never while the Arts exist in America, hold a mean
place among its Men to whom merit is Conceded.

BENJAMIN HENRY LATROBE, *Journals*, 3: 47.

IN 1798 LATROBE was traveling from Richmond to Philadelphia when
he first saw Washington, the future location of the permanent capital of
the United States. At the time it was neither town nor city. Latrobe was not
impressed, nor would he ever be. In 1790, Congress had passed legislation
moving the capital from New York to Philadelphia. Ten years later, the federal government would move again, this time to a ten-mile square on the
Potomac River designated the District of Columbia. Maryland and Virginia
had donated the land, and both states provided loans to the government to
make certain that it stayed. The Commissioners of Public Buildings had taken
it upon themselves to honor the nation's defining hero by naming the place
Washington.

Shortly thereafter, French engineer and hero of the American Revolution
Pierre L'Enfant was hired to develop a city plan, and his detailed map located
the meeting place for Congress on the site's commanding hill. A mile and a
half away he had sketched the president's home near Goose Creek, a marshy
swamp soon to be renamed Tiber Creek. The classical reference to Rome was
important to this generation of Americans. L'Enfant had also provided a plan
of grand diagonal avenues intersecting awkwardly with future city squares
and horizontal streets, an arrangement that would forever bewilder visitors.
In 1793, the president and other federal officials traveled from Philadelphia
to lay the cornerstone of the Capitol, where Congress would meet, afterward enjoying a barbecued ox. But turning intentions into physical reality
proceeded slowly. "Let us repair into the woods" became the wary expectation of legislators.[1]

Familiar with the grand political and cultural centers of Europe, Latrobe
considered the relocation from Philadelphia a mistake. The denseness of

London, with nearly a million residents, and Paris, with a half million, inspired his appreciation of population centers with compact living arrangements. So too did his early years in the planned Moravian communities of England and Saxony. Even after a decade in Washington, Latrobe urged an ornamental wall painter to stay away: it was better to work in Baltimore or Philadelphia rather than try to set up a business in "the infant and scattered establishment" of the new Federal City.[2]

Latrobe observed with distaste the republic's practice of partisan compromise and excoriated the arrangement northern Federalists had made to move the political center of the nation below the Mason-Dixon Line in exchange for southern support of the federal government's assumption of state debts from the Revolution. For what he called "this waste that the law calls the American metropolis" and "an imaginary capital," Latrobe held responsible the nation's revolutionary enthusiasms, a desire by Federalists to reelect John Adams by securing southern support and, especially, the whim of George Washington. "The idea of creating a new city better arranged in its local distribution of houses and streets, more magnificent in its public buildings and superior in the advantages of its site to any other in the world" was in fact

FIG. 3.1 View of District of Columbia and Georgetown. This eighteenth-century painting displays the rural nature of the new federal capital of the United States. Latrobe was critical of the move to Washington from the more developed urban center of Philadelphia. Library of Congress, LC-USZC4-530.

"the favorite folly of General Washington" who did little to assist the capital's development other than purchasing two "indifferent houses." Washington might know how to lead a nation into independence, according to Latrobe, but he knew nothing of the arts. At this stage everything was "badly planned and conducted," according to the critical architect who would devote years of his life to making the place a capital worthy of a great nation.[3]

In 1792, Washington and his secretary of state Thomas Jefferson had begun planning the public structures to house the government. Congress, symbol of the people's sovereignty and recipient of the first and longest article of the US Constitution, was the most important. As with so many aspects of the new republic, there was no American standard for legislative halls except for several brick state capitols, built during a period when the British colonial style was in favor. They generally resembled wealthy merchants' homes with a tacked-on cupola signifying the building's significance. In just such a structure, the former Philadelphia County Courthouse, Congress had met from 1790 to 1800. Instead, in the view of influential Americans, the appropriate precedents for truly monumental buildings lay in distant times and places. Jefferson, the amateur architect, understood this, and his design of the Virginia State Capitol in Richmond imitated the temple forms used in ancient Rome.

At the beginning of a new century, American leaders anticipated greatness and looked to Rome, not London, as an example. For Jefferson, far more than Washington, architecture had to proclaim the new nation's exceptionalism through its embrace of the classical tradition: "I am an enthusiast on the subject of the arts . . . as its object is to improve the taste of my countrymen, to increase their reputation, to reconcile to them the respect of the world and procure them its praise," wrote the man who became the country's third president.[4]

There seemed no better way to go about the process of creating such monumental structures than to supervise an architectural competition for a building to be located on Jenkins Hill, promptly renamed Capitol Hill in recognition of ancient Rome's Capitoline Hill. In Washington, Congress would no longer meet as in New York and Philadelphia in a Federal Hall or a Congress House modified for its purposes, as it had in the nation's first two capitals. Rather, a special building, to be called the US Capitol, would be constructed.

In the spring of 1792 an advertisement for a design competition appeared in newspapers from Boston to Charleston. It called for a brick building, with two large assembly rooms for the senators and representatives, capable of seating 300 persons, and several smaller meeting places. The winner would receive $500 and a lot in Washington, the runner-up $250. It was the kind of competitive arrangement that Latrobe, at the time living in London and learning his profession, would come to despise: it drew amateurs who provided elegant elevations and knew nothing of design, and it was subject to partisan favoritism from the judges.

Both Washington and Jefferson were disappointed with the applications. An early entry included a building that resembled an army barracks, another a clumsy courthouse. Still another featured a huge prairie chicken atop a poorly proportioned dome. Only one of the designers had any architectural training. Most were builders and carpenters; one was a furniture maker and another a territorial judge with no apparent experience, even in the trades that provided colonial Americans with their best buildings. The president informed the recently appointed commissioners that if nothing more worthy than these fifteen entries should appear, "the exhibition of architecture will be very dull indeed."[5] Then a late entry arrived, carried in person to Philadelphia by the English-born Dr. William Thornton from his plantation on Tortola in the British West Indies. Thornton's design of a portico framed by twelve Corinthian columns in front of a domed rotunda with two stone wings for the House and Senate satisfied both Jefferson and Washington, the latter proclaiming the plan "simple, noble, beautiful, excellently distributed and moderate in size."[6]

Thornton's design prevailed, but almost immediately its deficiencies surfaced: it would be expensive to build, the columns on the portico and rotunda were disastrously far apart, the important rooms lacked light, and a screen of columns obstructed the assembly hall. In mistakes that only an amateur could make, the staircases did not have enough headroom, and little light penetrated the Senate windows that were blocked by an arched ceiling. These shortcomings, the angry disagreements between Thornton and the supervising architects, and the difficulty of finding a labor force as well as obtaining sandstone delayed the erection of the building. But by 1799 the north wing for the Senate was mostly complete, and it was this part of the US Capitol, sitting in isolation on a prominent hill, that Benjamin Latrobe observed as he traveled north.

A year later Latrobe was living in Philadelphia when government records were loaded onto barges, and the 126 clerks and officers of the government and their families made their official move to Washington. By even eighteenth-century measures it was a small bureaucracy, and cynics joked that the entire government of the United States could fit on one barge. Most officials went by water down the Delaware and Susquehanna rivers to Havre de Grace, Maryland, then by stage coach to Lancaster and southward to Baltimore, finally arriving on the third day, if neither horse nor carriage broke down or stump, stone, or mud interfered. These were not unusual hazards: George Washington once spent two days stuck in the mud on his way from Mount Vernon to Philadelphia when his coach became wedged between two boulders.

The newcomers challenged the District's resources, as government officials hurried to find accommodations in a place with seven taverns, two hotels, and a few boarding houses. Secretary of the Treasury Oliver Wollcott correctly predicted the emergence of legislative dormitories when members of Congress (32 senators and 106 congressmen in 1800) could not find lodgings "unless they consented to live like scholars in a college or monks in a monastery, crowded ten or twenty in one house, utterly secluded from society."[7] With only four public buildings under construction, the departments of Navy, Army, Treasury, and State set up offices in temporary shacks, with their records insecurely stored in nearby warehouses.

In the fall, President John Adams arrived, only to learn a few months later that he had narrowly lost reelection. But for weeks no one knew who had won. The US Constitution failed to require electors to differentiate between president and vice president and an electoral tie had resulted between Thomas Jefferson and Aaron Burr, the anticipated vice president who refused to withdraw. Only in February after thirty-five ballots did the House of Representatives elect Thomas Jefferson.[8]

In his last message to Congress, which was still without a quorum, Adams insisted that "while the accommodations were not as complete as might be wished, yet there is great reason to believe that this inconvenience will cease with the present session."[9] Such an assurance was necessary because the idea of an ambulatory Congress moving from state to state, in similar fashion to judges who rode the circuit, persisted among those nervous about the concentration of power in one place. There was also talk of moving to Baltimore or returning to more civilized Philadelphia. Certainly the straggly village that a few residents were calling the Federal City hardly encouraged a sense of permanence.

When Abigail Adams, with her New England sense of frugality, had arrived to live in the vast, unfinished President's House, she promptly dubbed it the "Great Castle." Familiar with compact New England towns, she immediately located the city's principal failing: it was spread out with buildings too scattered for the communication of its officers. Many officials lived in

Georgetown where there was better housing, but this required riding a stage coach called the "Flying George" the three-mile distance along bumpy, rutted roads to the unfinished Capitol. The First Lady's new home on Pennsylvania Avenue had six comfortable chambers, but amid plaster and paint Abigail Adams found it convenient to hang her clothes to dry in the large, unfinished East Room. With few regrets, the Adamses returned to Massachusetts. John Adams left the morning of Jefferson's inauguration in March 1801, even before the new president declared in his conciliatory address that Americans were both Federalists and Republicans. In a subtle rebuke to his predecessor who had supported the Alien and Sedition Acts, Jefferson explained that reason and tolerance best combated error of opinion.[10]

Despite the Adamses' disdain, the federal city held future possibilities for ambitious entrepreneurs. Most assumed that the political center of the republic would bring commerce and attract, as Jefferson believed, foreigners, ambitious Americans, and manufacturers. Yet such private development would take years, at a time when the federal government had little money to spend on public works. The lots, owned by the government and intended to finance public buildings, were not selling. By 1804 there were only 109 brick houses and 200 wooden ones spread out over 100 acres, the latter mostly shacks for workers. But there was some progress.

Private builders were beginning to construct houses and hotels. A bookstore appeared on Capitol Hill, though many buildings there were still surrounded by thick brush and dense woods. Daniel Carroll, scion of Maryland's first family, a state representative to the Constitutional Convention, and one of the largest landowners in the District, was supervising the building of homes on Carroll Row, and he expected to make money from his ownership of a nearby brick kiln. English-born Thomas Law, the town's most fervent booster and husband of Martha Washington's granddaughter Eliza Custis, was constructing a row of houses on New Jersey Avenue. He was optimistic that he could sell the lots he had bought from the government.[11]

What Washington needed was people, commerce, and both private and public buildings. Without them, until well into the nineteenth century, Charles Dickens's dismissive label "the city of magnificent distances" applied. Popular Irish poet Thomas Moore, visiting in 1804, ridiculed America's pretentiousness about its capital:

In fancy now, beneath the twilight gloom,
Come let me lead thee o'er this modern Rome.

. . . And what was Goose Creek once,
Is Tiber now.
This fam'd metropolis where Fancy sees,
Squares in morasses, obelisks in trees:
Which travelling fools and gazeteers adorn,
With shrines unbuilt and heroes yet unborn.[12]

In his sweeping survey of the period, John Adams's great-grandson, the historian Henry Adams, vividly depicted Washington during these early years. Adams described a place, which was no more than an empty "fever-stricken morass," rising as a symbol of nationality "in solitude on the banks of the Potomac." Meanwhile "the half-finished White House stood in a naked field." A mile and a half away across a swamp "the shapeless, unfinished Capitol was seen, two wings without a body, ambitious enough to make more grotesque" its deserted surroundings. For Adams as for many Americans, the Capitol and President's House nevertheless represented the bold intentions of a new nation: "The conception proved that the United States understood the vastness of their task and were willing to stake something on their faith in it."[13]

In 1802, his Chesapeake and Delaware Canal enterprise undersubscribed, his private commissions stagnant, and his creditors insistent, Latrobe appealed to Jefferson for a job. His solicitation held a note of petulance and was written to impress the president with a national failing. In the United States, he wrote, he had devoted "time, talents and have incurred expence without any return. . . . The labor of the mind is not *here* supposed to be a *merchantable article*."[14] For the last twelve months he had been unemployed. His private resources were exhausted; his previous fees barely supported his family "in the enjoyment of those indulgences, and of that society in which I have been educated, and in which all my habits have been formed."[15]

In the spring of 1803, the sympathetic president, who had his own financial difficulties, responded. He appointed Latrobe to a newly created position—surveyor of public buildings. The title was borrowed from England for the man responsible for official buildings—in this case, the four federal structures under construction, but especially, given their importance and meager congressional funding, the Capitol and the President's House. The new arrangement of a surveyor and a second public appointee, Thomas Munroe, the Superintendent of the City, who administered payrolls, was intended to be an improvement on the previous system of commissioners.

Under that arrangement, during the 1790s three European-born architects, Etienne Hallet, George Hadfield, and James Hoban, had followed

Dr. William Thornton, who had proved incapable of any detailed design or supervising the process of actually creating a building. All three had fought with Thornton, each other, and the commissioners; all three had been fired for insubordination or inattention to duty. By replacing the commissioners with two appointive positions under his control, Jefferson expanded his influence on the architectural matters so important to him.

Jefferson's choice for surveyor was hardly surprising. He had known and admired Latrobe since the late 1790s when the two men had discussed a possible canal along the Rivanna River that ran through Jefferson's property but was not navigable. Latrobe had subsequently written Jefferson in hopes of his support for a commission for the design of the armory at Harper's Ferry and a new fort in Norfolk. Receiving neither, Latrobe held partisan politics responsible: "A man of my politics," he complained to Jefferson underlining his words for emphasis, "is not to be trusted in so important a case as the defence of the Country against the French."[16]

Both men were, at different times, officers of the prestigious American Philosophical Society. Often in absentia, Jefferson was the society's president for seventeen years and was living in Philadelphia as vice president of the United States when Latrobe was elected a member in 1799. A year before, just weeks after his arrival in Philadelphia, Latrobe had presented a paper to the society on the unique sand hills near Cape Henry, Virginia, the first of six papers he delivered there. Several were considered worthy of publication in the society's *Transactions*.

Some discussions among this intellectual brotherhood engaged the ongoing controversy between Jefferson and the French philosopher and naturalist Comte de Buffon. The comte had developed a theory of American degeneracy, insisting that all things in the New World, from the size of its animals to its plants and even its humans, were smaller and inferior to those in Europe, which, of course, Jefferson denied. In his *Notes on Virginia*, Jefferson had provided controverting evidence of the superiority of America's natural world—its huge mastodons, its remarkable birds, its flourishing plants, and especially its giant moose. After a long search for evidence of his contention he shipped a huge seven-foot stuffed moose to the comte. This same defensive mentality, applied to the need for exceptional public buildings, bound Jefferson and Latrobe together in a common endeavor.[17]

Their connection tightened when Jefferson asked Latrobe to design a dry dock for ships that the government could not afford to keep seaworthy but needed to preserve in these conflict-ridden days on the high seas. In the early days of his administration, Jefferson wished to reduce the size of the fleet but not destroy it, and what better way than to place these frigates retired from active duty in a building where they could easily be recalled in a national emergency. Latrobe responded with elaborate plans for a canal, locks, a basin, and a dry dock of timber arches using metal roofing and piers with individual colonnaded entrances, to be constructed near the Navy Yard on the Anacostia (East Branch) River. Jefferson had specified that the roof must resemble his architectural lodestar, the iron and glass domed grain market in Paris, the Halle aux Bles, and Latrobe had complied. But Latrobe's design, estimated to cost $200,000, was far too grand and expensive. Besides, argued several alarmed congressmen, there was no need for dry docks.

On one of his early trips to Washington Latrobe dined at the still unfinished President's House, where dinner began in midafternoon and the conversation lasted until seven. He sat next to Jefferson, he reported to his wife, noting the excellent dinner "cooked in the French style," with abundant wine, from sherry to champagne and even a few decanters of rare Spanish wine, a gift from the Spanish minister. A genial host, Jefferson said little during dinner, only "tending to the filling of plates which he did with great ease and grace for a philosopher." But after dinner the president directed the discussion, and Latrobe enjoyed "the mental treat of conversation that ranged from literature, wit, and a little business with a great deal of miscellaneous remarks on agriculture and building. There is a degree of ease in Mr. Jefferson's company that everyone seems to feel and to enjoy."[18]

With his acceptance of the surveyorship, Latrobe began his career as an architect of American public works, slightly exaggerating that he was the nation's *only* successful architect and engineer. Yet by any measure he was the nation's most talented, as well as its most experienced and best trained. Acknowledging his superiority, he wrote Christian that he had broken "the ice" for his successors: "what was more difficult destroyed the prejudices of the villainous Quacks in whose hands the public works had previously been."[19] A habitual complainer, he soon believed himself unfairly assailed by public opinion.

Seven years after his arrival in the United States, Benjamin Latrobe had signed on to design the US Capitol—an opportunity that became both an albatross and his great legacy. Certainly the building would never be his alone and that rankled. Repeatedly, as he organized the construction of the south wing for the House of Representatives, reworked the interior of the Senate wing and planned a space there for the Supreme Court and a congressional library, he dismissed his work as no more than a challenge overcome. Perhaps wary of the effect of his seeming ingratitude, he rendered the phrase in French, as not a triumph but merely "la difficulte vaincue."[20] In overcoming these difficulties, a resilient and determined Latrobe contributed his talents to the nation.

The US Capitol came with restrictions and the kinds of conflicts that challenged Latrobe's equanimity: he had to work within an external design that supposedly carried the approval of the national hero, George Washington, and a nearly complete Senate wing that was already deteriorating. Latrobe had to share his accomplishments with William Thornton and the three other architects who had briefly worked on the building before getting fired. He had to work within the uncertain budgets of the US Congress. Still he was designing during a special moment in American history when the leaders of the nation sought exceptional buildings. In the process, he had to remain faithful to the architectural principles that he intended to install, though the US Capitol would forever be a multi-authored, constantly modified structure.

Most important, he had to accept the direction of Jefferson, who even during the international crises that threatened the security of the United States, as Latrobe explained, took "a warm interest in everything that related to the design, arrangement, and management" of the building of the Capitol.[21] He had to gain agreement for the smallest of details from the president who practiced architecture as well as politics, a negotiating task Latrobe once described as "damned hard work."[22] He respected Jefferson: "My sincere wish is to be employed near you and under your direction."[23] At the same time he believed the president an amateur in matters of architecture. Yet he considered his compromises humoring the president as "a small sacrifice," given his personal attachment to Jefferson.

Still, they were a forfeiture of his autonomy. With the irony that increasingly saturated his letters, Latrobe lamented to his brother: "my magnificent appointment . . . [to] an office attended with enormous expense and a small salary, and which has hitherto furnished me with laborious employment in detecting the villanies and correcting the blunders of my predecessors."[24]

As a government employee, Latrobe barely supported his family. The expense of commuting from Philadelphia for four years, the rising costs of feeding and educating a family of five children, and his continuing speculations made it difficult to live on his salary of $1,700, even after Jefferson raised it to $2,000 in 1806. His salary never approached the 5 percent that he charged on private commissions; government service thereafter became "a ruinous connection."[25]

Problems began immediately when Latrobe delayed his departure from Philadelphia, until the president pleaded for at least a "flying trip," with the hope that repairs, rebuilding, and even the creation of the neglected south wing would be "put under full sail for the season." Congress had appropriated $50,000, and the president was optimistic that both the House and Senate could be completed in two years.[26] Until 1807 when Latrobe moved his family from Philadelphia, he was an absentee, continually urged by Jefferson to spend more time in Washington than his customary three visits a year. Dissatisfied congressmen, tired of being crowded into the library of the north wing, and senators, who dodged falling plaster in the Senate's poorly constructed meeting hall, found an easy target in Latrobe, who reciprocated by calling them "an assembly of clowns." His snobbery was evident when he discovered that one congressman was a butcher from whom he purchased his meat.[27]

Arriving for a preliminary investigation in late March 1803, Latrobe studied the US Capitol with its nearly complete north wing, an empty space in the middle, and on the south, the hastily constructed provisional chamber for the House of Representatives, nicknamed "the oven" because of its poor ventilation and resemblance to a gigantic Dutch oven. Within two weeks he had produced a fifty-six-page document of suggestions that may have disheartened the president who had promised representatives a proper home by 1805.

Latrobe's report on the Capitol was detailed, critical of Thornton's plan, and full of his own remedies. He had discovered multiple flaws in Thornton's design for the House of Representatives: the placement of the main floor required ascending a flight of stairs and then immediately descending more stairs to reach the legislative hall. There was not enough space for offices and committee rooms. The circulation was poor, forcing legislators to walk through a public lobby to reach their assembly room. The proposed 90-by-120 foot dome, rising 60 feet from the ground, could not be supported by the foundation walls. There was no coordination between the exterior wall of the south wing and the placement of windows and interior piers. The oval shape required cutting stone into complex individualized patterns.

Besides these elementary design errors, there were aesthetic flaws that Latrobe meant to improve, principally the elliptical (oval) shape of the House assembly room. "The eye is habituated to judge of circles and orthographical figures, but ellipses occur seldom. . . . They have a distorted effect." They were nothing more than an ugly unnatural remnant from an earlier period and had rarely appeared in Roman and Greek buildings. And on this point the ever-vigilant Jefferson agreed.[28]

More immediate than the change in design was the necessity of tearing down the poorly constructed walls and foundation of the north wing. In Virginia, Jefferson delighted in remodeling his home Monticello. But in Washington there was a need for permanence and observable progress in this very visible structure on a commanding hill. As deteriorating wooden walls were torn down, senators found themselves crammed into the north wing. Meanwhile, anxious residents of the town of 3,000 worried that the federal government, their insurance for prosperity, would move. After returning to Washington in the fall after his usual three months in Virginia, Jefferson was disappointed: the removal of the foundations was not proceeding quickly enough.[29]

For the next five years, Jefferson's practical requirements and artistic preferences collided with Latrobe's sometimes excessive, expensive perfectionism and his commitment to Greek, not Roman, precedents. The architect was a self-proclaimed "bigotted Greek" in his tastes, while the president admired buildings that followed the heavier Roman style that he had idolized in France. [30]Jefferson accepted replicas; Latrobe intended architectural expressions in a new style worthy of a nation rebuilding the world politically, inspired but not dictated by the past, as a painting to a model. And he had brought with him the talent to create architectural solutions that differed from those of the past.

Jefferson believed—and in fact had been warned—that Latrobe was extravagant; at the same time, Latrobe considered Jefferson an amateur who "fished his designs out of old books."[31] Jefferson, in Latrobe's judgment, was too cautious and never "pressed his opinions on Congress." Yet it remained "a small sacrifice to humor" the president. Latrobe "aspired" to be under his direction—"an instrument in your hands"—at the same time that Jefferson appreciated Latrobe's genius.[32]

The two men differed in temperament: Jefferson was ever diplomatic, calm, nonconfrontational, occasionally stubborn, but lacking the sense of presidential lese-majesty that would have doomed this relationship. Meanwhile, Latrobe, a professional architect but amateur politician, was filled with certainty, a distaste for authority, and a rebel's sense of persecution and injustice. Jefferson celebrated human nature and the virtue of human beings; the more pessimistic Latrobe believed "men owed each other mutual forebearance because all are imperfect and faulty."[33] Once, when Latrobe inadvertently addressed a letter to Jefferson criticizing the president's architectural taste, Jefferson simply overlooked the slight. In similar circumstances Latrobe would not have done so.

These differences in outlook tested but never destroyed their mutual respect because both men agreed on the larger enterprise of creating a heroic
structure that would be a focal point of the nation. They agreed that externally
the US Capitol must employ the temple design of the public buildings that
had been the people's meeting places in Greece and in Rome's Pantheon. It
had to be accessible, a place of dignity that did not glorify individual leaders.
Certainly it could not be hierarchical in the manner of cathedrals with their
pointed triangles, soaring spaces, and raised podiums for the clergy. It had to
be, as architectural historian Pamela Scott has written, a temple with a central
assembly room and smaller legislative rooms for committees where this new
secular religion of liberty would be installed. Finally, it had to be a structure
that improved and educated the taste of the country.[34]

Throughout Jefferson's two presidential terms, the two men negotiated
the details of the building along with the challenge of obtaining funding
from a frugal Congress. To save money, Jefferson urged wooden, rather than
stone, columns. Latrobe responded in a letter to John Lenthall, his on-site
clerk: "The wooden column idea is one with which I never will have anything
to do. . . . I will give up my office sooner than build a temple of disgrace to
myself and Mr. Jefferson. But he has too much good sense to persevere in his
conceptions, after hearing all that is to be said against them."[35] On this matter
Latrobe was persuasive. After negotiating their differences, they compromised
on a version of stone Corinthian columns in the style of the famed Choragic
Monument of Lysicrates in Athens.[36]

Learning that appeals to economy, practicality, and beauty were the most
effective ways to gain Jefferson's agreement, Latrobe used all three approaches
when their most significant disagreement emerged over light, specifically,
how to light the congressmen's assembly room in the south wing. Jefferson
insisted on skylights, small horizontal panes of glass between the ribs of the
dome as in the Halle aux Bles, whose lighting he considered the most daz-
zling architectural triumph in the world. Latrobe preferred lanterns, the vertical panes of glass of a cupola, arguing that the impractical skylights leaked
and clouded over. In a preview of the ideals of modern architectural practice,
Latrobe presented to Jefferson the conundrum he considered an unnecessary
choice: "Can beauty still be sacrificed to the *certainty* of practical security?"[37]
As in all his designs, he expected the lanterns on the Capitol would be beautiful as well as practical, because they would relieve the insipidness of the
building's rectangular mass.

Jefferson responded that he had never seen a cupola in ancient times; in
fact they were "one of the degeneracies of modern architecture."[38] Seeking

solidity in all matters architectural, Latrobe replied that the flickering light from skylights was too fragmented and dispersed, even to the point of creating a diversion in its episodic nature: "the spangled ceiling giving an air of gaiety that would destroy the solemnity" necessary for legislative deliberations. According to his architectural ideals, "As all the Architecture is solid and projected, its whole Effect will be lost by the destruction of *determinate shadows,* on which it depends. Every piece of Architecture, as well as of Sculpture, and every painting even, requires, to be advantageously seen, a *Unity of light.* I cannot conceive anything more harmonious, and even magnificent, than this room would be, if lighted by a large Mass of Central light."[39] But, of course, he would defer to Jefferson. On this matter the president refused to compromise: "It is with real pain I oppose myself to your passion for the lanthern and that in a matter of taste, I differ from a professor in his own art."[40]

But when the special glass ordered from Germany was delayed—the result of Jefferson's trade embargo—the headstrong Latrobe circumvented Jefferson and created a temporary roof that would accommodate lanterns. In a rare display of anger, Jefferson reacted to a matter he considered settled: "the plan established had been departed from, that it was wrong, and that it must be recurred to, by having the pannels immediately prepared. . . . I certainly should not abandon a plan which I believe will constitute one of the important beauties of the building on the hypothesis that it may occasion a dripping by condensed vapour."[41]

A contrite Latrobe was "mortified" that he had displeased the president. Acknowledging a wrong that must be repaired, though he seldom did so when he felt he had done his duty, as he felt he had in this instance, Latrobe prolonged the dispute in his letter of apology. He continued to make the case for lanterns, on the grounds that leaking skylights would destroy his reputation. He offered the argument to authority: in his experience as a professional architect, lanterns were the practical choice. For this conviction he offered the explanation popular with later architects: "For nothing in the eye of good taste (which ought never to be at warfare with good sense) can be beautiful which appears useless or unmeaning." "Magnificence," though he always strove for that, "is easily bought by expense and is infinitely less important than utility."[42] It went without saying that the Jeffersonian skylights failed the tests of good sense, beauty, and utility.

Declining to continue the controversy, Jefferson responded with friendly salutations and assurances of esteem and respect for the sensitive architect. The president held no "sentiment unfriendly to you. I saw a departure from the plan and it was my duty to bring it back to its course."[43] A few weeks later an elegant watercolor of the US Capitol, drawn with all three sections complete and signed B. H. Latrobe, arrived at the President's House, inscribed to Thomas Jefferson, a president who resolutely refused to accept gifts. As for the offending skylights, when frost cracked the putty around their frames, they leaked after rainstorms, as Latrobe had predicted. Eventually Latrobe designed a new way to deal with the moisture by sealing the glass panels on three sides in a wooden frame angled at the top to shed water.[44]

Latrobe hired the capable, English-born John Lenthall as his on-site clerk of the works. While the directors of the floundering Chesapeake and Delaware Canal Company kept Latrobe from moving to Washington, Lenthall hired both white workmen and cheaper, hired-out enslaved black men who could be rented from their owners for $60 a year. The existence of 3,500 enslaved in the Washington-Georgetown-Alexandria and nearby Maryland areas depressed the wages of free laborers to rates well below those in northern cities.

FIG. 3.2 Latrobe's 1806 Perspective View of the East and North Fronts of the US Capitol. Jefferson and Latrobe disagreed about the external lighting of the Capitol. After one of their disagreements, Latrobe sent this watercolor of the Capitol viewed from the northeast to the president. It conveys his overall concept for the building with two wings for the legislative bodies graced by two cupolas and a low saucer dome over the rotunda. Library of Congress.

At the same time, these historically overlooked African American craftsmen—skilled carpenters, iron workers, and laborers, some from nearby farms, others from Maryland's southern counties—helped to construct the most important public building in a nation that enslaved them.[45]

For both blacks and whites, employment in Washington was dangerous, given the unhealthy living conditions in primitive huts and the continuing threat of malaria and yellow fever. Congressional budgeting never permitted hiring for more than a season and even that was uncertain. Somehow the conscientious but irascible Lenthall found a labor force, while coordinating the delivery of materials, supervising the actual construction, listening to Jefferson's complaints about the increasing delays, and complaining about his own $3.66 daily wage, which, after Latrobe's intervention, Jefferson raised to $4.00.

Meanwhile Latrobe hired the experts: a special artistic painter George Bridport for the ceilings, the talented plasterer William Thackara, and another Philadelphian, the upholsterer John Rea, to make the heavy red and gold drapes intended to improve acoustics. He searched as well for materials. Of immediate importance was finding proper sandstone, the principal external building material of the Capitol. Latrobe insisted it must be handsome, available in great quantities, and malleable to the chisels and finishing of the nation's few expert stonemasons. He knew all about sandstone from his earlier excursions in Virginia where, after investigating the sand hills near Cape Henry, he concluded that the quality of its stone was the result of the winds along its coast in prehistoric times.[46]

In his role as surveyor Latrobe visited several quarries and was especially impressed with the sandstone from William Robertson's, near Aquia Creek in northern Virginia. One trip, requiring an overnight stay in Robertson's log cabin, came with a warning not to mind the rats. In Latrobe's account he was awakened by noises: "the hurry of animals was incessant." Soon "an uproar" across, around, and under his bed kept him awake until the intruders moved upstairs, having finished eating the basket of eggs under his bed. Then a rat, making its escape from the drawer of an overturned desk, bit his host, and "there was an end of all possibility of sleeping for the remainder of the night."[47]

Such lighthearted stories, a staple of his earlier journal entries illustrating the absurdities of human life, became infrequent as the turmoil of professional life overtook a man who considered himself "naturally of a most cheerful disposition," though, admittedly, "I find infinite satisfaction in grumbling and complaining."[48] Latrobe was a self-described "croaker," though "I have upon the whole enjoyed much happiness and success in the course of my life." It was the circumstances of his calling that occasionally made him miserable: "When shall my whole life cease to be exertion without thanks, labor without gaining a competence, vexation without a prospect of termination. Will it be when I am old, and decrepid, and impotent and blunted in my feelings? . . . We are wheels in the same machine and must move with the cogs that press us," he advised his religious brother, who thought otherwise.[49]

Both Jefferson and Latrobe agreed on the necessity of hiring Italians to carve the 24 columns, 2.5 feet in diameter and 147 feet in height, topped by intricate Corinthian capitals, intended for the interior of the representatives' assembly hall. They hoped to import the famed Carrara marble from Italy for the major statues, but this proved far too expensive. In Latrobe's architecture, columns with Greek capitals and handsome entablature (the material resting on the top of the columns including the cornice and frieze) emerged as one of the distinctive features of the meeting hall of the House of Representatives and in fact the entire US Capitol. But in its infant state the United States had only indifferent carvers.

When Canova, Napoleon's official court sculptor and in Latrobe's view "the best Italian and first European Artist," was not available, Latrobe appealed to Philip Mazzei, an Italian physician and horticulturalist. Mazzei had come to America before the Revolution and, intent on introducing Italian grapes and olives into Virginia, had become friends with Thomas Jefferson, who shared his interest in agriculture. Now, years after Mazzei had returned to Pisa, Latrobe enlisted his help "by direction of the President of the United States." Latrobe explained: "My object is to procure *a first-rate Sculptor* in the particular branch of *Architectural Decoration.*"[50]

In February 1806, two young Italian sculptors, Guiseppe Franzoni and Giovanni Andrei, both recruited by Mazzei, along their wives and children, arrived in Washington to begin their work, at first with clay and plaster models and then with more durable sandstone and marble. Years of labor awaited, both in Washington and in nearby Baltimore, whenever congressional spending faltered. While Andrei worked on the decorative frieze of figures personifying agriculture, commerce, art, and science, Franzoni began carving two symbols of Americana: Liberty, a serene, peaceful female, and the American eagle, the sign of national power.

Latrobe intended that these statues, placed behind the speaker's desk and in front of a window, would be the principal decoration of the legislative hall.

Both were immense—the seated Liberty specified by Latrobe was to be a precise eight feet, six inches tall and the eagle, fourteen feet from tip to tip of its wings. Expressing the European artistic superiority that irritated Americans, Mazzei had warned Latrobe that both statues should be done in Rome because there "the mind of the Artist is sublimed, if I can say so, by the sight of so many and so grand Objects."[51]

In fact, Franzoni's eagle, when finished in clay, looked foreign and did not suit. "It is an Italian, or a Roman, or a Greek Eagle and I want an American bald eagle," explained Latrobe in an appeal to his friend Charles Willson Peale, whose natural history museum in Philadelphia included all manner of the nation's beasts and birds as well as the mastodon excavated from along the Hudson River. Latrobe requested a drawing of the head and claws of the bald eagle for his Italian sculptor so that there would be no inexactness: "any glaring impropriety of Character would be immediately detected by our Western members."[52] What arrived was a box containing the actual head and neck of an American eagle, with the request that it be returned so that Peale could continue to use it in his popular lectures on America's exceptional birds. The result—"a scrupulously correct copy of the head of the bald eagle peculiar to our country"—was a realistic marble representation that took its place alongside Liberty.[53]

Throughout his surveyorship, Latrobe found his work undermined by the uncertainty of congressional appropriations. At the beginning of each building year he never knew how much money there would be and when it would be available. Doubts about payrolls affected the recruitment of workmen whose skills were marketable in other East Coast cities and who usually signed up for a year's labor at the beginning of the year, months before Congress voted on its appropriation bills. Latrobe began in 1803 with what Jefferson considered the generous amount of $50,000, approximately $1 million today; in 1804 another $50,000 was appropriated, with the expectation that such generosity would be sufficient. In 1805, Congress, with the House increasingly anxious to inhabit its permanent quarters, voted $110,000 for the south wing and $20,000 for other public works, including the President's House. In 1806, another $40,000 was voted; in just three years the still homeless House of Representatives had appropriated $270,000 for public buildings, most designated for the still unfinished Capitol.

Jefferson, anxious to keep his promises to legislators, refused any use of public money for his residence where, except for his food and wine expenditures, he lived frugally. But the building of the south wing and the repairs on the poorly constructed north wing drained whatever funds were available, and Latrobe was forever overbudget, overpromised, and, in the view of an increasing number of critics, underperforming.

Despite his explanations—the difficulty of procuring workers and materials, his illness at a critical point in 1806, the previous poor design, and Jefferson's faulty predictions about when they would be in the Hall of the House—congressmen held Latrobe responsible. Although Thomas Munroe was nominally in charge of the accounts, the more prominent Latrobe attracted the criticism. In 1807 Jefferson lectured the architect about a deficit of $51,500 and the responsibility of public officials in a republic: "The lesson of the last year has been a serious one: it has done you great injury, and has been much felt by myself. It was so contrary to the principles of our government, which make the representatives of the people the sole arbiters of the public expence, and do not permit any work to be forced on them on a larger scale than their judgment deems adapted to the circumstances of the nation." And then to lessen the sting, Jefferson ended his letter "I salute you with esteem and respect."[54]

In 1806, Virginia congressman John Randolph demanded a specific accounting of what he labeled "the sea of expense" to be expected because "artists are not good in money matters." Others noted that "the conduct of persons employed always fell short of promise." By 1807, Latrobe had become the subject of a week's debate, as Congress moved from anger to cynicism. Andrew Gregg of Pennsylvania believed that little had been done in seven years, and he had no hope that the Capitol would be finished in seven more. Some representatives wanted to abandon Washington for Baltimore or Philadelphia.

At a time in American history when state capitals moved frequently, the national government might follow suit. A few argued that the legislature should relocate to the largely completed President's House. But Philip Van Cortlandt of New York responded that the lack of money was the principal reason that the building was not finished. John Jackson of Virginia wondered how one room—the assembly hall of the House of Representatives that was in the process of becoming Latrobe's masterpiece—cost so much and took so long.

When Jefferson's son-in-law John Eppes attacked Latrobe as abusing the nation's trust, the architect feared that criticism from a family member represented the president's thinking until Jefferson assured him that Eppes spoke only for himself. Congressman Jackson wondered why gilded chairs and plated tables were necessary. He encouraged "the economy of old times," surely understood by a president with such simple republican tastes that he greeted his guests in old jackets and slippers. Ten thousand dollars was sufficient to build and furnish a splendid house, especially since in these perilous times, with the republic threatened by France and Great Britain, $20,000 was all that was spent on new fortifications.[55]

Legislators worried that the Capitol was becoming too grand and luxurious, a monument of extravagance similar to the palaces of monarchs. As for the architect, several congressmen noted, he was rarely in Washington. They suspected that he had gone off to find another job. On the contrary, said others, the work on the US Capitol proceeded slowly so that Latrobe could continue to collect his salary—another example of the corrupt use of patronage, a failing of the British government despised by all good patriots.[56] It was enough vitriol for the surveyor to contemplate resigning.

Unlike Jefferson, who often found himself the butt of harsh partisan complaints and sometimes responded by inviting his critics to dinner, Latrobe never let an insult go unanswered. In the fall of 1806 he took the unusual step of defending himself in a *"Private Letter to the Individual Members of Congress on the Subject of the Public Buildings of the United States in Washington."* More than 7,000 words long, the pamphlet was printed at Latrobe's expense and distributed to all 176 members of the Ninth Congress. Justifying his letter as a response to the "printed abuse" against him, Latrobe noted the multiple hazards he had suffered from the very beginning. The money from real estate lots in the city had been designated to support the building of the Capitol, a process intended to make its funding independent of uncertain congressional budgets. But only a handful of lots had sold.

Next Latrobe detailed the ways in which public funds had been used and the progress he had accomplished. He justified the delays as the result of obstacles that ranged from the difficulty of finding good sandstone to a recent illness that had prevented his presence in Washington. He complained of the initial competitive design process organized after a public advertisement that encouraged submissions from "all the personal vanity of those who think they have knowledge and taste in an art which they never had an opportunity to learn and or practice, and . . . of all those who know of design nothing but its execution." He expressed his disappointment when he first saw the Capitol: "All my ideas of good taste and even of good sense in architecture were shocked by the style of the building."[57]

Along with the insults to William Thornton, Latrobe lectured Congress on the "need for graceful and refined simplicity in architecture." He highlighted the perfection of "the chaste and simple buildings of the best days of Athens." But such ideas were novel to most congressmen. For those who had some knowledge and interest, Latrobe explained that his architecture was special: "All the books for the last hundred years up to 1760 are against me." Yet in a society like the United States the arts, including building, continued to improve, moving inexorably toward the beauty of simplicity. Just as the United States had established itself on revolutionary political ideals, so its architecture would follow similar progressive transformations. His letter was a tour de force, perhaps too long for busy congressmen to read, but sufficient for his own sense of personal justification.[58]

It did not amuse William Thornton. Latrobe and Thornton had been exchanging insults for over two years, at first privately when Latrobe's plan for the Capitol required changes in Thornton's defective design. Initially they had been friendly acquaintances; Thornton had showed Latrobe around the north wing of the Capitol. Later Thornton had invited the Latrobes to a party at his home; their wives had exchanged mutual calls in a relationship that helped establish the Latrobes socially. Thornton, an official in the Patent Office embedded in Washington's bureaucracy, had sent Latrobe his pamphlet on "Negro Emancipation."

But as Latrobe's changes in Thornton's design continued and he no longer muted his criticism, the relationship shifted to antagonism. Latrobe complained of the "radical errors," "imperfect sketches," "wholly impracticable parts," and general deficiencies of the Capitol, most attributable to Thornton. Jefferson, ever polite and nonconfrontational, encouraged Latrobe to call on Thornton, and a disastrous meeting took place. Following a subsequent exchange of angry letters, Latrobe found himself "at open war with Dr. Thornton . . . which according to the fashion ought to produce a *rencontre* with a brace of pistols."[59] A duel, the ritual of gentlemen anxious to defend their honor, might have occurred, like the famous one between Alexander Hamilton and Aaron Burr that took place a few months later.[60] With their mutual appreciation of a good insult, Thornton and Latrobe preferred words that ridiculed and mocked to pistols or swords.[61]

Latrobe's differences with Thornton emerged from his deeply held views about the theory and practice of architecture and his place in the profession he intended to develop in the United States. For Latrobe, Thornton was an amateur imposter who had only studied architecture for two weeks in the Philadelphia Library. He personified the incapacity of the untrained: "That you should be so very imperfect in the theory and wholly deficient in the practise of the Art, cannot astonish me who have from my childhood studied and for 15 Years practiced the profession and yet daily feel how very far my acquirements in the science and execution of this complicated art, are below those of many Men whom I have known. . . . It is impossible that you should ever be on a level with me, excepting in your own opinion." "Open hostility is safer than insidious friendship. . . . I now stand on the same ground from which you drove Hallet and Hatfield to ruin," he wrote, referring to the architects who had previously worked on the Capitol and who had been undermined by Thornton.[62]

Amateur or not, Thornton could never accept any modifications of his design, much less rejection by Latrobe. And so he responded to Latrobe's *Letter* with a so-called *Index*, purporting to be Latrobe's own commentary, though its author was no secret. It was delivered to congressmen on the final day of the March 1807 session. Noting Latrobe's "happy and original mode of stuffing private malice into a public report," Thornton, writing as Latrobe, offered apologies for not being in Washington "which excuse may extend to the whole work and apologies for the slow progress." There were technical comments especially about Latrobe's taste for simplicity: "On reflection," Thornton has Latrobe writing, "I must admit that the style of the Capitol is very plain. . . . I differ with every great architect for these three or four hundred years."[63]

The feud continued in the newspapers. With the Capitol an increasingly visible statement of Latrobe's competence as an architect, Thornton's attacks turned personal in a series of inflammatory letters assailing Latrobe's character in the *Washington Federalist*. Latrobe, according to Thornton, had come to the United States as a Moravian missionary, intent on proselytizing. In England he had done no more than carve chimney pieces. Latrobe, who had "mutilated" the Capitol with his changes, had also changed his name which originally included the surname Bonneval. "He says he is an American . . . but is an Englishman by birth." George Washington had not trusted him. "If Diogenes had now lived, he would never have blown out his candle on meeting Mr. Latrobe."[64]

After this challenge to his integrity, Latrobe filed suit for libel, hiring the high-profile lawyer John Law and demanding $10,000 in damages. In turn, the combative Thornton turned to another well-known lawyer, Marylander Francis Scott Key, who successfully delayed the case by replying that he was not ready to go to court. Finally, five years later in 1813, the judge called the case to trial. Latrobe won a verdict of libel against Thornton and was awarded court costs and one penny. A moral if not financial victory for Latrobe, the suit had at least stopped the mutual attacks. Latrobe advised his son Henry that "this plague is therefore off the list of those which have for some time beset me."[65]

Along with his work on the Capitol as surveyor of public buildings, Latrobe worked on the Naval Yard where he built shops, sheds, and storage buildings, all of which he dismissed as nuisances. An advocate of imposing entrances, he devoted more time to a triumphal arch. It was similar to those in Rome, with guard rooms between the inner and outer entrances, two Doric columns on each side, and topped by an eagle and an anchor carved by Franzoni. Known as the Latrobe Gate, it survives today at the entrance to the Naval Yard, and is a worthy specimen of Latrobe's intentions that public buildings, through their style and materials, express the nation's importance.

Latrobe was also responsible for the incomplete President's House and its landscaping. In his first plan he relocated roads, built a stone wall around the immediate private grounds, and graded the southern exterior. There he planned an informal English garden in the natural landscape style of the famous Capability Brown. As for the President's House itself, Latrobe continued to scorn it as "indifferently executed" and "a mutilated copy of a badly designed building near Dublin," referring to the unimaginative residence of the Duke of Leinster.[66]

The interior of the President's House failed Latrobe's tests for efficiency and beauty, the entrance hall no more than a "bloated stomach." He labeled Jefferson's scheme of a colonnade connecting the President's House and the Treasury and War Offices "a litter of pigs worthy of the great sow it surrounds and of the Irish boar the father of her."[67] Yet, bowing to Jefferson, he executed the colonnade which, over time, has proved a popular feature of the White House campus. He also developed plans for an improved interior with small oval rooms and for the exterior, the dramatic north portico. Although it was not built under his direction, the portico became the hallmark of an otherwise bland structure.

Later Latrobe worked with Dolley Madison on the furnishings for the House, choosing carpets, furniture, mirrors, and lighting fixtures. In 1809, Congress appropriated $14,000 for new furnishings for the President's House, and Latrobe drew on his past collaboration with his clients Mary and William Waln. For one of his most important houses in Philadelphia—what he constructed as his ideal "rational house"—he had worked with Mary Waln on the interior furnishings.[68] In doing so, far ahead of his times, he established the primacy of the architect over the entire building—from choosing the exterior material to the placement of rooms and their furnishings. In another progressive change he included women in the process. Supported by Latrobe, Mary Waln participated in decisions about the interior decoration of her

FIG. 3.3 Elevation of the East Front of the President's House. As surveyor of public buildings in the nation's capital, Latrobe was in charge of completing the White House as well as the Capitol. He considered the President's House a bad copy of an ugly building in Dublin. His eventual contributions, besides landscaping, were ideas for the portico on the north side and the columned bow on the south side. Library of Congress, LC-DIG-ppmsca-2368.

home, an early expression of what some historians call "domestic feminism." Of this process there was no better example than Dolley Madison.

Latrobe persuaded the ambitious First Lady to purchase American, not French, furnishings, and he designed chairs and sofas in the Grecian style, using lyres and vines as painted decoration for these classically influenced klismos chairs and settees. Rather than the traditional red, yellow, and gilded decoration for the walls, he used American colors—red and blue. With his wife Mary's help, Latrobe purchased the expensive mirrors that made Dolley Madison's parlor room a sparkling public stage for entertaining.[69]

Finally, in 1807, after four years of commuting, Latrobe moved his wife and their five children to Washington. Almost immediately after their arrival, he left for Richmond. He had been called to testify before the grand jury in the indictment proceedings against Aaron Burr, who was accused of a treasonous conspiracy to foment revolution in the American West with the help of the

Spanish. Officials, especially Jefferson, believed that Burr's intention was to establish an independent empire. Latrobe had known Burr in Philadelphia and Washington, and the two shared common interests in land speculation and western development.

It was Burr who encouraged Latrobe to compete, unsuccessfully, for the commission to design New York's city hall. Later Burr solicited Latrobe to survey the site for a proposed canal around the Ohio River falls in Louisville. Another request came in 1806 when Burr asked Latrobe to recruit 500 Irish laborers, recently unemployed after the failure of the Chesapeake and Delaware Canal Company. Burr's enemies believed that these workers, once in Ohio, would be recruited as soldiers in a possible military conspiracy against the federal government. Burr offered Latrobe land in Louisiana, which he refused.

Latrobe's involvement with Burr, while tangential, was sufficient to warrant a subpoena and a trip to Richmond. There Latrobe willingly explained that his "connexion with Burr, [was] a connexion which called merely for statement, not defence."[70] The architect was not called to testify as a government witness. His main contribution was to inspect the rooms in the tavern where Burr was temporarily sequestered and to add several safety features such as wooden bars and a stronger door to ensure that Burr could not escape.

The Latrobe family arrived in Washington in time to observe the celebration of the completion of the Assembly Hall for representatives where in the fall the Ninth Congress of the United States would convene. True to Latrobe's principles, practical matters had been taken care of in the basement: there were more committee rooms as well as "water closets in the most retired part of the story."[71] In the assembly hall, Franzoni's plaster versions of Liberty and the American eagle were complete, awaiting their more permanent versions in the Vermont marble Latrobe considered as excellent as any in Italy.

Liberty held a classic liberty cap in one hand and in the other, a scroll representing the US Constitution; at her feet a footstool represented the disgraced English monarchy. In this south wing of the Capitol, Latrobe practiced his ideals of simplicity: there was little decoration save for Franzoni's statues, and on the opposite wall the frieze by Andrei of four figures representing art, science, agriculture, and commerce. Instead the glory of the space rested in elements of architecture: the proportions and shape of the room, the grandeur of the marble columns placed on a raised bank around the room, the placement of the windows, and even the saucer dome, albeit with Jefferson's skylights. Like Latrobe's Bank of Pennsylvania it was so simple and so beautiful.[72]

The editor of the *National Intelligencer* praised the room as "a chef d'oeuvre of architectural skill," no surprise to those who had looked at the plans and were acquainted "with the talents of the Architect." It was "the handsomest room in the world occupied by a deliberative body. . . . [O]n entering it, the

FIG. 3.4 This painstaking digital recreation of Latrobe's Assembly Room for the House of Representatives conveys the splendor of Latrobe's interior design. Its vast space also reveals the reasons for the complaints by House members that they could not hear each other's speeches. The British destroyed this room during their attack on Washington in 1814. Latrobe rebuilt it in 1816. Richard Chenoweth, Architect.

spectator feels a new and strong sensation of pleasure, from the splendor and elegance of all that surrounds him."[73]

Jefferson and Latrobe exchanged compliments over their success in conveying the nation's greatness through architecture. Such a room would provide a teaching tool to improve American taste. As Latrobe wrote Jefferson: "It is no flattery to say that *you* have planted the arts in your country. The works already erected in this city are the monuments of your judgement and of your zeal, and of your taste. . . . As to myself, I am not ashamed to say, that my pride is not a little flattered, and my professional ambition roused, when I think that my grandchildren may at some future day read that after the turbulence of revolution and of faction which characterized the first two presidencies, their ancestor was the instrument in *your* hands to decorate the tranquility, the prosperity, and the happiness of your Government."[74] Jefferson replied with his ultimate praise: the US Capitol, besides being "a durable and an honorable monument of our infant republic," would be favorably compared "with the remains of the same kind in the antient republics of Greece and Rome."[75] Latrobe, he believed, was the only person in the United States who could have executed such a building.

But there was also criticism characterized by Latrobe as "abuse," especially regarding the acoustics and the heat. Congressman John Randolph could not hear the speaker and found the hall "admirably suited to everything except that purpose required for debate." Latrobe dismissed the perpetually cranky Virginia congressman as "sick, disappointed and always crazy."[76] But when others grumbled about the distracting echoes, Latrobe responded that the debates were sufficiently audible to be accurately reported. Still he ordered heavy drapes to cloak the sound that reverberated in a vast space measuring 110 by 86 feet with a height 55 feet. By late fall there were complaints about the cold, after which Latrobe delivered an ingenious solution by applying steam heat delivered through iron pipes. Even for those elected officials without specific objections, the Capitol seemed too grand and luxurious for a nation that had recently overthrown a monarchy steeped in such lavish materialism.

It was customary to celebrate the completion of public buildings with a feast honoring the workmen, and Latrobe organized such a festive evening in the fall of 1807. Nearly two hundred of those who had worked on the building— chiseling, lifting, carrying, moving, hammering, mortaring, and plastering—enjoyed the music, drinking, and toasts. But to Latrobe's irritation John Lenthall, the clerk of the works, never appeared: "Your seat remained empty like Banquo's, but neither you or your ghost appeared." Over the last year of construction, the relationship between the two men had deteriorated. Lenthall complained of being overlooked, underpaid, and rarely informed of Latrobe's intentions. He had not attended, he explained, because Latrobe, whether from frugality or snobbery, had not invited all the workmen, a group that did not include the enslaved but did include white laborers. For Latrobe, Lenthall's reaction had "contrived to spoil the pleasure of the entertainment for *me* at least"—another ruined success for the architect.[77] By the end of the year the relationship had been repaired, and Latrobe was again writing to his "dear friend" Lenthall. So it continued until 1808.

That year Latrobe turned his attention to the north wing of the Capitol where two branches of the federal government still coexisted: the legislature and the judiciary, along with the Library of Congress. Earlier he had supervised the necessary repairs in a structure that had been sloppily constructed: the roof leaked after only a few years, the timber had rotted, the plaster was falling, and the walls (in the idiom of the day) were "swagging." With the south wing complete Latrobe intended to do more than repair: he would alter the interior, according to a plan that Jefferson had approved. Work began after the Senate moved to the first floor and Latrobe turned the chamber into a hippodrome—an intimate theater like those in ancient Greece similar to the one he had just completed for a semicircular lecture hall and domed amphitheater for anatomy classes at the University of Pennsylvania.

First, he redesigned a space for the Supreme Court to give that body a permanent room below the Senate. The awe-inspiring design for the Court featured a shallow dome with extraordinary conically shaped vaulting, the latter Latrobe's specialty. There would be room there as well for the US Circuit Court whose members earlier had found Long's tavern on Pennsylvania Avenue more convenient and warmer than its location in the north wing. Latrobe had hopes that his design would be carried out for an elegant congressional library with Egyptian-style decorations and three levels of stacks. By September, all the room's arches and vaults were complete as well as its half dome. It was time to lower the buttressing framework that Lenthall, well known for his understanding of the mechanics of vaulting, had installed in a novel, cheaper arrangement, approved, but not entirely endorsed, by Latrobe.[78]

As the workman lowered the centering, there was a loud crack and then, in a catastrophic architectural failure, the arch and vault collapsed. With that, part of the Senate floor above fell. The four workmen underneath escaped, but Lenthall, a single step from safety, was crushed by tons of mortar and brick. "That he at last fell victim to his zeal for the public service, which always outstripped all regard to his own interest, convenience and safety, is . . . deplored by all who acted with him," wrote Latrobe in his explanation to the Washington newspapers.[79] With Jefferson, Latrobe was more candid: in public he must accept responsibility, but in fact Lenthall's "anxiety to save expense, and afterwards, his fears of the failure of his project were the real causes of the fall of the Vault."[80]

As for the other arches and vaults above the Senate, they were sound. "Let those who wish for satisfaction visit the building," dared the beleaguered architect to his critics.[81] The arch and vault were promptly and inexpensively rebuilt in a three-bay arcade with stone columns and piers, but the disaster destroyed Latrobe's already tenuous standing with Congress. And it irritated Jefferson when he asked for an additional $700, claiming compensation for extra duties after Lenthall's death.[82]

By the spring of 1809, Latrobe had also lost his presidential leverage. After two terms Jefferson had retired to Monticello from what he called "the splendid misery of the presidency" with "unfeigned joy."[83] His successor, James Madison, had less interest in architecture and more concern about Latrobe's extravagance with public money. In fact the new president had been warned by Jefferson that with Latrobe "the reins must be held with firmness."[84] Congress, ever suspicious of Latrobe's estimates, paid little attention to the architect's reports and requests, considered even more frivolous once the Capitol was mostly complete except for its center section.

Congress had more critical issues to consider: American neutrality was constantly challenged on the Atlantic Ocean by both the British and the French vessels that harassed American shipping and, in the egregious violations by Great Britain, impressed supposed British nationals serving on better-paying American ships. Meanwhile Jefferson's controversial efforts to isolate the United States from international turmoil with his embargo and limitations on trade had reduced the customs fees on which the national budget depended. As war loomed, Congress established a committee to investigate the expenses of the Capitol. Rather than charging him with malfeasance, as his enemies hoped, the committee vindicated Latrobe.

In his defense Latrobe offered his own calculations. The north Senate wing had cost $457,000; the south House wing for which he was entirely responsible $329,000, the differential a clear indication of the benefits of his good design. The center, connecting the two wings, remained unbuilt, though Jefferson hoped that Latrobe would design the middle building "embellishing with Athenian taste the course of a nation looking far beyond the range of Athenian destinies."[85] To one critic, Thomas Law, who asserted that everybody condemned his design, Latrobe maintained that he was indifferent to

both praise and censure. The larger point went to the expectations of the republic: "It may indeed be said that as good laws may be made in a Wigwam,
as in the Capitol, and that all decoration is useless, and all history mere idle
amusement." But he did not believe that Law or many Americans thought so.[86]

In fact, Latrobe had revised a building into a vision of democracy. The
Capitol, as architectural historian Jeffrey Cohen has pointed out, was functional, rational, and transparent. It needed no expert for explanation, no con-
noisseur for appreciation. A building graced by his segmental geometries and
practical vaulting, it explained itself, without theatricality and ostentation.
The Capitol expressed democracy physically.[87]

For the next three years Congress cut Latrobe's budgets, sometimes entirely, sometimes by two-thirds. Even his authority was limited when the
word "alter" was removed from the legislative description of his tasks. Latrobe
might "repair" public buildings but could no longer change and transform
them. Yet ever hopeful, the architect presented optimistic estimates of future
work, especially on the exterior of the west side, where he intended to better
integrate the massive Capitol with the valley below.

In 1810 Latrobe anticipated an appropriation of over $40,000. His famed
corn cob columns, their capitals ingeniously carved to display American
maize, had just been installed. "This Capital during the summer session
obtained me more applause from the Members of Congress than all the
Works of Magnitude, of difficulty and of splendor that surround them," he
informed Jefferson.[88] Two centuries later they remain a much admired feature
of the building. Latrobe followed these with representations of magnolias
carefully carved by Franzoni into the small columns in the Senate gallery. But
these imaginative examples of how classical styles could be transformed to express a homegrown American culture failed to persuade Congress. It denied
the entire $47,432 requested.

In 1812, Latrobe lost his position as surveyor. Congress agreed to pay
the outstanding debts on the Capitol and President's House, Franzoni's and
Andrei's expenses to Italy, the completion of sculptural work, and Latrobe's
remaining salary. But they included no future appropriations for the "late surveyor." Latrobe's estimates of expenses and completion dates had often been
unrealistic, and the collapse of the arches had increased his vulnerability.
After nearly a decade of work on the Capitol and President's House, Latrobe
was no longer in charge of the nation's public buildings.

Latrobe acknowledged the personal failings that inspired his critics. He
considered himself, possibly correctly, the most unpopular public official in
Washington. "I find myself an object of suspicion and hatred and persecuted

by the most unmanly abuse in the public papers."[89] But no one except Thornton attacked his architectural designs or accused him of incompetence. And the charge of extravagance was unfair, he believed, when the costs of the north and south wings were compared to his advantage. In a telling self-analysis, Latrobe believed his unpopularity arose from "a haughtiness of deportment and despotism of manner," a European inheritance associated with all artists. These traits he could and would not change, but he did admit his failure to consult congressmen. "Still my works speak for themselves. They will live after me, and my children will have no reason to be ashamed of their father," he predicted.[90]

Like Jefferson, Latrobe was convinced that buildings transmitted political ideals and that the US Capitol was the visible statement of those visions. Latrobe used stone to establish the permanence of the republic and its resources, masonry to suggest durability, saucer domes to display significance, and the classical architectural vocabulary of columns, capitals, porticoes, and temples to connect the infant United States with previous societies admired for what America aspired to be—a powerful, enduring nation. The message was clear: the United States established a new era in human history represented by its unique and powerful Capitol. The architectural energy apparent in his Hall of the Representative compared favorably to any European assembly hall. Latrobe's contributions to the city and the nation were so significant that in 1814 his buildings became the target of invading British forces.

No longer a salaried public employee, Latrobe cultivated clients among officials in Washington who wanted showpieces in their local communities. For Congressman Thomas Worthington, a central figure in Ohio politics, he executed an example of his rational domestic house in Chillicothe, then the capital of Ohio. Constructed from native sandstone, the result was a two-story, hip-roofed central building with wings projecting forward from the principal front.

In Kentucky Latrobe designed the wings and reconfigured the interior of Ashland, the Lexington home of the Speaker of the House, Henry Clay. He provided plans for Kentucky senator John Pope, in one of his few surviving domestic homes. Unable personally to oversee its construction, he sent specific instructions to the builder, and though modified into a museum, the house remains a striking example of Latrobe's adventurous designs.

Pope's country villa outside of Lexington, Kentucky, had a dramatic circular domed space on the second floor, set in the center of a square plan. Ever practical and sensitive to the growing importance of separate spaces for women, he had given "the husband his Castle on the ground floor, the wife,

FIG. 3.5 Pope House. This important Latrobe house survives today. Built for Senator John Pope and his wife Eliza in Lexington, Kentucky, in 1811, Latrobe created a private "rational" home with a circular domed space in the center of a square plan, with a rotunda on the second floor. Also notable were the convenient placement of the service rooms. Library of Congress, LC-USZC4-118.

her breakfast parlor or housekeepers room . . . her kitchen, scullery, store-room, larders, pantry snug around her." Later he acknowledged that "too many closets can never be made for an American lady."[91]

Latrobe designed a spring house and outbuildings outside of Baltimore for his friend, former South Carolina senator Robert Harper, as well as an addition to the Talbot County, Maryland, home of Secretary of the Navy Robert Goldsborough. Such buildings spread his ideas about domestic architecture throughout the United States.

When Latrobe first visited Washington, he immediately diagnosed what the community would need if it was ever to take its place alongside Paris and London as one of the global centers of the world. The instant, legislatively created federal city had no commercial base, and the business of government was too small to stimulate such growth. Washington lacked the kind of internal improvements that fostered trade. The federal government could not create an immediate city because Washington competed with nearby Georgetown and Alexandria, two well-established communities that Latrobe, in one of his inimitable analogies, compared to "a pair of fat twins, who are suckled by a consumptive mother."[92]

Given the scarcity of engineers in the new republic, local companies, their charters newly approved by the US Congress, turned to Latrobe for advice and commissioned surveys for roads, bridges, and most important, a canal. In his capacity as an engineer he refined his understanding of how an integrated system of internal improvements could transform a town into a worthy capital and how such a capital could unite a spacious nation.

He was not, as Latrobe explained to one local promoter who had dismissed him as "a travelling Engineer," like some of those "French pretenders" who had come to the United States looking for work after the Revolution. He was "an American of the fourth Generation. I am a *travelling Engineer* only by having *travelled home.*"[93] His family had been in the United States for nearly a century. Still, as he informed Peter Buel Porter, a congressman from western New York, he knew that French and British engineers, more talented and experienced, might be available for projects in the District of Columbia: "The only advantage I may be supposed to possess over any foreigner, is that to an Europaean education in my profession, I add 15 years experience in its practice in our country, an experience necessary to modify Europaean ideas to the resources, and to the manners of those to whom the direction of public works must be committed as well as of those by whose labor they must be executed."[94]

He had learned from Jefferson as well as from the artisans who had worked on the Capitol. He understood the cultural differences between Americans who, with their brief national history, preferred hasty, temporary construction using the abundant wood found in their forests and Europeans who built for permanence using stone and mortar. Latrobe had learned that state and local governments often resisted underwriting improvements, and that Americans held "an erroneous dread of bold measures, and the fear of uselessly expending money in works hitherto unknown among us."[95]

After fifteen years in the United States he had also developed an aesthetic philosophy appropriate for a developing nation, most of whose citizens were not much interested in the arts but instead were preoccupied with making money. In 1811, as his tenure in Washington was ending, Latrobe traveled to Philadelphia to deliver a lecture to his fellow members of the Society of Artists of the United States, a new organization promoting American culture. The occasion was an opening exhibition in College Hall on Fourth Street. Latrobe had contributed three framed drawings for the exhibition—a perspective of the US Capitol, a view of the Virginia State Penitentiary, and a landscape of the Schuylkill River. After members viewed the various paintings and displays, Latrobe began a three-hour oration on the beneficial synergy between the arts and government in a free society.

Appealing to the authority of history, Latrobe established connections with Rome and Greece where the arts had served freedom. (No doubt an audience that at times donned Grecian robes for its meetings was sympathetic.) In Rome, for example, the best buildings and sculpture, as well as engineering projects such as its famed aqueducts, accompanied and strengthened the republic. But in the United States, according to Latrobe, the arts had never attained influence, the result of erroneous claims that public support was too expensive, that such support would corrupt a young republic, and that the arts were useless and elitist. On the contrary, he pointed to his own Bank of Pennsylvania, Philadelphia Waterworks, and Centre Square Engine House.

In his conclusion Latrobe connected the fine arts to domestic happiness, "charmed leisure," generosity, and patriotism.[96] It was a popular lecture among a segment of the population, and he sent copies to friends, including Jefferson. But the topic was then, and would remain, a controversial one. Neither state nor federal government would ever provide the kind of support for the arts that Latrobe, remembering the patronage of Georgian England, hoped for. His own professional struggles indicated as much.

Nor did the government provide sufficient support for internal improvements. The most critical improvement for Washington was a canal through the center of town, designed to link the Potomac and Anacostia Rivers. L'Enfant had envisioned such a plan. By 1804 several entrepreneurs had organized the Washington Canal Company that proposed a waterway beginning south of the President's House on the Potomac River, running along Tiber Creek uphill to the Capitol and then turning southeast where it would enter into the Anacostia, thereby connecting Washington's two waterways. With London and Paris as examples of cities where canals had facilitated trade, such an improvement seemed an excellent accelerant for commercial growth and personal communication. The development of wharves along the way held out possibilities for improved local transportation on packet boats as well as for commerce. With such a system in place, the capital city might compete with Georgetown and Alexandria.

The company's officers turned to Latrobe, first for a survey and then for plans that he provided for $300. In 1804, in the customary manner of raising money for private ventures, the company's proposals were made available to potential investors who could purchase shares. But even Latrobe's elegant drawings and a promotional pamphlet by Thomas Law failed to encourage sufficient subscribers. The plans lay dormant for five years. Meanwhile, Jefferson warned Madison that if the overly ambitious Latrobe was involved, he might propose a gigantic canal, perhaps even of the proportions of the 153-mile Languedoc Canal in France that connected ports on the Atlantic coast to the Mediterranean. For Latrobe the failure to support funding was another sad example of what he described to his brother as "projects that are set on foot, and never compleated, of national works begun without consideration, carried on with a short-lived enthusiasm by ignorant or fraudulent agents, and then dropped with disgust or dragging up hill against a public lassitude or impatience."[97]

Revived in 1809, the canal company again turned to Latrobe. This time he insisted they appoint him engineer and pay him a salary. He would no longer provide the free advice that board members solicited even at social events and that he warned his students to avoid. In a letter to Elias Caldwell, president of the Canal Board, he explained the profession: "that an Engineer is not merely an overseer of Laborers working under the direction of Managers, but a Man whose means of subsistence and fame depend on his reputation to whose skill and integrity the most important undertakings of Mankind must necessarily be confided, and who therefore must be allowed a certain power, without which no man in his senses will incur responsibility." It was the same message he preached to American builders, as he compared the work of engineers to physicians and lawyers who were paid for their "skill and knowledge and integrity." Neither architects nor engineers in America were rewarded in such a manner.[98]

The board offered Latrobe payment in company stock. Convinced of the financial possibilities of the canal, Latrobe purchased more shares. But after his appointment, a few promising investments, and the near completion of the project, the canal became as frustrating an endeavor as the Chesapeake and Delaware Canal had been. Both needed what was beyond the comprehension of most legislators—substantial public subsidies. The board also interfered, insisting on wooden locks that deteriorated and were located as far downstream as possible, where, as Latrobe pointed out, they would be subject to tides. As work on the canal proceeded, there was a constant need to remove silt in order to keep the channel open. Storms ruined the locks, and the canal never became a money-making venture. When, hard-pressed for cash, Latrobe tried to sell his shares to pay his doctor, they were worthless. The canal limped along, never making money for its investors until in 1870, full of trash and sewage, it was filled in.[99]

From his ventures in canals, roads, and bridges, Latrobe developed an understanding of the benefits of internal improvements to the nation. In Washington he had become a fixture in a circle of friends that included poet Joel Barlow, inventor Robert Fulton, surveyor William Tatham, and engineer Turner Carmac. All had either been born or traveled abroad; all held more cosmopolitan views than insular Americans who dismissed publicly supported ventures as unnecessary and unconstitutional. They were modern men, full of innovative ideas and ready to use their enlightened ideas to alter and manipulate the environment. Often they met in the Capitol Hill home of Treasury Secretary Albert Gallatin.

Latrobe called the Swiss-born Gallatin the most complete man in America. He had fought in the American Revolution, taught French at Harvard, and been elected to the Pennsylvania legislature. In 1793 the state legislature elected him to the US Senate, which refused to seat him on the grounds that he had not been a citizen for nine years. Gallatin then ran as a congressman and was elected to the House of Representatives, which had no such restriction. There he served several terms before Jefferson named him to his cabinet as treasury secretary in 1801.

In a town suspicious of a political economy underwritten by the national government, this circle of friends refined their arguments that investment in internal improvements—today called America's infrastructure—was a patriotic cause. They made the case that improved transportation would bind a large nation together. In the increasingly insecure Atlantic world these improvements would contribute to national security by providing the means of rapid communication and travel, important functions during military operations. In capital-short America, Latrobe and his circle of like-minded innovators concluded that government must invest in mixed public-private ventures.

Both Gallatin and Jefferson believed that, given optimistic projections for budget surpluses from land sales, in the future federal funds would be available. In his second inaugural address in 1805, Jefferson, considered a supporter of a light and simple government even after his executive action purchasing the huge swath of land in Louisiana, had encouraged federal subsidies for improvements in peacetime and with changes in the constitution, funds for "rivers, canals, arts, manufactures, education and other great objects within each State."[100]

Always hopeful for government support, Latrobe had become even more so as private investment in the Chesapeake and Delaware Canal faltered. With his encouragement, the company petitioned Congress for support on the grounds of the canal's military, commercial, and strategic benefits. The petition, one of the first of its kind, was tabled by an unsympathetic Congress worried about the constitutionality of investing taxpayer money in commercial ventures. Still, the idea had its supporters. A few years later, Congressman John Quincy Adams introduced a resolution requesting that the secretary of the treasury prepare a report on congressional constitutional power to aid in "the opening of roads, removing obstructions in rivers, and making canals."[101]

To gather information, Gallatin sent questionnaires to officials throughout the United States. He also asked Latrobe, the nation's canal expert, to provide such an evaluation. What followed was classic Latrobe: a careful, 8,000-word report on the nation's geology and its potential for canals and roads. If properly located and constructed, by using rivers that flowed horizontally across mountains, according to Latrobe, such canals and rivers could create a coastal inland waterway from Maine to Georgia and a western system linking the Hudson and St. Lawrence rivers, through the Great Lakes to the Allegheny and Ohio rivers. It was a modern concept, fulfilled years later in the Inland and St. Lawrence Waterways. "Neither in Europe, nor in our own Country," wrote Latrobe, "do I know a line of inland navigation which by so short a distance and at so easy an expense unites such extensive and productive ranges of commercial intercourse." Gallatin included the Latrobe report verbatim in his pathbreaking "Report on Roads, Canals, Harbors, and Rivers," sent to the Senate in March, 1807. But the Senate adjourned without taking any action.[102]

Latrobe was not surprised. He had never had much respect for legislators ever concerned with their reelection and parochial local interests. They had too often challenged his work on the Capitol to earn his respect. "Congress . . . will do nothing that has *character* and *force* in it." "The first object with a majority of the members is to prepare for the next election: the second to promote the local interests of their district or their state, and if then any energy of mind is left for national objects, it wastes itself in projecting schemes for saving money."[103]

Nor was the president immune from Latrobe's criticisms: "Would not all this be otherwise, were our very virtuous president [James Madison] *to read, learn, and inwardly digest* the words of the constitution: 'He *shall* from time to time recommend to Congress, etc, etc.' But his opinion of *Executive* duty makes, I fear, a mere machine of him."[104] Still Latrobe did not give up. He continued to lobby for national improvements, visiting congressmen, sending the Gallatin report to influential friends in New York and Virginia, and haranguing newspaper editors to support internal improvements.

In 1810 it was Latrobe who wrote the internal improvement bill introduced by Senator John Pope and Representative Peter Buel Porter of New York. And it was Latrobe who worked out a proposal that as a protection for taxpayers, Congress should contribute only after the private companies had sold and secured payment on two-thirds of their shares.[105] He had hopes for the bill: "I have canvassed both houses with the Members of the New York delegation who are most zealous for it and we have a majority of *promised votes,* and *none determined* to oppose."[106] Although he denied any personal interest in the bill, if it passed he would resume collecting his lucrative annual salary of $3,500 as engineer of the Chesapeake and Delaware Canal and his speculations in nearby land would gain substantial value. But the bill stalled in the Senate, its ideas resurrected fourteen years later in Henry Clay's American System, a program for economic development based on a federally financed system of roads and canals.[107]

By 1813 Latrobe's prospects in Washington—public and private, engineering and architectural—had disappeared. It was time to move westward, where he might find new possibilities for a substantial income and other avenues to improve the nation.

4

Beloved Mary and the Little Folks

No one enjoys the happiness and indolence of home more than I do.

BENJAMIN HENRY LATROBE, *Journals*, 2: 253

IN 1808, MARY ELIZABETH LATROBE delivered the last of the couple's six children. She had been married to Benjamin Latrobe for eight and a half years and pregnant for half of them, a familiar condition for married women of her generation. Her last child, a daughter named Louisa, in honor of her husband's favorite sister, was stillborn. Writing to his father-in-law Isaac Hazlehurst, Latrobe described the loss of "a very fine Girl," adding clinical details absorbed through fatherhood. Only five of his nine children survived infancy. This baby had been dead about three weeks, the result of "the umbilical cord wrapped around the neck of the infant three times. . . . Suffocation of course ensued. This sort of occurrence has never yet been explained by physicians."[1]

Both parents were despondent. Latrobe, however, found a dreary consolation in the knowledge that "the infant has escaped all those evils which render the happiest on earth [in] a state of trial and probation." His wife, a believer in the Christian promise of resurrection, felt the sorrow "but not as those who have no hope." Meanwhile her husband was relieved that his wife had survived, noting that she was "as well as she has ever been on such an occasion."[2] Having lost his first wife in childbirth, he knew firsthand its dangers.

When the couple's five-week-old daughter Juliana—Mary's first child— had died in 1801, Latrobe designed an exquisitely simple marble tombstone in the cemetery of St. Andrew's Church near Mount Holly, New Jersey. As he described to Christian, the marble monument depicted a butterfly of the yellow and black Machaon species escaping from its chrysalis. He intended to comfort both himself and his wife with this remembrance of their first child. After three daughters died in infancy, Latrobe tried to explain his sorrow: "These little creatures are in fact emanations of ones soul, and hang by invisible but strong ties to the parent stock." They were insignificant in the great order of things, incapable of solving a problem in Euclid, he wrote, but they caused shattering grief. Three years later he "still dropped a tear" over Juliana's death. [3] Never the aloof parents of historical analysis who supposedly regretted, but did not grieve over, a child's death, the Latrobes represented a new sensitivity toward children.

At a time when one-third of all children died before their fifth birthday, Latrobe monitored the illnesses of his children closely. Before five-month-old Mary Agnes "breathed out her innocent soul," he described her violent fevers and the toll on her mother, "my excellent wife," who was still nursing the baby and now found "the nutriment which flows for her infant to be wasted and dried up."[4] No clinical particular of his wife's deliveries escaped a man who throughout his life studied medical matters. During the delivery he observed the nine-hour labor of his wife, the size of Mary Agnes's head (larger than his

FIG. 4.1 Juliana's tombstone in St. Andrew's Cemetery, Mount Holly, New Jersey. Latrobe lost four of his nine children to early childhood diseases. He designed this tombstone of a butterfly escaping its chrysalis as a remembrance of Juliana, the first child of his second marriage who died in 1801, aged five weeks. Devon Graf, Photographer.

son John's), the earlier laceration of his wife's uterus, and the taking of twelve ounces of blood from his wife that he believed delayed the delivery of the child until "the *Os Uteri* could be put back."[5]

Neither Mary nor Benjamin Latrobe considered limiting the number of their children, no matter what their economic circumstances. In this period the uncertainty of an infant's survival encouraged replacement children. After the first Juliana died, the name that honored her maternal grandmother was used again, shortened to Julia. Even when he was the father of four, Latrobe hoped that if he lived a few years longer, he would be able to welcome a half dozen more babies. The vaunted Latrobe fertility—his brothers and sisters all had six children—remained "a great blessing if you all feel toward your little folks and their mothers as I do."[6] Later, when Mary was forty-one and had not been pregnant for several years, her husband lamented that there were no prospects for another child.

Fatherhood was a choice that expressed the significance of family in his life. Even before effective contraception was developed, everyone from French peasants who practiced coitus interruptus—*le retrait* as it was called—to middle-class American couples using condoms and spermicides understood that parenthood might be voluntary. During the early nineteenth century, children were becoming expensive projects rather than useful junior farmhands. As a result, fertility rates dropped steadily in the United States. But for Christians like Mary Latrobe, it was the purpose of marriage and the nature of sex for women to bear children. They were the heritage of the Lord. For her more secular husband, children removed "the mortification of selflove" and provided solace and recreation from a turbulent professional world.[7]

Latrobe had an additional reason to father a large family. Having been raised in a Moravian collective that substituted stern communal living for the intimacy of a nuclear family, he chose the latter arrangement. His fictitious connection to French royalty with dynastic ambitions intensified his allegiance to his family. More than once Latrobe wrote that his children would never be ashamed of his buildings and might even, as he expected they would, take pride in them.

Before her marriage, Mary had insisted that her husband's two children, still living in London with relatives, immediately come to the United States. In the fall of 1800, eight-year-old Lydia and seven-year-old Henry arrived and were by all accounts seamlessly incorporated into a new household in a new country. Mary excelled in what is often difficult family business: her own children had no idea that Lydia and Henry were their mother's stepchildren. As

Latrobe described his wife's mothering: "To [her own children], she is as we all are, sometimes hasty, & always unceremonious, while to Lydia and Henry she mixed the truest affection, with much more consideration of their own wishes & feelings.... With such a stepmother no apprehensions of neglect or severity could find room and in fact from the first hour of their meeting, little Henry attached himself to her with particular fondness."[8]

The Latrobe household, despite its uncertain finances, included domestic servants. In this period only the truly poor lived without servants. Southerners used slaves, and few northern middle-class families lacked either a young farm girl who had moved to the city or an immigrant Irish woman to clean, scrub, launder, and cook. While middle-class American women like Mary Latrobe were expected to manage their households, they did not anticipate performing the actual drudgery of housework.

In the case of the Latrobes, Kitty McCausland, the American-born daughter of an Irish immigrant, worked in the household from 1802 until her death in 1815. Small, red-haired, and fierce-tempered, Kitty slept with the children, cooked, and cleaned for the household. Wrote an exasperated Benjamin Latrobe to his son Henry in 1815, "Kitty, grown old, as cross, as faithful, as good a Cook and as troublesome neat as ever. Plagues John as she did you and spoils Ben."[9] When Kitty died in a horrific kitchen fire, all the Latrobes mourned her.

There were slaves as well in the extended Latrobe household, usually a young male who tended to Latrobe's coach and horses. By 1814, Jack had replaced David Smith and another young slave Francis, acquired from Robert Harper, served when the family returned to Washington. Latrobe's students—among them Robert Mills, William Strickland, and Lewis de Mun—lived with the family at various times. As their mentor, Latrobe charged fees for his instruction but forgave them in return for his apprentices' services.

Home, wherever it was in his family's nomadic existence, emerged as Latrobe's shelter from a heartless world. There, as a father and husband, Benjamin was ahead of his times in his emotional relationship with his wife and his children. "I am," he exaggerated in 1804, "so happy in my family at home that I have no time to think much of my vexations."[10]

The public world that led to his chronic insolvency might disturb his equanimity, but his private life provided comfort and distraction: "What should I do without the sedative, of the kindness and example of my beloved Mary?"[11] In one of his many letters to Christian with whom he shared these intimate feelings, Latrobe explained, "Round the blaze of my own fire, by the side of my excellent wife, is all the happiness."[12] Benjamin Latrobe was by nature an affectionate husband and father; by conviction he was an engaged one and in both relationships he was a modern man who treated his wife as an equal partner managing a different sphere from his.

As a widower in Virginia he had criticized the genetic gamble risked by the local gentry who married their cousins. Latrobe believed that such intermarriage magnified deficiencies because of the similarities among kin who felt a natural sexual affection. The best marriages, he thought, were those between partners who differed in disposition and temper. Certainly he and Mary qualified—he sensitive, high-strung, and given to swings of unrealistic exuberance about his prospects, offset by melancholy periods and violent headaches; she calm, serene, and an efficient homemaker who could run the household on slender resources; he punctilious in his profession but forgetful even of his age and forever losing his glasses. "She is besides one of those women who without expense have the art of making everything that belongs to them wear the appearance of exquisite taste. Cleanliness and order reign from my Garret to the cellar and I am myself surprised at the unseen Art by which all is produced," he boasted to his brother.[13]

Nor did Mary waste money on what her husband deemed "frippery... unless I undertake to provide her some she will pass for a woman only by her dress. I have resolved to spend 14 to 15 Dollars on her mantle piece, as she saves me twice as much a Year in beads, feathers and Gewgaws."[14] In her husband's mind Mary had character. She was "benevolent," at the same time that she demonstrated "firmness in the practice of what she deems right. She is a *woman of honor*."[15]

Latrobe considered marriage a lottery. When his friend Charles Willson Peale married for the third time, Latrobe calculated that the possibility of a happy marriage for his friend had declined, citing a recent study on chance and probability. In any case, Latrobe knew that he had won twice. Meanwhile, Mary, whose letters to her husband have not survived, proved an adaptable spouse. After two years of marriage, in a comment that indicates the transformation of her life, she described her status to her brother as that of "a domestic animall, full of family concerns."[16] She had traded her earlier comfortable life in Philadelphia's high society, when she had accompanied her mother to fancy teas with Martha Washington, Mrs. General Knox, and the wife of the Episcopal bishop, for frequent moving and at one point the isolation of Iron Hill. Her father complained to his son-in-law; she, ever supportive, did not. For Mary Latrobe, the absence of her husband was more troubling than living in a refurbished log cabin.

In Philadelphia, Mary eased the couple's way into society. She was also the source of an important commission. Mary Wilcocks Waln was among Mary's closest friends. After her husband William Waln grew rich from the China trade, the Walns hired Latrobe to build a house that became one of the architect's early efforts to create what he labeled a rational American home, adapted to the climate and manners of Americans. In the Waln home the placement of the kitchen, the attention given to a kitchen parlor, and the location of service rooms reflected Latrobe's growing attention to the practical needs of women.

Latrobe's admiration for his wife's efficiency in running their household encouraged his sensitivity to an architectural style that responded to domestic convenience. When Mary Waln, despite episodes of poor health, traveled to New York to buy fabrics and furniture for her new home, she represented Latrobe's efforts to accommodate female taste. During his work on the President's House, both Latrobes collaborated with Dolley Madison on the interior decoration: "Mrs. Latrobe is so good as to run about for me and aid me with her taste and judgment in those articles she understands better than I," explained Latrobe to the First Lady.[17]

In their first years in Washington the Latrobes, residing in a rented house halfway between the Capitol and the Navy Yard, enjoyed the busy social life of a small community of government officials, civic leaders, and foreign dignitaries. Mary led the way. As an intimate of Dolley Madison's in Philadelphia, she provided social respectability and an understanding of the parlor politics that her husband lacked. In Washington there were new friends—the families of two secretaries of navy, Robert Smith and Paul Hamilton, the Russian minister Andrei Daskoff and his American wife, and the former South Carolina senator Robert Harper and his wife Mary. Latrobe reached out to foreign visitors, some of whom he brought home to the Sunday lunches that became his wife's preferred means of hospitality. Some acquaintances enjoyed Mary's company but found her husband haughty. In 1807, Robert Mills's future wife, Eliza Barnwell Smith, described a social occasion with the Latrobes and their daughter Lydia. "The ladies made an agreeable impression upon me, but Mr. L. is accused of being rather too pompous in manner and conversation," criticism with which she agreed.[18]

When her husband's prospects dwindled after seven years in Washington, Mary faced another move. Convinced of promising prospects as an agent and investor in a steamship company organized by the inventor Robert Fulton, Latrobe again uprooted his family, this time to Pittsburgh, a place

FIG. 4.2 Waln House. Among Latrobe's contributions to American architecture was his development of what he called a rational house designed in the context of American customs and tastes, with attention paid to the convenience of housewives. Constructed in 1806–07 in Philadelphia, the Waln House integrated interiors and furniture, with Mary Waln a principal influence. Latrobe's elegant simplicity is apparent in this view of its exterior. Library Company of Philadelphia.

where Latrobe, ever the snob, found "only a few families worth visiting."[19] When he lapsed into a depression as the venture failed, Mary intervened. She encouraged her connections in Washington to hire Latrobe to rebuild the damaged US Capitol, requiring another family move.

Latrobe acknowledged Mary's tolerance for their vagabond life: "My wife with the tenderness and kindness of a woman has the Spirit of a Man, and is ready to strap on my knapsack, God Bless her!" Still he grumbled that as the creator of so many important American buildings and engineering works he "ought not at 46 Years of Age to have to ask it of her."[20]

Returned to Washington in 1815, the family, as always, rented—this time a $400-a-year, two-story, four-bedroom house in northwest Washington with land "to keep our horses and a cow and an immense garden." Latrobe was pleased: it was now his intention to "to live as much out of society as possible," as cheaply as a gentleman could.[21] Yet the location of the house meant that his wife was too far away for the convenient visiting that she had grown up with and that was the essence of female socializing. At least with the aid of a telescope that her husband arranged, she was not too far away to observe her husband on Capitol Hill and watch her beloved return home.

Latrobe's financial problems never came from any personal excess. While he ordered his clothes from a well-known Philadelphia tailor, he specified that they not be "too flashy [but] fashionably made in moderation." [22] He drank good claret and ate expensive figs, but these were hardly budget-busting luxuries. Rather, his financial difficulties came from bad investments, often in projects he was working on.

As a consequence, residential permanence perpetually eluded the Latrobes. From Washington, the family moved again, this time to Baltimore. Near the end of her husband's life, Mary established a household in distant New Orleans, far away from her beloved Hazlehurst relatives. Despite these migrations, all undertaken with prosperity just around the corner, Latrobe was never what every wife coveted—a reliable breadwinner.

Everywhere the albatross of debt intruded. Once Latrobe hoped to take his wife to a health spa in Virginia but found he could not afford it. There were times when the family was forced to sell its furniture. In 1814, Mary and Benjamin Latrobe "learned what it is to look forward to the inability not of educating but of feeding our children."[23] Several times Latrobe acknowledged that there was not a dollar in the house. And he was humiliated on those occasions when economic circumstances required Mary to take up the work of servants. In Pittsburgh as his finances spun into insolvency, Mary was forced to cook, clean, and wash, undertaking what her husband complained were "the meanest of domestic offices."[24]

Through all their difficulties the couple shared an interest in both music and art. Some of Mary's watercolors were included in a Philadelphia art exhibit. She sang, in a soft soprano voice her husband compared to that of an angel, the songs he collected for her, including some of Christian Latrobe's hymns. But after Juliana died, she could no longer finish his brother's cradle song before weeping when she came to the line "Spare, Oh Spare the babe."[25]

Mary Latrobe was not a submissive, domestic wife. Besides her influence on her husband's understanding of how buildings should fulfill female domestic needs, she held strong opinions about politics. Once she skewered President Madison "as a little shriveled spider in the midst of a large flabby cobweb shaking in the wind." (Meanwhile her husband characterized the president as "honest, weak and yet obstinate, with a total ignorance of mankind.")[26] Curious about the new wave of religious revivals, later dubbed the Second Great Awakening, Mary Latrobe insisted her husband arrange a visit to a Methodist camp meeting in nearby Montgomery County, Maryland.

There after listening to the groaning and shouting, she dismissed the religious frenzy as absurd and the preacher as a fraud. [27]

Companions and parents, Mary and Benjamin were also lovers, sustaining a sexual attraction—what Latrobe called a "chemical affinity"—throughout their marriage. He always thought of his wife, as he informed his son Henry, "con amore." He wrote a friend in England that his remained "a love match on all sides."[28] He praised his wife's "virtue," but he also took note of her physical appearance, convinced that while her figure, after delivering six children, was fuller than it had been when they first married, it was still the finest in Washington.[29]

No doubt absence made their hearts grow fonder, for these two were often separated. His letters throb with the ardor of "your most tenderly affectionate husband"; "believe me unalterably yours"; "I have, my dearest Love, not a moment to say more than what you already know, that I am yours soul, mind, affections, talents, person forever." His reward from his travels was always "your arms and kisses." During one lengthy separation, he wrote, "You don't know, but you can guess how much I want You." And again, "I want to press you to my bosom and hang over your sweet dear face with tears of affection." "My feelings for you disqualify me for business."[30] Latrobe's architecture was based on an aesthetic of austerity and restraint; his personal life was marked by a passionate intimacy with his wife.

As a widower in England, Latrobe had been a chaste man, resisting any sexual involvement with Henry and Lydia's "very pretty nurse maid." In the United States he criticized philanderers like "the insatiable libertine" Alexander Hamilton as hypocrites.[31] In his journal he referred to reproductive organs in Latin or Greek, as if embarrassed by their English synonyms. He despised Thomas Moore's poetry for its sexual innuendoes and complimented Virginia women for their delicacy in such matters. It was in his marriage, and only there, with a woman of unlimited physical affection for him, that he found sexual satisfaction.

Only briefly after their marriage in 1800 did Benjamin and Mary Latrobe ever live alone. Even on a wedding trip that lasted nearly two months and was the longest holiday of Latrobe's life, they spent several weeks with Mary's parents at Clover Hill, the Hazlehurst country home in New Jersey. Isaac and Juliana Hazlehurst had been reluctant to surrender their stay-at-home daughter. Later Mary delivered most of her children at Clover Hill; her son John spent weeks with his widowed grandfather, and there were frequent visits, some to recuperate from illness. Latrobe embraced his American in-laws with spontaneous, exuberant affection. They replaced the family left in England: Mary's parents became "my dear father and mother" and her brothers his. Expecting a visit from his brother-in-laws Isaac Jr. and Samuel Hazlehurst, Latrobe joked about their intended visit "to this very fine city, tho' scattered" where "a saddle of venison was waiting. . . . So don't let it rot / and stink before fit for the spit or the pot." He and Mary had "Beds as well as Board /We can afford."[32]

When his brother-in-law Robert died in 1804, Latrobe provided a sentimental inscription for his tombstone highlighting Robert's virtue and wit. After both his father-in-law and brother-in-law Samuel complained of his constant moving and his indebtedness, Latrobe accepted their concerns as well intended. As for his failure to repay a loan from the Hazlehurst company, Latrobe pleaded "the imperfection of human nature," explaining to his father-in-law what both knew to be true. "Consider that if I am an imprudent and refractory Son, I have been an affectionate husband."[33]

Heritage was crucial and so the couple named their infants after relatives— John after Mary's eldest brother dead in Charleston from yellow fever, the two Julianas after Mary's mother, Mary Agnes and Louisa after Latrobe's sisters, Benjamin after his father and grandfather. In all his children's names their father inserted Boneval, inexplicably removing an "n." If he had been born a Boneval in France, he conjectured, "I should have been greedy of military fame, and probably have lost it in pursuit of love. Ambition and love have had an humbler course, and I have certainly been supremely happy . . . though also supremely wretched."[34]

Latrobe indulged in what Christian described as family vanity, and so the Bonneval connection survived, a sustaining myth for Latrobe in a country where inherited distinctions collided with the denial of hierarchy and the celebration of personal ascension. "We are *jammed* between our republican principles and our aristocratic wishes."[35] In an application to a school administrator, Latrobe described his son Henry Sellon Boneval Latrobe as "of an excellent disposition, good habits and good talents," besides which his son was "descended from French Ancestors of respectability, my older Brother being at present the representative of the House of Boneval."[36] Occasionally he signed his name B. Henry Latrobe B. and Benjamin Henry Boneval Latrobe.

Latrobe intended to retain, as best he could, an attachment to his original family, hoping in his early years in America that at some point he could travel to England or perhaps his beloved Christian, a Moravian leader in a church dedicated to overseas missions, might visit the United States. Eventually, after ten years of separation, Latrobe accepted the impossibility of ever getting "a peep at you. . . . We are now both arrived at an age in which we may very reasonably give up all hopes of again seeing each other again on this side of the grave."[37] For remembrance's sake, he commissioned Charles Willson Peale's eldest son Raphaelle to create a miniature portrait on ivory which he dedicated as a gift "to my brother Christian."

In his forties he advised Christian that they were both old, an accurate assessment given that eighteen was the median age in the United States. Still he hoped that Latrobe cousins and nephews, spreading across three continents and six nations during the nineteenth century, would remember each other through letters and reminiscences. Meanwhile, Christian remained convinced that his brother's emigration had been a mistake. Given his interests and personality, Benjamin, insisted Christian, did not fit into a country "still unripe and in the process of fermentation and without any qualification that enriches."

In a letter to his brother John, Christian explained that Benjamin had become an American, but "only with difficulty" did he "lower himself to the level of an American mind or mode of thinking. . . . He wants all of us to move to America."[38] The idea of emigration was an absurdity to this cultured leader

FIG. 4.3 Raphaelle Peale Miniature. Painted on ivory, this small likeness of Latrobe was intended as a gift for his brother Christian. It is notable for its depiction of Latrobe's curly hair. Courtesy of the Maryland Historical Society, 1956.90.1.

of the Moravian church who never came to the United States. But in 1835, Christian's son Peter visited his American cousins in Baltimore where they shared stories of their ancestors. Later generations granted Latrobe's wish with their unusual level of familial self-consciousness apparent in a taste for genealogy and reunions.

Latrobe kept in touch with his English relatives through an informal international postal service, whereby English visitors returning home and American friends traveling overseas carried letters. Three thousand miles of ocean could not "put asunder the ties of affection" he felt for Christian: "You are my brother in feeling, in reasoning."[39] He filled his letters with news of both his work and his family and questioned Christian about their siblings. Christian reported that Anna Louisa had married a respectable Moravian clergyman, Frederick Foster; John Frederick, a physician, married a baroness in Livonia and was forgotten by the American Latrobes. His younger sister

FIG. 4.4 Latrobe Family Reunion. In this photograph taken at the National Arboretum in 2004, members of the Latrobe family from three continents gather among Latrobe's twenty-two columns removed from the US Capitol when the east front was expanded in the 1950s. Latrobe was a committed family man and the extended Latrobe clan maintains a strong attachment to their familial heritage as evinced by frequent reunions and attention to genealogy. Kathy and Charles Latrobe.

Mary Agnes remained unmarried in Yorkshire. Eight years older, Benjamin had barely known her in Fulneck, but still, she was a Latrobe.

When Mary Agnes married at the age of thirty-three, in Latrobe's view she made a disastrous choice in John Batemen, a Yorkshire clothier. Of course, Latrobe acknowledged to Christian, his view of Batemen's inferiority clashed with American notions of equality and was "unconstitutional" in the United States. Still it arose from a "very unreasonable reluctance to see the Characters and talents of our incomparable parents transfused into the blood of the Bateman's, and that the bed of our Sister should be ascended, by a man coming from a workshop fuming with a concoction of *urina humana* and *faeces porcorum....* We cannot descend to the Bateman's."[40]

After ten years in the United States, Latrobe still retained his snobbish instincts. He admired the possibilities of advancement in the nation; he even supported a political system run by what he called "*an unlettered majority.*" It was in social settings that he found America's wealth-based class system obnoxious: "I have dined at the same table at the house of our richest Merchant [in Philadelphia] with a man who formerly dressed my wife's hair and another who supplied her with shoes."[41]

On the other hand, in a nation that presumed in its republican ideology an equality based on virtue and capacity, not pedigree, Americans had nevertheless established social ladders. To Latrobe's chagrin, their definition of mechanics and artisans included builders and engineers as well as architects. As Latrobe described to a member of Maryland's aristocracy, Richard Caton, "A Lady, otherwise accomplished, the daughter of a man who made his fortune in a coasting Vessel, did me the honor to wonder at my *genteel and saucy* air, considering that I was only an Engineer and not a Gentleman; a secretary of State, on my admiring a very wonderful piece of mechanism in his presence, was astonished at my surprise, considering that I was so great a *Mechanic,* and could probably execute a better one myself, and Richd. Bland Lee, told me, that he wondered at the professional claim of respect which I asserted—as if my profession *were equal to that of a Merchant.*"[42]

The deteriorating relations between Great Britain and the United States tested brotherly bonds. Both Christian and Benjamin were ardent nationalists. Both offered justifications for the actions of their respective nations in a decade of renewed controversy that climaxed in the War of 1812. Latrobe reminded his brother that he had not a drop of English blood in his veins, that his mother had been American and his father Irish, and that therefore Christian had no reason to support the "brutish" policies of Great Britain. As the British practice of stopping American merchant ships and impressing sailors deemed deserters continued, Latrobe informed Christian that the English were the aggressors. In an era when tests of nationality and citizenship were determined on the sea, he argued that the British violated American sovereignty by claiming the right to determine who was British. [43]

Worse, the English justified their bellicose behavior with the fiction that they were intent on fostering the prosperity of America. "It makes me sick.... You hate us all in as far as we carry off part of the profits which you might put in your pockets."[44] Latrobe compared the English to the wolf of ancient lore who complained that the lamb drinking in the stream below him had muddied the water. Since the time of Queen Elizabeth, he continued, in one of his longest, harshest letters to his brother, the English had sought to monopolize the Atlantic trade and to be "Lords of the Ocean."[45] As an example, Latrobe cited the British fleet that had recently bombarded neutral Denmark, destroying property and killing women and children.

Despite Jefferson's policies of limiting trade and the exposure of American ships, the British had become increasingly aggressive along the shore of the Chesapeake Bay, an area Latrobe knew well. There they were raiding farms and setting off Congreve rockets, the much-feared iron tubes filled with gunpowder that could travel a mile. In the summer of 1807, the *Chesapeake-Leonard* affair proved Latrobe's point. As he informed Christian, without cause the British frigate *Leonard* had attacked the *Chesapeake*, destroying the ship and carrying off four American sailors.

In response, Christian cited an incident that outraged the English: it was the Americans who were the aggressors in an unprovoked night attack in the Atlantic by the forty-four-gun American frigate *President* on the much smaller HMS *Little Belt,* causing thirty-two British casualties. There were other confrontations on the seas, one involving the aggressive American commodore John Rodgers. He should be hanged, according to Christian, who also attacked American congressmen as uninformed and parochial. Even in the midst of his public battles with Congress over appropriations for the Capitol, Benjamin found time to defend the legislators he often criticized. They were not mathematicians nor metaphysicians nor could they conjugate Greek verbs, but, as he explained to Christian, they were honest farmers who understood the interests of their nation. (In fact, they were mostly lawyers.) Latrobe hoped that Christian would "moderate your ire against the country to which you owe your existence" and stop attacking Rodgers, an admirable American and one of Latrobe's oldest and most intimate friends.

Latrobe could not resist pointing out the contradictions in his brother's position. On the one hand, his brother was an official of a church that preached doctrines of peace, so he hoped that "the prayers of our excellent father will not be in vain. . . . [But] in the next paragraph you hang Rodgers at the Yard Arm and talk in the true style of the Church Militant during the Crusades. Did I not know you to be benevolence and liberality itself *in fact*, you would alarm me for your character by *your words*." As for his own views, he believed that God had created all nations upon earth. "All are bad enough, but mankind are pretty much alike all over the world."[46] Privately he acknowledged the uses of war for Americans: it would make "a nation of us."[47] Despite the sharp exchanges, the connection between the brothers, sustained by their memories and news of their families, survived even the British destruction of one of Latrobe's masterpieces, the US Capitol.

Mary and Benjamin Latrobe intended to be self-described "liberal parents," tolerant of their five surviving children's aspirations. "I have no idea of anything this side of the grave more calculated to attach the mind to sub-lunary happiness than a household with happy children," he wrote. They were "my little selves playing about me . . . little mixtures of myself and of my wife and what idea could be more consoling." Both parents despised harsh physical punishments and instead offered unwavering affection to the "little darlings who are the best, if not the only things worth living for."[48] Having missed the early childhood years of Lydia and Henry, Latrobe delighted in playing with and instructing his new brood. "I think my little John is a little wonder! Everyone else thinks him only a fine and engaging child," he acknowledged.[49]

According to his Papa, three-year-old John had already learned the alphabet and would have learned it sooner had his imagination not run away with him. As reported in a homeschooling episode in Latrobe's journal: "Come here John and say your letters to me," at which young John after A and B declined to say C and instead offered as the third letter an O with a piece broken out of it; G the same, H was a gate and Q a round O with a tail to it and so forth. Such ingenuity from his son was sufficiently extraordinary to be described at length in his father's journal.[50]

A poem of Latrobe's described another happy domestic scene, tinged with his persistent melancholy:

Impromptu for my Juliana's Sampler

Watched by her Mother's glistening eye
Her needle Julia plied;
Uncounted flew the moments by,
While grew her sampler's pride.

The little hands with guileless art
That wove each lettered row,
While her bright eye, and playful heart
Still gladdened over the show.
When age shall dull that mother's eye
And all but love be fled
Then shall those hands with riper joy
Strew roses over her bed.[51]

Homeschooled, Julia did not have the educational advantages of her brothers. But she did attend dancing school when the family lived in Washington. To sew and dance and perhaps learn French were all talents sought in young girls who would find their future in marriage rather than in a learned profession like boys. But when the family moved to a new rented home far from dancing school and Julia could no longer attend, she meticulously described the dance steps in her notebook in order to practice at home: "Positions: Bend and slide the foot and spring into the third position." On the cover of her tiny notebook her father drew an elegant watercolor of a dancing woman.[52]

Latrobe's letters to friends and family were filled with news about the children, their health, their dispositions, their intellectual prowess; even their teething was worth mentioning. The level of detail indicated an engaged father. To his father-in-law, Latrobe described fourteen-month-old Julia "running around everywhere on all fours with great rapidity and walking around the room by the chairs and bed, but not yet venturing onto the open floor."[53]

To Christian he occasionally confided realistic assessments of their characters and abilities. Lydia had her mother's "unevenness of temper along with excellent qualities of solid value." Yet his eldest daughter, he confessed, had "inherited the miserly disposition of some of her maternal relations."[54] Henry was a "fine, steady fellow," while Julia, "the finest of the flock," was his pet. John had the "wit and good nature of his mother and the vivacity of his father's family," and the youngest, Benjamin, governed the house "despotically," solemnly declaring that he would never learn his letters. In this child-centered household, "He [Ben] is one of the wildest and boldest fellows I ever saw—though good natured enough but as fierce as a lion."[55]

Lydia created the first family crisis and test of the couple's permissive principles. In 1804 Latrobe's business partner Nicholas Roosevelt announced that he—age thirty-seven—and Lydia—age thirteen—were in love and intended to marry. Her father erupted: "On the subject you have written to Mrs. L we had better *talk* than *write*. Perhaps it will be better still to *laugh—13 Years and 6 months*."[56]

Roosevelt had been a frequent visitor to the Latrobe household in Philadelphia. He came to discuss the steam engine project that propelled the municipal waterworks and that might provide additional opportunities for a profitable investment. At the time, Lydia was a student at the Jacques Academy, a local girls' school run by a French émigré. No one suspected that a child of thirteen and a man twenty-four years her senior could find romance. Certainly her father did not. "But before I dreamed that anything serious was meant," Latrobe explained to his brother, "things were so far settled between them as to put out of my power to prevent their union save by an exertion of authority to which I hardly conceive I have a right."[57]

Latrobe, like other men of his generation, was not prone to psychological musings as to why a young girl, separated from a father in childhood, might be attracted to a business partner only three years younger than he. Instead, Latrobe dismissed the affair as incongruous, a violation of principles of propriety as well as his hospitality. Later financial entanglements would destroy the friendship between the two men, but in 1804 Latrobe considered Roosevelt, a man of "good moral character, of one of the oldest families in the State of New York, has a very handsome fortune, and inhabits one of the most enchanting Country seats in New Jersey, on the River Passaic. He calls himself 33, but is suspected to be a Year or two beyond that."[58] (At the time Roosevelt was 37.) In every respect save his age Roosevelt would have made a suitable husband. But the idea of such a union with a child, his daughter, tested Latrobe's commitment to the American custom of free mate choice without the intrusion of parents. "Neither my principles nor my disposition permits a forcible separation of the parties," though he did insist on a delay.[59]

A brief compromise was reached; the two lovers would have no contact during a probationary period. But Lydia, angry at her father, still corresponded with Roosevelt but then abruptly, while living in Washington, broke off contact with him and entertained attention from other men. She found no one whom she preferred to Roosevelt including, according to family lore, the dashing naval hero David Porter who had shown interest in Lydia. In 1808 Roosevelt renewed their courtship. Four years after Latrobe had first learned of their romance, Lydia Latrobe and Nicholas Roosevelt were married in her parents' rented home in Washington.

It was a family affair save for a few friends, among them Dolley Madison. When the time came for the bride and groom to leave, Lydia clung to her stepmother and had to be forcibly separated by her father and carried to

Roosevelt's carriage. It was a bad beginning to a happy marriage that survived despite Roosevelt's financial difficulties. Still at odds with her father, Lydia named her first child after a friend, not her stepmother, as her father expected. "Call her what you please," he admonished, "I shall always call her *Mary*."[60]

Committed to steam energy as the innovation of the future, Nicholas Roosevelt developed a steam engine that could effectively power sidewheels on vessels and, along with Robert Fulton, he intended to demonstrate its commercial possibilities and make money. His pregnant wife insisted that she, their infant daughter, and a nurse join him in an epic voyage down the Ohio and Mississippi Rivers to New Orleans. The dangerous journey included an earthquake, attacks by Indians, and flooding.

The most exciting event took place in Louisville. There, in October 1811, Lydia delivered a son named Henry Latrobe Roosevelt after her brother. Grandfather Latrobe was pleased: "The family of Boneval of which you are a descendant have always had eccentric journies thro' life. Few have died where they were born: The French in Turkey or Ireland, the Americans in England or Russia, the Europeans in America. He who was born in a Steamboat must surely have a singular course in life."[61] While Latrobe wished his daughter well, he could never forgive her marriage to a man who had cheated him in their mutual financial affairs. To his son Henry he acknowledged that Lydia had not "married to please me." Still, crucially for her father, she would "do honor to any family and any Station in society. Yourself and the rest are all I could wish for."[62]

When Latrobe was living in Virginia in 1797, one of the trustees of a newly chartered school in the panhandle region of western Virginia bordering Maryland asked him to evaluate its bylaws. Ferdinand Fairfax, who had met Latrobe in Richmond, had been impressed with the young architect's ideas about education and wanted his opinion on the school's proposed curriculum and management. The Charlestown Academy, which opened in 1798 and survived until 1905, was one of a number of institutions chartered by state legislatures after the American Revolution. Along with their educational mission, they were intended to instill patriotic ideals in the nation's male youth. With time on his hands, Latrobe provided a detailed program, and in the process his contrarian theories about education emerged.

The classical languages and literature played a featured role in the Charlestown Academy curriculum, as they had in Latrobe's own education and in most American academies. But despite his own fluency in ancient Greek and Latin, Latrobe found the classics to be inappropriate as "the head of your studies." It was not that "these beautiful languages" should not be taught; instead Latrobe argued that they should not be the central focus of the curriculum. To be sure, there were many benefits to the study of classical languages, among them the discipline of engaging in "the dry laborious study of words" and their utility in decoding scientific language. And once fluent, a man might enjoy Xenophon, Livy, and Cicero.

For a man who found the guiding principles of his architecture in Greece and Rome, his demotion of the classics in boys' schooling seems contradictory. There was, however, a subtle connection: while his buildings employed classical concepts, they were by no means simply replicas of ancient structures. Instead they were made suitable for the United States—its climate, its political culture, and its ideals. Similarly, education must be grounded in the national context.

According to Latrobe, the conventional emphasis on classical languages in most academies had little relevance to young Americans. "Learning, in fact, within the remembrance of every one who is above thirty, was another word for Greek and Latin." Yet, it was ridiculous to make an American boy learn "useless works and acquire command of a language which he will never be required to speak or to write." Instead, a newly ordered political society without a king or established hierarchy demanded a different curriculum with emphasis placed on more practical studies in the areas of mathematics, physics, writing, science, and even modern languages. American education should be engaging and useful, never boring, outdated, and irrelevant. And most young boys were bored by learning dead languages and reading remote ancient plays. Besides irrelevancy, a classical education created another problem in a republic: it produced an elite. "A republic would be illy served if its schools were only contrived to create a privileged class of men furnished with language . . . which cannot be applied to the common transactions of life."

Instead Latrobe proposed a practical program that dismissed his own training and undermined that of Oxford and Cambridge. These elite English universities, he complained, were "immense hospitals, in which lingers, decrepid and mortally wounded, what remains of Greek and Latin ignorance in England." As "America took the lead in the practice of improved political theory in the organisation of a community," so it must set an example, as he intended to do in the design of his buildings, "of a rational education of her citizens." Such schooling would devote more time to natural history and mathematics and would prepare students for professions and vocations, as he believed his Moravian education had not.[63]

As to the Charlestown Academy's proposed regulations for punishment of its students, Latrobe found them far too punitive. The creation of a Book of Disgrace for offenders was mere revenge; it was better termed a Record of

Misconduct. Corporal punishment was immoral; punishment must be moderate and reasonable. Restricting it to those under sixteen indicated just how irrational and unfair it was. "As an American republican I may ask, what right has any human being to prescribe laws to the actions of any other unless they be injurious to him?"[64] From such logic emerged Latrobe's riff on school as a society—a little political entity—with individual rights and responsibilities that replicated those in the nation. "Let politicians do what they please." Schools would teach Americans "principles for the grounds of equal laws, equal justice, and equal rights."[65]

No doubt reflecting on his own dismissal from the Moravian seminaries of Niesky and Barby, he argued that expulsion was the most effective solution for improper conduct. "Does a boy fear the ferula as much as temporary separation from his Schoolmates," a question to which he answered no. Years earlier, after his own rebelliousness had ended in separation from his classmates, he had written his former "brother" Johann Friedrich Fruauf, who remained at Barby, a fond letter sent to "my dearest friend." Never did Latrobe comment on any chagrin or shame experienced by his expulsion from two Moravian schools, but he did admit to missing some of his classmates. Others were only hypocrites, what he dubbed "half friends."[66] Twenty years later at the end of his lengthy analysis of the best curriculum and management for the Charlestown Academy, Latrobe found in Latin an appropriate closing. He wished the school "Esto Perpetua"—May it be perpetual.

In 1815, a congressional committee consulted Latrobe about designing a national university. The subject had preoccupied American leaders from Benjamin Franklin and Benjamin Rush to George Washington and Thomas Jefferson. Latrobe agreed with their vision that a self-governing people required civic schooling: education was the taproot of a democratic popular culture. And at the apex of the educational system stood a national university supported by Congress that trained political leaders. Latrobe's friend Joel Barlow had described just such a university in his *Prospectus for a National Institution*.

Similarly, in his annual message to Congress in 1815, President Madison encouraged the establishment of a national seminary of learning in the District of Columbia. It would be, in Madison's words, "a monument of Congressional solicitude for the advancement of knowledge without which the blessings of liberty can not be fully enjoyed or long preserved." It would serve as a model for other seminaries, "a nursery of enlightened preceptors and a central resort of youth and genius from every part of [the] country." Its graduates would return home and "contribute their national feelings, those liberal sentiments, and those congenial manners to our Union."[67]

Latrobe responded with a sketch of buildings arranged in a quadrangle on the Mall west of the US Capitol. The university would look upward to the Capitol in a physical setting that conveyed the relation of education to the nation's political culture. He proposed a porticoed central building flanked by wings intended to house dormitories, classrooms, and a library. Opposite the central building on the eastern end of the university, Latrobe sketched a chapel and nearby a "sheet of water" that eventually became the Capitol Reflecting Pool. Latrobe's concept, similar to that of Jefferson's academic village at the University of Virginia, reflected a commitment to the importance of faculty and students residing in intimate proximity in households, a more democratic, student-oriented educational vision than existed in European universities. But Latrobe's ideas remained on paper when a congressional bill involving the funding of such a venture was postponed and was then forgotten.

After Lydia and Henry arrived in the United States, Latrobe faced the challenge of educating his own children. He continued to believe that his own training in Moravian schools was a great misfortune. It had equipped him for either the life of a gentleman or that of an impoverished clergyman, but not for his role as a professional architect and engineer. It had not taught him how to manage his money in a country where there were endless unmonitored investment opportunities. Instead, as he had proposed in his plans for the Charlestown Academy, he intended a more practical education for his sons, at the same time that he proudly compared his more advanced understanding of mathematics as a young boy to that of Henry's. In any case the lesson learned and applied was that his eldest son needed to be prepared for a profession from which he could gain his livelihood.

Initially Latrobe hoped for the law, "the profession which governs this country."[68] He intended that at some point Henry would travel in Europe and study law in the famed London inns devoted to legal studies. Yet he discovered that his eldest son "would rather I believe become acquainted with *things* than with *words*."[69] In any case, as part of his education his son had to be exposed to the accomplishments of gentlemen—music, drawing, and dancing.

Actively managing his son's education, Latrobe removed Henry from a boys' academy outside of Philadelphia and sent him to a Catholic institution in Baltimore, informing its head, Reverend William Du Bourg, that while it might seem ridiculous to push forward a boy of eleven, the course of his own education had been as rapid. He intended that his son "enter upon Mathematics, Natural history and philosophy, improve in classical knowledge, and learn French, Spanish and German." It was the very definition of schooling that he had earlier complained created a privileged class: "Education produces superiority of influence in those who possess [it] over those who want it: that is educated Men are of themselves an aristocracy governing the majority . . . ergo, education is an anti-republican machine by which the few coerce the many; ergo it ought not to be suffered in a republic."[70] But such a philosophical contradiction between preferred common schooling for the benefit of society and the practical reality of privileging one's own children in entitled settings often led leaders of the republic, like Latrobe, to surrender their principles.

In his application letter Latrobe explained that Henry's distant ancestors had been Catholics—a claim that was only accurate if his Boneval heritage was authentic. In fact, the Latrobes of Languedoc had been fierce opponents of the Catholic Church during the Reformation in France. Still, Henry's birth mother and "present excellent mother" were both Protestants, though Henry was ignorant of church dogma, according to his father.

The fact that his parents chose a Catholic school of high academic reputation indicated their tolerance. Besides, with his Moravian past in mind, Latrobe would "rather see [his son] do honor to the benevolence of our Creator, by the cheerfulness of a Catholic than disgrace the benignity, the mercy and the justice of God by the Religious Gloom of some Protestant sects."[71] In an inaccurate paternal boast, Latrobe calculated that his own talents were "very inferior to those of my son, [I had] a disposition much less *sober* and persevering, and opportunities for folly and dissipation which he knows nothing of."[72] In any case he promised that his children "shall not want instruction, nor yet an example of industry as long as I live.[73]

At the time, Latrobe had begun business negotiations with John Carroll, the first Roman Catholic bishop in America. The ambitious Carroll had been collecting funds for a great religious edifice in Baltimore—a cathedral, given Carroll's status in the church. Familiar with Latrobe's work he had asked the architect to review initial plans for such a structure designed by Latrobe's nemesis, William Thornton. As usual, Latrobe found much to criticize and offered his own design free of charge, save for expenses. The bishop was delighted, although it would be a year before Latrobe completed what would eventually be the first of seven designs.

While he was corresponding with Latrobe, Carroll was also promoting the school Latrobe had chosen for his son Henry—St. Mary's Academy in

Baltimore. If the church was to succeed in Protestant America, there must be priests to tend the flock. It would be, in Carroll's estimation, impossible to import enough priests who spoke English; instead seminaries like St. Mary's must be created to train native clergy. Established in 1791, St. Mary's was run by the Sulpicians, a French order dedicated to educating Catholic priests. Located in the city that was the center of American Catholicism, the school was at first unable to attract enough potential seminarians. For it to survive, its head, Reverend William Du Bourg, began accepting young men of every creed who wanted more than simply the routine curriculum of a boys' academy. The institution promised courses in modern languages, science, and mathematics taught by well-trained Sulpicians, and, additionally, attention to the morals of its students.

Rechartered by the Maryland legislature as a college in 1805, St. Mary's began offering AB degrees. It soon attracted young men from Maryland's best-known families, both Protestant and Catholic, including the Jenkinses, the Warfields, the Ellicotts, and the Carrolls. Henry was in the school at the same time that Dolley Madison's son, John Payne Todd, boarded there. Besides the local aristocrats, more than half of the student body in his class had been born outside the United States, many in St. Domingue where civil war had forced migration. Some émigrés had settled in Norfolk, as had Latrobe when he first arrived in the United States. Others came to Baltimore where they established a community along South Street and sent their sons to St. Mary's.

Henry graduated from an institution that his father described as the best but most expensive school in America, with a tuition of $46 a session and annual boarding fees of $100. By attracting the sons of notable Maryland families, offering a demanding curriculum taught by well-trained academics, and avoiding efforts at overt conversion, the college showcased Carroll's strategy that American Catholicism should demonstrate indifference to the influence of a foreign pope while offering services to all Americans, no matter what their faith. Latrobe was attracted to the institution's cosmo-politan nature and international student body. He appreciated the school as well for providing what he thought his father had denied him—helpful connections. [74]

Henry lived in a four-story U-shaped building with a superb botanical garden in its courtyard. There were eighty students in his class, only one-third American-born. (Henry listed his birth place as Middlesex, England.) He studied mathematics, natural history, and science, all St. Mary's specialties. Six days a week he spent an hour and a half in mathematics class and two hours a day in classes devoted to philosophy and rhetoric. He became fluent in French; the French flavor of St. Mary's had been one of its attractions for his father. He read modern languages such as Spanish and German, though not ancient Greek. He studied Latin, for it was still important for gentlemen. He learned to play the violin and took drawing in a program closely monitored by his watchful father, who apologized to Du Bourg for his "parental anxiety." [75] At one point Latrobe, deploring his son's "extreme bodily inactivity" insisted he take dancing in order to make him more active, no matter what the extra fees might be.[76]

After two years Henry asked his father permission to move from his "cell at college" to a boarding house in Baltimore's Fells Point or, perhaps, to the home of Latrobe's friend Maximilian Godefroy, the French-trained architect who taught fine arts at St. Mary's and designed its Gothic chapel. Latrobe declined, agreeing with his son that such a move might permit *"less restraint"* and *"more fun* . . . But of the benefit of the restraint, and the injurious consequences of the *fun,* you have no idea. Therefore you must be content."[77]

In his role as his children's ever-present tutor, Latrobe chided Henry for his failure to understand the difference between facts and theories. In one exchange between father and son, Henry had accepted the theory of evolution promoted by the French diplomat and ethnographer Benoit de Maillet,

FIG. 4.5 St. Mary's Buildings and Gardens. Latrobe's sons—Henry, John, and Ben— attended St. Mary's College in Baltimore. At times, Latrobe had difficulty paying the tuition, but committed to the importance of education for his sons, he sent them to St. Mary's. This sketch shows the dormitories and classrooms as well as the garden of the institution. Library of Congress, HABS MD,4-BALT,18-1.

who argued that all life had begun in the ocean. Man, de Maillet claimed, had started as a fish. The evaporation of the seas had allowed organisms like sea men and mermaids to adapt to conditions on land. When Henry promoted this romantic theory, his father initiated the kind of intellectual conversation unusual for fathers of his time.

In a long letter, Latrobe pointed out the errors in fact and reasoning that undermined Maillet's theory. Then he expanded the discussion into the larger theme of the difference between fact and fiction, a topic that for years had been an interest and to which he brought modern insights. As an example, Latrobe used the wildly varying accounts in the newspapers of the recent *Chesapeake-Leonard* affair, noting the misrepresentations that emerged from the biases of the observers. Finally, he recommended that Henry read his friend Constantin Volney's lectures on how to establish the validity of both scientific and historical information.

Latrobe expected to pay for his children's education with his first wife's inheritance from her parents. Her share—held in trust for Lydia and Henry after her death—was anticipated to be nearly 3,000 pounds. Latrobe, as usual in monetary matters, exaggerated the amount to 10,000 pounds. But the Sellons—especially Lydia's brother who managed the estate and went bankrupt—refused to send any money. After a series of polite letters, Latrobe turned to a London attorney to collect the money and even sent Christian to negotiate with William Sellon, who conveniently was never at home.

If Latrobe could not collect his children's inheritance, he could not pay Henry's tuition at St. Mary's. And so began a battle with Du Bourg, who at the time was struggling with the school's insufficient funds. Latrobe removed Henry for a year and believed when his son returned that the school would remit the tuition and provide a scholarship. Instead he discovered that Du Bourg had been charging interest on the unpaid amount. The disagreement simmered. By 1809, two years after Henry's graduation as the valedictorian of his class, Latrobe owed $945. When Du Bourg sent the school's financial agent to collect, Latrobe was outraged at this "dunning by threats." Eventually, he signed a bond payable to the college, to be paid in a year. This proved impossible, in part because Congress had not paid him, and so a friend ended up covering the bond. With the debt resolved, Henry's younger half-brothers, John and Benjamin, attended St. Mary's, as did several of Latrobe's grandchildren.

In 1809 Henry began the next phase of his education, this time as his father's assistant working on the US Capitol with the official title of clerk of the works. Latrobe justified his choice of a family member as a saving for

Congress. John Lenthall had been paid $1,400; sixteen-year-old Henry's salary would be $800. Henry's education, Latrobe explained to President Madison, "has been specially directed to the objects of my profession, he is an excellent draughtsman, a good accountant." He had worked in Latrobe's office during vacations and "would be, independently of personal motives, the best assistant I could procure."[78] Henry soon took on additional duties as his father's agent in other projects—the Washington canal, surveying a proposed road to Rockville, Maryland, and reviewing the financial possibilities for a Virginia copper mine powered by a steam engine. Acclaimed by his father as "all I could wish for," he was "an excellent lad; he sticks to his mother when not in the office. . . . [W]hile not without faults, he has no serious vices." In any case, according to his father, unlike Philadelphia, Washington offered few opportunities for a young man's dissipation.[79]

In 1811 a great financial opportunity for father and son emerged. For years Latrobe had developed contacts with prominent officials in New Orleans. He knew William Claiborne, governor of the Louisiana territory, and had recently designed a five-ton monument sculpted by Guiseppe Franzoni that honored Claiborne's deceased wife and daughter, who had died from yellow fever, and his brother-in-law, who had been killed in a duel. Latrobe had worked on the plans for a lighthouse to be built in the mouth of the Mississippi River and had designed the city's custom house.

New Orleans was investigating the possibility of a much-needed city waterworks, considered an especially crucial improvement, given the yellow fever epidemics that annually swept across the city and that seemed connected to foul drinking water. At a time when doctors treated symptoms, it was left to laymen to explain causes. Some observers believed yellow fever was caused by foul drinking water, an explanation that spurred the organization of water companies. Others, including Latrobe, believed that the disease originated in the filthy air—the miasma—and that drinking alcohol made one susceptible to the disease's ravages.

Aware of Philadelphia's successful waterworks, the New Orleans Waterworks Company turned to Latrobe. With Robert Alexander, a hard-drinking friend described by Latrobe as "half Carpenter and half Gentleman," he developed a plan, similar to that in Philadelphia, of a steam-engine powered municipal water system. To finance their civic improvement, partners in the company intended to raise the needed capital of $240,000, with 240 shares offered to the public and the city, at the cost of $500 a share, and Latrobe owning the other half as compensation. An exuberant Latrobe predicted a personal goldmine: he needed only 2,000 houses in New Orleans to pay

$10–$20 dollars a year after the initial expenses. Given the burgeoning population of New Orleans, an exclusive contract with the city would be worth $40,000 a year. "We shall surely succeed and be the richest men in America," he predicted.[80] But first the partners needed to secure a franchise from the city, and to that end Henry was dispatched to New Orleans.

Henry arrived in early January 1811, just before the start of the largest slave rebellion in American history.[81] Five hundred enslaved men and women from nearby plantations armed with guns and axes were marching on New Orleans, only to be slaughtered by army troops and a hastily gathered militia on the outskirts of the city. No doubt Henry saw and smelled the brutal consequences of defeat: the chopped-off heads of the enslaved on poles along the roads, the rotting bodies along the canals. When word of the uprising reached Washington, his father worried.

But by the end of the year there was good news. The rebellion had ended and Henry had been successful in their business affairs. He had also joined what his approving father called "the best society." Fluent in French, Henry had persuaded the city council, most of whose members were French-speaking Creoles, to sign a contract. His father was elated: "I would rather commit this immense concern to Henry than to any man I know of ten years older."[82] Despite Henry's early success, the waterworks proved to be the most prolonged and frustrating engineering project in Latrobe's career.

For the next six and a half years Henry lived in New Orleans, a city that seemed an exotic foreign country to Americans who valued its strategic location and enjoyed its well-established temptations. Settled in 1719 by the French, bargained away to Spain after the French and Indian War, briefly returned to France, and then sold in 1803 to the United States by Napoleon, the city's tangled ownership reflected the global importance of its location on the Mississippi River and its access to the Caribbean as well as the interior of the United States. In 1810, New Orleans's population of 17,242 —6,331 whites, 4,950 free people of color, and 5,961 slaves—had surged with the arrival of St. Domingue exiles. Henry lived in a place where Anglo-Americans were a minority; most residents were of French, Spanish, and African heritage, the so-called Creoles born in the Louisiana territory.

New Orleans retained its French identity, its temptations, and its racial definitions, no matter who was in control. The city established a fluid racial system of three castes, unlike the rest of the United States. In New Orleans there were free whites, the black enslaved, and what the French classified as *gens de coleur*—mixed-race residents, who were the source of an algebraic vocabulary of archaic color classifications such as mulatto, octoroon, and quadroon. The source of the mixed-race inhabitants was no testament to republican ideals of equality; rather, it resulted from imbalanced sex ratios.

There were many more white men than white women, and in time there were more biracial women than biracial men. French legal codes prohibited marriage between free whites and persons of color; they did not explicitly prohibit interracial cohabitation outside of marriage.

Nor did they prohibit freeing the children of such unions or self-manumission by those who bought their own freedom and entered into a world of limited privileges. In this freewheeling community where men outnumbered women and nearly a third of the city's population was mixed race, it had become the practice of French and Spanish men to have secret sexual affairs in the form of concubinage in which a white man provided a house and support for his mixed-race mistress and, sometimes, children. Some said it was cheaper to have such an arrangement than to live in a hotel. In any case the liaisons between white men and their female consorts was sufficiently institutionalized to earn the neologism "placage." These women were placed, often with their mothers' approval, not kept.

Initially Henry was attracted to the gambling casinos along Bayou road. In New Orleans men bet on the races; they gambled at cards in the taverns; they played billiards in the tippling houses in what is today the French Quarter. As Henry confessed his indiscretion to his father, after a few "bumpers" he had lost $800. Informed of his son's debt, Latrobe blamed himself for dispatching a "warm-hearted Boy of eighteen into so dangerous a scene as New Orleans." The father paid the son's debt and forgave his son. Latrobe considered Henry, as did Henry in return, a friend: "It cannot be a greater comfort to You to call your father your friend than it is to me. . . . How happy then is a father who in his own Children, has surrounded himself with that sincerely friendly circle, which the very nature of society savage as well as polished renders it vain for him to collect elsewhere."[83]

Still, after the drinking episode, the weekly letters from his parents came with specific warnings. Henry was admonished to beware friends who took him to taverns, to never fall into debt, and to avoid "dangerous liaisons." To the French-born New Orleans merchant and civic leader, Jean Blanque, Latrobe acknowledged his fears: lacking the cultural amusements of Europe—its music, fine arts, learned societies, museums and gardens that had absorbed him as a young man—in "the young cities of our continent and without that precious resource . . . a young man of an ardent mind and sociable disposition could not be anywhere in more danger of acquiring morals and habits forever destructive of his happiness, than in the luxurious climate of New Orleans."[84]

By the time Henry had been warned to avoid "dangerous liaisons" he was living with a free woman of color and had fathered several of her children. It was a relationship that he kept secret from his parents.

Perhaps he met the mother of his children at one of the famous quadroon balls where mixed-race women and white men danced, flirted, and sometimes initiated permanent sexual relationships. Possibly she arrived in the flood of emigres from St. Domingue. During Henry's years in New Orleans, despite the disapproval of Governor Claiborne, the balls continued to flourish, advertised in newspapers and held in large ballrooms along Conde (now Charles Street) and nearby St. Peter Street.

Henry had made friends in several communities. He was well known among the French-speaking civic leaders. He designed houses with a partner, the French-born architect Arsene LaCarriere Latour, and he enjoyed unusually close ties with the black community. At first simply an acquaintance of sculptor Florville Foy, Henry became a close friend of his son Prosper, a successful marble cutter, and the mixed-race Prosper chose Henry to be his son's godfather.[85]

Professionally Henry was thriving in New Orleans both as an engineer and an architect. His father, given to contradictory views on the relation of work to social standing, believed his son was succeeding because he had not been educated, "as I was, to believe it beneath a Gentleman to earn an honest livelihood."[86] Flush with cash, young Henry offered to repay his father for his education, an offer Benjamin Latrobe declined. He would be mortified "to know you had paid a single cent for your own education." The first object must be for Henry to maintain his own credit and stay out of debt. "I am an old financier and shall not be entirely at a loss altho' I may now and then be tightly pinched," responded the father to his son's offer.[87]

When the water project stalled because of limited funds, a delayed steam engine, and the interruption of navigation during the War of 1812, Henry built the first version of the city's famous Charity Hospital, a warehouse, and a market, and in 1816 a new building for Davis's Ballroom. Henry also served as an engineer in Andrew Jackson's forces during the British invasion in 1815, placing artillery and constructing a line of defense during the battle of New Orleans. According to his proud father, he earned General Andrew Jackson's praise.

Parental advice continued throughout Henry's years in New Orleans. Increasingly warnings centered on avoiding the epidemics that swept through New Orleans. "Take care of your health, my dear boy," "God bless you my dear boy take care of your health above all things for the rest I fear nothing," and the more specific "*Never sleep with your windows open. Be very temperate in your drink.*"[88]

Eleven years younger than Henry, John Hazlehurst Boneval Latrobe found his schooling as closely monitored by his "Papa" as Henry's had been. As a child, when John cut his second tooth it had been worthy of note, along with his father's fervent hope that his son would never replicate his father's life and "eat the bread of dependence upon it."[89] To accomplish such financial independence required a practical education. When John was a precocious four, Latrobe intended to send him to Joseph Neef's new school along the Schuylkill River outside of Philadelphia. There the Alsatian émigré instituted his permissive principles of equality between teachers and students, along with an advertised curriculum in which students learned old things in a new way, by understanding rather than memorizing. This modern approach to the needs of the child and learning a trade rather than conventional knowledge of the classics appealed to Latrobe, but the family moved to Washington before John could be enrolled.

Instead the second Latrobe son attended Reverend Robert Elliot's free public school. But after John became infected with "vermin" [head lice], the result, his father informed Elliot, of "promiscuous intercourse with Children whose parents are not very attentive to cleanliness," it was time for a different school.[90] Besides, according to Latrobe, John's playmates were of a lower class, not "sufficiently endowed in their domestic habits and ideals" to be suitable companions. Latrobe moved his son to John McLeod's school across the street from the family's rented home on Ninth Street, between G and H streets.

Latrobe described John as "a boy of wonderful powers. He will be a tall fellow—hate dancing till he is 16—without being awkward."[91] At fourteen John looked eighteen; indeed as an adult he became a massive presence. John, according to his father, employed "sesquipedalian verba," words a foot and a half long. It was a family trait to use big words. When the family returned to Washington from Pittsburgh, John and his younger brother Benjamin studied at the Jesuit-run Georgetown College where they learned "little or nothing. I shall take John home with me after the holidays and teach him myself in the Office, hoping at 15 or 16 to send him to Princeton."[92]

But Princeton was expensive, and on the advice of his friend Robert Harper, Latrobe considered the advantages of the US Military Academy at West Point. Earlier he had applied to the academy for an appointment as professor of engineering, hoping to improve his chaotic finances with a fixed salary. Now he sought a place for his fourteen-year-old son. Latrobe explained to his father-in-law that it was time to consider "what part he [John] is to act in the world. The respectability of the family on both sides forbid our looking to any profession but that of a Gentleman for him. If he is to be a Lawyer or a Physician he must receive a College education of 3 years at least. . . . If a Merchant, his time in a respectable counting house will be equally expensive for us." Latrobe hoped his son would choose some profession other than architecture and engineering. But, like Henry, "his talents indeed point to my own, as well as his inclination."[93] Still, wherever John went to college and whatever his future, his father intended to serve as an ever-present guide, as he felt his own father had not been.

A West Point education cost nothing and the institution was, in Latrobe's judgment, "of the very first kind." The academy, with its refurbished engineering department after the War of 1812, included courses in civil engineering that Latrobe considered essential to the development of the United States. In addition, he hoped military discipline would correct John's few faults—his indolence and his occasional bad manners. In September 1818 John Latrobe entered West Point as a cadet and two years later he was the head of his class.

Latrobe never imagined a formal education for Julia, though she was "a little faultless daughter," "who beats John in everything he attempts to learn."[94] From his years in London, Latrobe was aware of Mary Wollstonecraft's pleas to educate women in *Vindication of the Rights of Women*. The English feminist's arguments on the significance of educating women for the benefit of both men and women and ultimately society had also been the talk of Philadelphia. But Latrobe saved money by homeschooling his youngest daughter. In any case Julia would eventually need to find a husband, not a profession. Throughout her childhood she delighted her father with drawings of animals, poetic doggerel, and cardboard replicas of his buildings.

In 1806, Latrobe had been in Virginia searching for stone for the US Capitol when he learned that three-year-old John and one-year-old Julia were desperately ill from dysentery, one of the many efficient child killers of the nineteenth century. He left immediately for home, stopping briefly in Baltimore. There after learning that his design for the Cathedral had been tampered with, he had "a very disagreeable dispute" with one of the trustees of the Cathedral. Then during a ride on the Baltimore-Philadelphia coach the horses threw the coachman and only after a struggle was Latrobe able to control them. He had been, as he described the event to his brother, "in danger of my life."[95]

Upon arrival in Philadelphia, sleepless and anxious, he endured a psychic experience: "I appeared to have *two* separate minds, *one* perfectly easy and quiet, perhaps a little torpid . . . the *other* agitated by some evil not recollected without difficulty," which in his precise retelling of the episode in his journal erased sentiments of distress and compassion. In this state he felt nothing and could make only superficial inquiries about John and Julia, who were improving. "Is this my husband?" asked his wife of the man who usually displayed such warmth and concern for her and the children. Meanwhile Latrobe feared for his sanity, describing both bodily pain and being "wholly deprived of my reason. I thought I would never have command of my senses again."[96]

Three days later he succumbed to a violent case of dysentery, no doubt contracted from the children. For ten days, two of Philadelphia's best-known physicians treated Latrobe, who later remembered "violent exertions of mind, excessive spirits, weakness to fainting of body and the peculiar horrible Pain of dysentery." Dr. Albert Kuhn, considered by Latrobe to be "old school," had received his formal training at the University of Uppsala in Sweden and the University of Edinburgh. Dr. James Reynolds, an Irishman known in Philadelphia as much for his republican politics as his medicine, had taken on Latrobe's case as a volunteer. Latrobe believed Reynolds did so in order to experiment. Both physicians agreed that "a most violent nervous fever" affecting his senses had attacked him.

Both physicians employed the torturous therapies of their time; both operated under the basic philosophy that health came from a proper balance of four bodily fluids—blood, phlegm, yellow bile, and black bile. The purpose of their treatment was to obtain the proper balance and harmony of humors disturbed by an illness. To that end Kuhn prescribed massive amounts of castor oil, in order to clean out his patient's overloaded bilious system. Reynolds employed the popular therapy of blood-letting, removing twenty-eight ounces of blood from each arm, on the theory that this would reduce the fever, after which Latrobe promptly fainted.

Meanwhile Latrobe endured vivid dreams, possibly the result of the opium that his doctors were also prescribing. As he later described his condition, scenes of Mahomet conversing with angels, artisans making machinery, and a masquerade dance of millions "hurried through my brain." Then after ten days, his fever broke overnight; the bloody flux of dysentery disappeared; and the patient improved, though now subjected to an assortment of emetics and purgatives—musk, castoreum, and assafoetida. Eventually Latrobe was well enough to move to Clover Hill.

Latrobe had always been interested in matters of health and sickness; they were part of the human condition that attracted his curiosity throughout his life. And diseases, a constant threat to his children, found a careful observer in Benjamin Latrobe. Earlier he had described his father's symptoms before his death in 1796. In 1801 Latrobe chronicled the medical history of another relative, his mother's brother, Frederick Antes, who died after a two-week illness.

Latrobe's daily notes in his journal on the progression of Antes's disease are meticulous. He catalogued the medicines given to Antes—doses of calomel and the powder from ground Mexican and Middle Eastern plants, ipecacuanah and jalop—along with a concoction of snake root promptly vomited by the patient and later, a few drops of Rhenish wine. He detailed the physical symptoms of his uncle's decline—the "furred tongue," lowered pulse, passage of stools and painful kidney stones and finally, "at 11 on September 20, the temporal artery ceased to beat." Four hours later Frederick Antes died "without a groan or convulsive motion."[97]

Although Latrobe believed patients to be poor reporters of their medical histories—they only wanted to get well and had no medical knowledge—he considered himself an exception. He read medical texts and scrutinized his family's medical history and inherited conditions, concluding that the Latrobes suffered from a predisposition to kidney disease. He routinely assessed the training and reputation of the physicians who treated his family. His engineering background and professional efforts to improve water quality inclined him to consider matters of public health. Not alone in his interest but unusual in the depth of his knowledge, he represented a generation that no longer interpreted illness and death as the will of God but as matters for human intervention.

In 1816, Latrobe sent a letter to a well-known Washington physician, Dr. Henry Huntt, detailing the chronic and most debilitating medical condition of his life—what he called his "hemicranias." What doctors at the time labeled remitting opthalmia, modern medicine would diagnose as migraine and/or cluster headaches.[98] At the time Latrobe had read an account of a case in London similar to his that had been treated successfully with opium. He sought Huntt's advice. He offered a detailed description of the frequency of his attacks (usually two a year), their onset with a painful throbbing around the eyes followed by vomiting, numbness of one side of his body, sensitivity to light, and after a week or ten days of suffering "excessive lowness of spirit and a tendency to hysterical affections."[99]

The headaches had begun when he was seventeen. He had been hiking in the Carpathian Mountains with friends. He felt an excruciating pain in his eye, fainted, and tumbled down the mountain. Later he associated these attacks with a mental state of anxiety and "vexation" or perhaps too much food and wine, though Latrobe was a temperate man.

He explained to Huntt that he had tried the entire interventional arsenal of nineteenth-century medicine—bleeding, cupping, blisters, and baths, though he had declined salivation, the dangerous administration of mercury on the tongue. He had taken as well the internal medicines doctors prescribed, including calomel, jalop, and bark. But he had not taken opium since it made him restless and anxious. It is not clear what advice Huntt offered in return but Latrobe continued to suffer throughout his life. His descriptions are colorful: once he described a headache arriving "on the N. East side of my head." During another episode he could neither read nor write and existed for fifteen days on tea and toast. In one episode in Washington the disease attacked his eyes and forehead for six weeks. During this siege "I could not bear the company of anyone, not even of my wife." After his recovery he offered the grim message of a chronic sufferer: "*Valeant, quantum valere possunt.*" [May they be in good health, as far as they can be in good health.][100]

Besides Latrobe's hemicranias, his household was rarely free of some disorder. The children suffered the familiar diseases of chickenpox and measles. Mary Latrobe endured chronic episodes of severe rheumatism and was treated with laudanum, sometimes as many as 120 drops a day. The entire family was often ill from bouts of bilious, malarial fever. Like many Americans, the Latrobes depended on Tissot's herbal drops, the all-purpose medical factotum of this age. The constant presence of sickness and the uncertainty of survival disposed a man who had rejected the religious faith of his fathers to accept the poet's complaint that we are "*poor playthings of unpitying fate.*"[101] When Latrobe noted in the final paragraph of his letters that the family was well, it had significant meaning for this generation.

There was one scourge that seemed a special curse. Latrobe had first confronted yellow fever in the United States when he arrived in Norfolk and saw the yellow flags that warned of its presence. He had confronted the disease again in Philadelphia, where with various degrees of severity it visited annually in the summer and fall. Yellow fever had killed Mary's brother John in Charleston; it had killed his friend the Venetian physician Giambattista Scandella in New York as he was preparing to return to Europe. It had affected Latrobe's travel plans and several times had delayed the transport of materials for his architectural projects. And it had also influenced his career. Believing that yellow fever originated in bad water and the excessive accumulation of filth and the cloud of miasma that arose in the summers from such debris, Latrobe had built his waterworks in Philadelphia as an effort to end the pestilence. In the meantime, he cautioned Henry to "fly" to Pensacola if yellow fever appeared in New Orleans.

5

Breaking Points

*In two years I must be a great blunderer if I do not realize
a handsome fortune here.*

BENJAMIN HENRY LATROBE, *Papers*, 3: 459.

FINALLY, IN THE fall of 1813, two years after he had lost his job as surveyor of public buildings, Latrobe and his family left Washington. He had
wanted to go earlier but could not pay his creditors nor afford the cost of
moving. At the time, Latrobe had a few private commissions and was still the
unpaid engineer of the Washington Canal Company. But after his dismissal
as surveyor, his family barely survived on his small salary from the Navy Yard.
Much of the money from his previous commissions he squandered on an investment in a power-loom enterprise organized by a Connecticut inventor,
Samuel Blydenburg, whose device promised an exponential increase in finished cotton goods over hand-loom weaving. But Blydenburg proved more
talk than action. Other investors dropped out; Latrobe remained and lost
more than $2,000. Subsequently there were overdrafts at banks and unpaid
doctors' and blacksmiths' bills. A chronic matter earlier, Latrobe's finances
became an intractable preoccupation as he reached middle age. He necessarily engaged in the "money hunting" that he had earlier decried as an unfortunate American characteristic.[1]

Yet by Latrobe's unrealistic calculations, after paying his creditors, he was
worth over $20,000: the charter for the New Orleans Waterworks under his
son Henry's direction accounted for $25,000, though it was far from com-
plete; the profit on future steamboats amounted to $16,000. But these were
paper assets, and at the time Latrobe could not scrape together enough money
to "get from hence."[2] He had contributed to his financial perils with his risky
investments, although he insisted he was not a speculator. "I never risk anything on mere hope and chance. To induce me to enter a project I must see
my way thro' it."[3]

On the other hand, his financial situation was beyond his control when the government proved as lax as private clients in paying his accounts. The Navy Department had not reimbursed him for a steam engine that had cost $2,000, and it took three years for the government to pay him the $300 he charged for the design of a US Naval Hospital that was never built. By any measure he was a hard worker; in fact, one of Latrobe's failings was that he took on too many projects and never finished them on time. So often did he blame the delivery process, however uncertain at the time, for the late arrival of a promised design that his explanations may have been fictitious.

To a fellow émigré with whom he shared thoughts on books and ideas, Latrobe described his life as little more than drudgery. He had no time to read books, though they furnished him with the "idea that I was born for something better than to be a slave for bread."[4] Frustrated and broke, he informed Christian that he had accomplished enough in Washington for his professional reputation to survive. Personal money matters now must dictate his life, and for them he must leave the city and recreate himself in a different setting.[5]

Soon Latrobe enlisted a new patron. He had known the inventor Robert Fulton through their mutual connections with poet and diplomat Joel Barlow and his wife Ruth. The Barlow home—Kalorama —had become a gathering place for Washington's intellectuals, politicians, and businessmen, an American version of a Parisian salon. While in Paris, Barlow had met a fellow expatriate, Robert Fulton, an itinerant inventor trying to interest Napoleon in his inventions for a submarine and a torpedo he called an underwater cannon. It did not help when Fulton launched one of his steam-powered maritime creations on the Seine River with an engine so heavy that the vessel immediately sank. Back in the United States, he continued to work on his vision for steam-powered ships.

In Washington Latrobe visited the Barlows often, even apologizing for the frequency of his visits. In their parlor he and Fulton, who was in Washington to register a patent, had discussed their mutual interest in the subject of circular saws for boring holes in wooden fence posts. Both men shared the Enlightenment pleasure of investigation and invention. Later they exchanged letters about new forms of canal locks. Both advocated the development of canals and roads, and their astute observations on American transportation had been included as appendices in Secretary of the Treasury Gallatin's 1808 report on internal improvements.

But what brought the two men together in a business relationship was the steam engine—the wondrous invention that by powering ships on America's rivers provided multiple benefits. Advocates for internal improvements like

Latrobe and Fulton believed that steamboats would bind the vast republic into a union, thereby reducing the secessionist opportunities for adventurers like Aaron Burr. By promoting the settlement of the interior of the country, steamboats would extend America's internal markets and expand the national economy. Not to be overlooked, their developers would get rich.

Latrobe had learned about steam engines in England as an apprentice in the office of John Smeaton. He had observed the process of heating water and using the resulting steam as a form of power in a society previously dependent for energy on human and animal muscle and on harnessing the force of streams and rivers. He had observed its success in providing steam-powered water to London through the Chelsea Waterworks.

The concept of steam engines was simple; its complex application required the building of a machine with boilers, condensers, cylinders, connecting rods and pistons. By using coal or wood to heat water, the machinery would create steam, and, through a pipe from the boiler to the cylinder, deliver the steam's power. In the case of navigation the challenges were twofold: how to put a heavy engine onto the wooden frame of a boat without it sinking, and how to apply the captured steam power to some sort of mechanism that would propel a boat.

As countless versions of steam engines appeared, Latrobe continued to prefer the low-pressure British version developed by Isaac Watt and Matthew Boulton over a new, smaller high-pressure model engineered by Connecticut-born inventor Oliver Evans.[6] In the United States where there were only three operating steam engines in 1800, Latrobe's innovative application employed this new technology as an energy source for his waterworks, despite the reservations of many Philadelphians. Initially, however, he was suspicious of its application to ships.[7]

In one of his papers to the American Philosophical Society Latrobe answered an inquiry as to whether improvements had been made in the construction of steam engines in America. His conclusion in 1803 was classic Latrobe—precise, thorough, and technical. It was also contentious, as he publicly criticized Evans's steam engine and thereby initiated a lifelong battle with a leading American inventor. Years later Latrobe still felt so strongly about the matter that he petitioned Congress to void one of Evans's patents. In his remarks to the society Latrobe concluded that Americans had added innovations to steam engine technology. In his judgment these did not yet rise to his standard for *improvements*.[8]

After his success with two steam engines in Philadelphia, Latrobe had ordered another for the Washington Navy Yard. Its manufacture was overseen by an English-trained former employee of Watt and Boulton, James Smallwood, who had emigrated to the United States. In a role similar to that of Latrobe in architecture, Smallwood had transmitted English methods to a technologically underdeveloped country. Installed by Latrobe in the Navy Yard, the machine successfully powered a multi-use hammer, a rope that dragged logs from a dock, and a sawmill.

Latrobe was not an inventor or even one of the many contending American fathers of the steam engine. His relation to the new machinery remained that of an adopter and promoter—a consulting engineer who applied the invention to pump water and drive machinery. "You misjudge my profession," he informed Secretary of the Navy Robert Smith, "if you suppose I have anything to do with steam engines other than to use them when I want them."[9]

Still, his training as an engineer, his knowledge of geometry, his understanding of materials, and his unremitting curiosity and commitment to innovation complemented his work as an architect. He was forever interested in the application of new technology, and he accelerated the use of steam power in the United States. "My way *generally* is to stick to that which will *certainly* succeed, because tested by experience and to let others make the new experiments."[10]

Weary of Washington and in need of a job, Latrobe appealed to his friend Robert Fulton. By 1812 Fulton was no longer a failed inventor; he had become a successful entrepreneur after his steam-powered *North River,* later renamed the *Clermont,* churned up the Hudson River from New York to Albany and back at a pace-setting six miles an hour. Crowds along the river cheered this strange, smoke-disgorging vessel. Fulton had a legislative monopoly on steamboat travel on New York rivers and along that state's coast, with penalties supposedly charged for any infringement. Like his patents, his exclusive privileges were constantly challenged by those he dismissed as pirates. Initially without competition, his partnership with the wealthy Robert Livingston, scion of a landed New York family, flourished. The combination of a rich partner and a talented inventor created an immediate commercial success. Turning his attention to the west, Fulton envisioned a vast national network of steamships using the great river passages of the interior, especially the Mississippi and the Ohio. And he insisted that his patents gave him exclusive control of all steamboats on American waters, arguing that inventors must be protected by monopolies.[11]

He and Livingston hired Latrobe's son-in-law Nicholas Roosevelt to build the *New Orleans*, the first vessel powered by a steam engine to complete what turned out to be a four-month trip down the Mississippi to New Orleans. Later Fulton fired Roosevelt for his sloppy invoices and failure to attend to his duties. Now rich and commercially successful, at first Fulton failed to respond Latrobe's pleas for a job: "I believe you have forgotten that there exists such a personage as myself. I have however not entirely forgotten you," persisted Latrobe in letters to a man he considered his friend.[12]

A few months later Fulton offered not the partnership that a man with capital might have commanded and that Latrobe hoped for, but an arrangement that nevertheless promised financial stability. Fulton needed an agent to supervise the building of a steamboat in Pittsburgh. He calculated the profits from one round trip from Pittsburgh to Louisville carrying forty passengers and sixty tons of goods at $6,600; four round trips a year would increase profits, at least on paper, to $26,400; if there was a second boat, minus expenses and after investors were paid, profits would amount to a handsome, steady income of $3,600 a year for Latrobe. And while the boats were being built and outfitted with a steam engine, Latrobe would earn a salary of $2,000 a year, at a time when urban clerks and skilled artisans never made more than $400 a year. "You have now my friend to compare this prospect of certain fortune with your prospects at Washington and be guided by your own judgement," advised Fulton.[13]

As a self-proclaimed professional man, Latrobe believed that he brought important attributes to Fulton's project including "a perfect knowledge of business, integrity, industry and an ability to oversee mechanics."[14] From Latrobe's perspective theirs was much more than just a business arrangement; the two men were joined together in the time-honored bonds of male friends. Even if he made his fortune on "your western Waters," Latrobe informed Fulton, he would not feel "more towards you than I shall do if I never see [that fortune.]"[15] But the collegial affirmation of friendship transcending the pursuit of wealth suggests the opposite: Latrobe expected, as Fulton had intimated, that he would become rich. By the fall of 1813 Latrobe had accepted Fulton's offer and even had a name for the steamboat he would build in Pittsburgh: he called it the *Buffalo*, "as befitting an <u>American</u> vessel."[16]

To avoid lawsuits, Latrobe could not leave Washington until he paid off his creditors. He needed cash as well to pay the cost of transporting four wagon loads of books, instruments, silver, and furniture. In an embarrassing request for a loan from Fulton, he exaggerated his financial resources, balancing his "estate" comprising nearly $10,000 of liabilities against assets of $48,000. The latter included land worth $3,000, the future New Orleans waterworks that he estimated as worth $25,000, and $14,000 in cash owed him.

Latrobe even counted seven shares of the dormant Chesapeake and Delaware Canal stock as an asset. By any measure his prideful accounting overstated his wealth, most of which depended on future success and had little relation to his current status. He still blamed his Moravian upbringing for his inability to deal with his finances: "My habits and education have imperfectly instilled into me the grand system of pecuniary ethics which governs us Americans."[17]

Along with Latrobe's past, his profession contributed to this deficiency. Buildings were long-term projects, as was their often-contested and delayed reimbursement, frequently for materials and labor costs advanced by the architect. Consequently, Latrobe became accustomed to including future claims—however uncertain--in his financial reckoning. Despite his persistent efforts to educate Americans about the orderly payment of fees and the understanding, so crucial to the economics of architects, that they must be paid for the design of even unbuilt structures, there remained no acknowledged American standards about the process. Nor was there any organization or group of colleagues to assist in transforming architecture into an established profession with regular practices. Latrobe also lived in a nation where the emerging system of capitalism encouraged risk-taking and the associated credit system depended on unreliable promissory notes, fake bills of exchange, and discounted bank notes. One had to be careful. Latrobe was not.

The result was an ongoing personal crisis as Latrobe's sense of himself as an elite professional increasingly clashed with his economic circumstances. Ever hopeful about his financial opportunities, this time in Pittsburgh, he informed his brother, "If I live to finish what I have undertaken & which will occupy three or four years, I shall very probably be able to sit down at my leisure & deliver the Oar at which I have pulled so lustily and so long to my son Henry."[18] Meanwhile his specious, futuristic accounting provided a means to bridge the gap. Still, as he admitted to Fulton after claiming assets of over $40,000, "This side of the grave there is not a poorer man."[19]

Fulton sent $1,500 as a loan to pay off his debts, and in the fall of 1813 the family left Washington, "bidding an eternal adieu," as Latrobe darkly catalogued the culture of the nation's capital, "to the malice, backbiting, and Slander, trick and fraud and hypocrisy, lofty pretensions and scanty means, boasts of patriotism and bargaining of conscience, pretence of religion, and breach of laws, starving doctors, thriving attornies, whitewashing of Jail oaths, upstart haughtiness, and depressed merit."[20] The Latrobes visited Mary's widower father at Clover Hill before turning west. To his father-in-law who objected to losing his daughter to faraway Pittsburgh, Latrobe promised that the family will "be very little further from you than we are here. Two days journey is the whole distance."[21] But their first trip proved otherwise.

It took the Latrobes twenty-two days to travel the 350 miles from Philadelphia to Pittsburgh. The family journeyed in a large olive-green carriage, with a special space in the back designed by Latrobe for the children—ten-year-old John, nine-year-old Julia, and seven-year-old Benjamin. Peacock, Latrobe's beloved horse, for whom he expressed "brotherly affection," was tied behind.[22] Kitty McCausland, the family's all-purpose nanny and cook, had left earlier to prepare the large brick house on Market Street that the family rented. The roads were miserable, more navigable than passable. It rained and snowed, and even in October, there was ice in the Allegheny Mountains as they passed through Dewitt's Gap. They were greeted by a violent thunderstorm as they approached Pittsburgh, a western city of nearly 5,000.

Pittsburgh was the sixth community that Latrobe had lived in since his arrival in the United States and the first that was not along the Atlantic seacoast. Given its advantageous geography astride three rivers and its natural resources of coal and water power, the city served as a popular link to the west. Earlier it had been an obvious location for a colonial fort. As the nation expanded, it had become the largest community west of the Alleghenies and east of the Mississippi River. During the first two decades of the nineteenth century, Ohio, along with five other states west of the Alleghenies, joined the Union. Along the journey Latrobe observed eighteen families traveling west and memorialized these migrants in a handsome watercolor featuring their Conestoga wagons: "The road is thronged with them. The sceptre . . . is indeed departing from New England," he concluded.[23]

Latrobe's profession had always required mobility, but he expected to stay in Pittsburgh for at least five years, making his fortune from steam-powered commercial vessels, while his son Henry oversaw the profitable waterworks in New Orleans. The most gifted architect in America now began a new life overseeing the miracle of commercial boats powered by steam engines. Ever versatile, Latrobe now worked as an engineer and, in the unfamiliar capacity of a business man, as the agent of Robert Fulton's Ohio Steam Boat Company.

To a friend Latrobe described the natural beauty of Pittsburgh, a place "on a tongue of Land between two rivers both beautiful" with steep surrounding hills. It was the confluence of these two rivers—the slow-moving Monongahela and the rapid Allegheny as they formed the Ohio—that was crucial to the city and to Latrobe's mission. After acknowledging the physical beauty of the place, he explained to a friend: "but—there is always a BUT—" and in the case of Pittsburgh, it was the perpetual cloud of smoke

FIG. 5.1 "View of Village of Bloody Run." En route to Pittsburgh across the Allegheny Mountains, Latrobe observed Americans moving west. Later he completed a watercolor of a Conestoga wagon carrying migrating families into western Pennsylvania and Ohio. Note his depiction in the foreground of the infantrymen of the War of 1812. Courtesy of the Maryland Historical Society, 2003.14.

that obscured the sun. Without wearing a mask outside, residents had sooty faces, with the soot like "a fat blacking which lights on everything and everybody." And the sliver of land along the Monongahela where many boatyards were located frequently flooded. The place was all water and mud and smoke; the members of his family, he joked, were perpetually "well-smoked."[24]

An early site of the nation's industry, at the time Pittsburgh boasted 130 separate "manufactories," employing 1,500 men in saw mills, a salt mill, a brewery owned by his son-in-law Nicholas Roosevelt, and a flour mill powered by one of Oliver Evans's high-pressure steam engines. The city exemplified the process of technological acceleration; steam engines required iron parts and boilers, thus stimulating associated industries. In this emerging western powerhouse of coal, foundries, glass factories, and shipyards, as Latrobe described, "here are no poor, and cold and hunger are unknown. Those who do not grow rich—even I—must be either stupid, lazy, or drunken."[25]

The nation was in its second year of war with the British when the family settled in Pittsburgh. Earlier military assaults targeting Canada had been unsuccessful as Americans learned that invading Canada was more than a matter of simply marching across the border. Newspapers were full of General William Hull's humiliating surrender of Detroit, though the Americans had been more successful in naval warfare. Latrobe considered Hull a traitor—worse than Benedict Arnold.[26] He also considered the war a patriotic endeavor that would enhance the nationalist instincts in what he earlier described as "our illcemented Union."[27] After the British triumphs in Spain and Napoleon's defeat at the battle of Leipzig, the British redirected their vast military and naval arsenal against the Americans. By 1813, the number of their troops in this second war against the United States had soared to 52,000. The number of ships in the Chesapeake Bay grew to a rumored 100.

Long a critic of American preparedness and its generals but ever a fervent patriot, Latrobe had offered his services as an engineer to Captain Elias Caldwell's Light Horse militia troop before he moved to Pittsburgh. Earlier he had approached General Henry Dearborn about improving the defenses of Washington and had been informed that engineers "were of not much use in our Army; anybody could dig a fort."[28] Before he left the capital, Latrobe was one of a handful of Americans to warn of a British land invasion as the Chesapeake Bay became a safe harbor for the British fleet and a dagger directed at Washington. In fact, the situation kept him awake at night, "*Me*, who have no interest but a national one," at a time when most of "our great Men . . . go on quietly as if these British Ships were in the Thames."[29] Latrobe would be in Pittsburgh when his warnings came true and the British army advanced on Washington, setting fire to his great masterpiece, the US Capitol, in the summer of 1814.

The war both complicated and enhanced his project in Pittsburgh. The British threat of an invasion and successful blockade of the Atlantic coast stifled trade, with national exports plunging from $61 million in 1811 to just over $7 million in 1814. Personally affected, Latrobe had been unable to ship the parts for a steam engine to New Orleans for his municipal water project. With Louisiana now part of the United States and New Orleans a thriving port with access to the Caribbean and South America, river and coastal traffic was quicker and more efficient than travel on the nation's interior roads. Americans were turning to an alternative mode of transportation stimulated by the war—their vast internal river system. As Latrobe described in an article in the *National Intelligencer*, "between New Orleans and Washington [by using rivers] there will be when the road from Cumberland to Brownsville [Pa.] is completed, *only seventy-two miles of land carriage,* and that over a capital turnpike road," the latter the kind of carefully surveyed and constructed road he had recommended when he lived in Washington.[30]

With river travel rising in importance, there was an impetus to shift from energy provided by wind via sails to the more reliable power provided by steam engines. Capable of traveling six miles an hour on the Ohio and Mississippi rivers and powerful enough to go upstream and overcome swift currents, these ships had to be sufficiently low-hulled to navigate rocky shoals and shallow summer waters. On the other hand, making Latrobe's work more complicated, wartime inflation increased the cost of wages and materials— especially iron, coal, and timber—necessary for the construction of this new generation of ships. Labor was scarce, though the war did bring some unusual opportunities, which Latrobe took advantage of.

Six prisoners of war, captured at the successful American defense of Lake Erie, remained jailed in Pittsburgh under an informal parole system based on the understanding that officers were gentlemen and, having given their word, would not try to escape. Shortly after his arrival, Latrobe had been hired to build a temporary prison barracks for which he collected $300. There he met the British prisoners of war. Soon several were invited to the Latrobes for Sunday lunch and some evenings. According to Mary Latrobe, they were "elegant and well informed and their misfortunes give them a claim on all good Christians. . . . My husband talks politics most outrageously with them and defends our Administration. I step between them and point to the [amputee] Purser's crutches."[31] One prisoner taught young John Latrobe the British manual of arms.

Among these prisoners were several artisans and a shipwright. By using them in his boatyard, Latrobe saw an opportunity to improve a local workforce so deficient in skills that he had imported a shipwright—William Hurley—from the east. To legally employ British prisoners, Latrobe solicited the help of John Mason, the US commissioner of prisoners. After receiving a special order, he soon had the men at work for the benefit of the country that they had recently been fighting, in what one tactfully described as an unnatural war. A few months later, this time for a friend, Latrobe requested that a prisoner who had been a glassblower in London be paroled to work in a local glassworks factory.[32] In Latrobe's reading of the partisan politics he disdained, none of the citizens of Pittsburgh would complain: they were all Federalists, even the Irish among them, who opposed the war and would hardly object to the hiring of a few British soldiers.[33]

At first, in the fall after his arrival in 1813, his work went well. But then Latrobe lay ill from a bilious fever for a month, as he explained to his impatient employer. Recovered, he thanked Fulton "most truly and sincerely for placing me here.... After 25 Years toil for the public, I shall at last owe ease and competence to the friendship of an individual."[34] By December he was searching for a foundry to build the steam engine that would power the *Buffalo,* but he soon encountered a series of problems. Latrobe had expected to use the already established yard of another Fulton-funded enterprise, the Mississippi Steam Boat Company, where another steam-powered vessel—the eponymous *Vesuvius*—was nearly complete. But there was no room.

So busy were the city's other engine shops and boatyards that for a time he was unable to find space to locate his operation. Nor could he find a place along the Monongahela after being told to abandon one location when its more profitable, short-term business making iron tools expanded. Promising a weekly report to Fulton, he instead wrote of the weather, other ventures in the city, the high cost of iron, the availability of timber from the vast forests along the Allegheny, and the proper proportions of steam engines to wooden ships. He included summaries of his expenses and casual mentions of his balance sheet. But, as Latrobe would soon discover, Fulton demanded precise accounting reports and weekly vouchers, not Latrobe's long digressions.[35]

In a letter to his wife's uncle, John Livingston, Fulton defined his requirements. He expected "precise details on the state of the works," submitted on the first of every month. Agents must keep regular books of all receipts and disbursements and vouchers for every cent spent. Materials, especially iron, must be weighed and posted on the expense ledgers, and of course, agents were responsible for every cent of their accounts. "As you grow rich," Fulton advised, "let me make you an active accurate man of Business."[36]

Latrobe solved one of his problems by leasing property where he built a forty-foot-long wharf, a warehouse, foundry, boiler, carpenter shops, boat shed, and saw pit, costing $5,000. He designed an ingenious horse gin with gears to drive various operations. Later, when this elaborate workplace became an issue, Latrobe argued that its built-in efficiencies decreased the cost of the *Buffalo.*

Even his son John thought otherwise. Describing a place where he played as a child, years later John acknowledged that there were no better shops in Pittsburgh than those of his father. Still his father's great fault, if indeed it was a failing, was that "he always wanted to do things in the best way, and he sometimes in consequence incurred the charge of extravagance; nor did he deviate, on this occasion, from his usual course, in the building he erected for the steamboat company."[37] In his new role as a businessman, Latrobe explained to Fulton that his works could later be sold for a profit: "If I have ventured too much I can get back again a *handsome gain*."[38]

By the winter Latrobe exulted to his son Henry that he was "here over head and ears in great things. The steam boats and two barges on the Stocks, 4 gangs of brick makers at work, Smiths, patternmakers, filer and turners, Ship joiners and boiler makers all as busy as possible; a country seat for Mr. Beltzhoover ordered, 6 houses offered in the town . . . besides 5 or 6 steam engines talked of," the last for a rolling mill, a flour mill, and a woolen mill in nearby Steubenville.[39] By early spring the 120-foot long, 300-ton *Buffalo* had been framed, sealed, and mostly caulked. This was progress indeed, but most of the projects described by Latrobe had nothing to do with the *Buffalo* and his employment by the Ohio Steam Boat Company. John Livingston, completing the *Vesuvius* nearby, reported to Fulton in New York on Latrobe's extracurricular enterprises.

A month later Fulton cut off Latrobe's credit; as a result, no one in Pittsburgh accepted his drafts. So began an agonizing conflict that lasted for months. Fulton charged that Latrobe spent money without authorization and too much of it at that. For example, there was an unexplained expense of $920 in February and the $5,000 for the workshop. In Fulton's indictment, Latrobe was not only over budget but he also spent too much time on other projects. He used tools paid for by Fulton and the Ohio Steam Boat Company to build a flat boat for himself, in addition to the approved freight boat *Harriet,* diplomatically named for Fulton's wife. Latrobe neither sent timely vouchers nor itemized his accounts, as Fulton required. He had never repaid Fulton's $1,500 personal loan. And though Latrobe had promised to do so, he had failed to raise money from investors for another possible joint project—the Potomac Steam Boat Company. No one in Washington had confidence in him, although Latrobe had persuaded President James Madison to buy five shares of that stalled enterprise.[40]

At first surprised, then hurt, and eventually angry, Latrobe responded that the initial budget established by Fulton had been too low. To spend only the specified $23,000 for the boat "*compleat*" was impossible when similar boats Fulton had financed cost nearly twice as much. Besides, much of the expense was beyond his control: "The enormous price of Iron, of steel, of tools, and Anvils, Vices, &c, I cannot regulate. . . . The Mississippi boats with the same engine have cost $45,000. . . . [I]f you will give me time, I will buy your Shops, tools, &c. for the[ir] value and you shall have security in *Land* and *wharf,* and *Warehouse*."[41] He begged Fulton not to close down the enterprise with the *Buffalo* so near completion: it would be ready for launching in May. As to the matter of his records, "I keep a regular and very fair set of books. My Vouchers are in the most perfect order; not a cent charged without a regular receipt."[42] But sending the information had proved difficult, and he had been unable to get his records into "a more compendious form" for John Livingston to carry to New York.[43]

The disagreement between two of the early republic's creative geniuses—one of buildings, the other of boats—festered, with a partial reconciliation during the late spring. Latrobe organized a meeting of the prominent residents of Pittsburgh to raise money. Fulton, in New York where his monopoly on New York waters was being contested, was distracted by legal battles over his patents and monopolies. Then in April, as crowds cheered along the Ohio, Livingston's steam-powered *Vesuvius* rolled free of her stocks and began her first voyage as a commercial vessel between Pittsburgh and New Orleans. Latrobe rode his horse along the road that skirted the river while measuring the speed of the vessel at a commendable eight miles an hour.

At Fulton's request, Latrobe described the event and its importance to the commerce of the nation in an article published in the *National Intelligencer*. "It does not require the ornament of metaphor to impress upon the public mind the incalculable advantage of an intercourse by water, effected in large vessels, which move with certainty and rapidity through an extent of internal navigation embracing a space almost as large as the whole continent of Europe. . . . [This mode of transportation], so often before attempted and laid aside in despair, has become *practical* and its principles reduced to mathematical certainty." Latrobe closed with praise for Fulton to whom the nation owed a debt of gratitude for his inventions.[44]

A month later Latrobe's *Buffalo* was launched—"a very desperate attempt," given the shallow water in the Monongahela River that would drop even lower during the summer. "I had to decide, whether I would risk an injury to so capital a boat, or risk lying in the stocks till November."[45] John Latrobe remembered watching the *Buffalo* slide stern first over the wharf, then stop until one half of the boat hung precariously over the ten-foot drop. It seemed as though it might break in two.[46] But the downward motion continued until after a loud noise the bow of the *Buffalo* dropped into the water, with only a small bump on the side to mar the occasion. The vessel floated level; there was no sign of any tilting. "My father drew a deep breath . . . when he saw that all was safe."[47]

But the *Buffalo* was not complete: it lacked the essential element of an expensive steam engine. Meanwhile Fulton had stopped paying the vouchers that Latrobe insisted he kept as "regular as a band of soldiers."[48] For weeks during the summer Latrobe suffered from one of his debilitating hemicranias. Recovered by the fall, Latrobe sent a twenty-one-page letter to "my angry friend" in which he outlined expenditures to Fulton that were not over $22,000, though his workshop on the Monongahela had cost an extra $5,000, and the engine would add an additional $6,000. "Mr. Fulton sent me estimates of what *ought* to be the cost of the boat, I sent him accounts of what it actually was."[49]

Latrobe preferred to calculate future possibilities: four trips between Pittsburgh and Cincinnati calling at various towns along the way—Marietta, Steubenville, and Point Pleasant with passengers and goods—would produce an annual profit of $43,000.[50] It was idiocy to leave the vessel incomplete; he would surrender his own share of the profits and mortgage the *Buffalo* in order to continue. Besides, he had put $6,000 of his own money into the project.

By the fall the break between Latrobe and Fulton was irreparable. Legal action replaced angry words. Fulton dismissed Latrobe, rebutting his former agent's accusations with his own: how had Latrobe, who had been unable to leave Washington until Fulton lent him the funds to do so, been able to amass thousands of dollars in a few months to spend on the *Buffalo?* Why hadn't Latrobe, who supposedly cherished his honesty, used this money to repay "a debt of honor"? Fulton concluded with a devastating personal insult in his final letter to Latrobe: "Few men know their standing in life because there is a delicacy about informing them. I had many advisors from Phila. and Elsewhere [tell me] not to engage in any business with you [and] that trouble would be the result." He ordered Latrobe to turn over all assets to the company including the *Buffalo.* If he did not, "the consequences may be extremely unpleasant to me and unhappy for you."[51]

Latrobe mustered his own weapons in this battle. First, there was the matter of protecting his integrity: "Any attempt to injure [my character] will be in vain for it will and can be effectually resisted." Still, if he was treated as an enemy, he would "act only for myself." Efforts to injure his financial interests would also fail. Using Pennsylvania's mechanic's lien law, enacted a few years earlier to protect workers from employers who did not pay their wages, Latrobe found a friendly sheriff who agreed to an attachment of what Fulton considered the property of the Ohio Steam Boat Company—the *Buffalo*, the *Harriet*, and his shops. Meanwhile, as an employee-creditor owed money by Fulton's company, Latrobe turned to the courts to apply protection. Until the suit was decided, William Hurley, the shipwright Latrobe had hired, took charge of the boats. But in November, the Court of Common Pleas of Allegheny County dissolved Latrobe's attachment, ruling that Latrobe did not qualify as a mechanic, which in better days he would hardly have contested. The court determined that he had contributed neither materials nor labor to the construction of the *Buffalo* and therefore lacked standing to place a lien on the property.[52]

While his suit was moving through the courts, Latrobe offered an olive branch to Fulton—"an amicable inquiry and impartial investigation" undertaken by Henry Baldwin, a prominent lawyer in Pittsburgh. Facing economic disaster and personal humiliation, Latrobe continued to believe that his only mistakes were in accepting Fulton's design for too large a boat to be built on too small a budget. "My crime is that I could not accomplish impossibilities, had to call for more money, and thus fell into disrepute. . . . Why do you threaten me with disgrace when you are uncertain whether what I say is not true, that I have a sufficient voucher for every item of account and legal proof of every Statement I ever made?"[53]

But Fulton no longer answered his letters, telling friends that he could hardly have ruined an already penniless man. In response, Latrobe excoriated his former friend: "Fulton has acted the part of a Madman by me, and by all his agents, with every one of whom he has quarreled. He is a spoiled Child and . . . sometimes a little crazy." Referring to Fulton's project for a steam-powered warship, to be named *Fulton the First*: "If his Fultons do no more than his torpedoes, *Fulton the First* will be also Fulton the last."[54] Latrobe informed his previous antagonist William Thornton, now in charge of the US Patent Office and registering patents of his own in an extraordinary conflict of interest, that Fulton's patents were fraudulent, especially his claim for the innovation of side paddle wheels on steam-powered vessels. The credit for that invention belonged to his son-in-law Nicholas Roosevelt.

Still, Latrobe was ashamed "that I had not sufficient penetration to see under [Fulton's] exterior of plausible generosity and enlarged views, the selfishness, and low cunning of his character. I have been his dupe, and am now suffering the punishment of my credulity."[55] The man with whom he had earlier believed himself so compatible that he suggested they might plan to live near each other in old age had reduced his family to poverty. To his previous benefactor, Latrobe threatened "the day of retribution will come to you."[56] Two months later Fulton suddenly died.

Latrobe had been confident that his financial problems would be solved as soon as the *Buffalo* made its first trip down the Ohio. Instead his ventures in Pittsburgh chilled his exuberant expectations about his future. He lapsed into one of his painful hemicranias. Meanwhile the orphaned *Buffalo* remained at a dock along the Monongahela, a visible reminder of another unrealized opportunity. The vessel was later sold at auction, and, furnished with a steam engine, ran profitably between Pittsburgh and Louisville before exploding and killing seventeen passengers in 1820.

In his dealings with Fulton, Latrobe had learned little from past episodes in which both his public and private architectural work had been challenged as too expensive, grandiose, and slow and his expense accounts considered insufficient. Partly this was the fate of an émigré whose formative years had been spent amid the handsome buildings of Georgian England whose costs were guaranteed by rich patrons and royalty; partly this was the result of attitudes in the early republic that favored the simplistic over the polished, the inexpensive over the costly, the temporary over the permanent, and, in Latrobe's view, the mediocre over the superior. But his own stubborn refusal to adapt to a new culture was also in play. In Pittsburgh Latrobe again depended on future possibilities, such as the uncertain value of his expensive shops. Too late he realized the consequences of his failure to provide the kind of accounting that Fulton demanded, that had made the inventor a commercial success, and that American businessmen increasingly required.

Latrobe's assessment of his conflict with Fulton incorporated both realism and magical thinking: "My industry has indeed been unremitting, my talents sufficient for their employment, but my habits, and habitual sentiments, and modes of acting as well as of thinking have been altogether ruinous. I see a thousand openings for a most splendid fortune which I have passed by, inviting as they were. My chivalric honesty has prevented my amassing a fortune even in this place."[57]

Latrobe continued to believe that he had never injured Fulton; on the contrary, he insisted, he had acted ethically, always serving the inventor.[58] He had kept to the moral high ground. To his son Henry, he crafted the episode as a lesson in character and finance. Henry should learn from his example: "among the lessons of self denial which are necessary to virtue and to happiness, not only the restraint of passion but of benevolence is to be learnt. The latter to my and Your disposition may be difficult, but it must be practiced, at the expense of pain. *Speak truth and stay out of debt* are precepts which include almost all the virtues."[59]

Certainly Fulton was a difficult, egocentric employer. Latrobe was not the only one of his business associates to call him greedy, fraudulent in his patents relating to the application of steam engines to boats, and obsessed with obtaining legal privileges that assured his financial success. At a time when the American patent system required little more than registering a design with the Patent Office and certifying that it would do no harm, and when development-oriented state legislatures readily granted monopolies, Fulton took advantage of an immature system to deny competition.

Doggedly litigious and often exaggerating his originality in order to claim protection, Fulton was frequently in court and was rumored to have hired more lawyers to protect his interests than anyone in America. By any measure Fulton benefited financially by obtaining privileges extended by state governments, although there were increasing challenges to monopolies as being hostile to the public interest. Still it would be more than a decade before such state-sponsored monopolies were overturned in *Gibbons v. Ogden*, the Supreme Court's landmark ruling that the federal government had the authority to regulate interstate commerce.[60]

As a practical matter, Fulton may have been less interested in Latrobe's *Buffalo* after two other boats he had financed were completed in Pittsburgh. He no longer needed the *Buffalo* and so cut his financial ties to Latrobe. Whatever the explanation for the break with Fulton, Latrobe suffered. By Christmas he accused Fulton of reducing his family "to absolute distress to the sale of furniture to buy firewood and coals."[61]

To a fellow victim, lawyer and steamboat agent John DeLacy, whom Fulton was trying to put in prison for debt, Latrobe admitted that "I and my wife have suffered and are suffering a state of wretchedness of which we never before had any idea."[62] He considered bankruptcy, assigning all his property to a trustee and "walking out whitewashed," by a judge who had probably been insolvent himself, after which he would begin again "in a small house, build[ing] as a contractor or common carpenter and so get[ting] on as well as I can. But who will employ me? It is a great misfortune to be born and educated a *Gentleman*: at least on this side of the Atlantic."[63] In these financial straits, he faced practical dilemmas: what would he do, how would he feed his family, and where would they live?

In this desperate period another crisis emerged. Because Latrobe was well behind schedule on his waterworks project, his contract with the New Orleans City Council had expired and required an extension. It was in this arrangement to supply clean water to the city of New Orleans that Latrobe's hopes for financial prosperity now rested. Just before the miserable Christmas of 1814, Latrobe explained his difficulties to the city council—first, the war with the British had "upended" commerce. It had also interfered with the manufacturing of the steam engine parts he had intended to send to the city. Latrobe reminded the council that he had already spent more than $30,000 in the construction of an engine house in New Orleans, a similar structure to the one so often praised in Philadelphia. He prayed for the indulgence of the council and made "a pledge of my honest intentions to fulfill my engagements to You." Later that year he received word that he had been granted a two-year extension, the first of three.[64]

During his eighteen months in Pittsburgh Latrobe had both public and private clients who hired the famous architect to design buildings for them. There is little documentation for these structures and it is uncertain, save for Latrobe's mention of them in his letters, whether some of them were ever built. But after Fulton cut off his credit, these commissions provided the funds he promptly invested and lost in the *Buffalo*.

The largest and most enduring was his design of the US Allegheny Arsenal along the Allegheny River, a government building inspired by homeland security needs during the War of 1812. Latrobe's design featured a central arsenal building with a shed for guns and handsome pavilion homes for the commandant and officers. The arsenal, which survived as a government building until 1926, displayed the simplicity that in Latrobe's mature work never reduced to homeliness but rather emerged as understated elegance. The plans reveal how, in this case for a multipurpose public building, Latrobe solved several problems in residential design that he had struggled with throughout his career. According to the experts on his domestic architecture, Michael Fazio and Patrick Snadon, these were "the convenient provision of a kitchen . . . without resorting to traditional outbuildings; the hierarchical distribution of primary and secondary spaces; the elegant accommodation of multiple room shapes . . . and the creation of interior scenery."[65]

As for other commissions, there were the usual challenges with his residential clients in the Pittsburgh area. These included an unrealized design for a house for a Mr. Riddle, who after a disagreement refused to pay Latrobe's fee and then built the house using his plans, and a "country seat" for the large landowner Daniel Beltzhoover, who disputed his fees and later sued. He designed a warehouse for John O'Hara, a mill for Mr. Cowan, stores for foundry owner Mr. Beelen, and a structure for the circus that delighted his children and for which he was paid $500. The most famous Latrobe home in the area was a commission for William Foster's house in Lawrenceville, Pennsylvania, where his son, songwriter Stephen Foster, lived as a child.

Latrobe complained about the nature of some of these jobs: "I [am] an Architect and *builder* for I build now stores, pig pens, country seats, barracks, shops and anything that brings money."[66] For years he had joked that he could succeed as a mechanic or a blacksmith or even selling wood. To Dolley Madison he had declared, "The Motto of my family, of my art, and of my duty

FIG. 5.2 The US Arsenal on the Allegheny. While in Pittsburgh working on a steamboat, Latrobe took on extra jobs, including a commission for a military complex consisting of an arsenal, commandant's house, and powder magazine. The arsenal displays the clarity of conception, excellent masonry, and simplicity of his designs. Library of Congress, LC-USZC4-103.

is *tutto si fa, tout se fait,*" loosely in English "we will do anything." (The traditional Latrobe motto was the more ennobling "He who searches finds.")[67] Years later John Latrobe described these jobs as the humble functions his brilliant father was forced to undertake. Pittsburgh, like Richmond, Philadelphia, and Washington, could not provide enough architectural commissions to sustain a family of five. As Latrobe complained, the place was not sufficiently developed as "a scene for my profession as yet." And without Fulton, he lacked the capital to build an income-producing steamboat.[68]

In his capacity as an engineer Latrobe oversaw the construction of a steam engine for a mill in Steubenville, intended to run its cotton and woolen operations. But his absences overseeing this operation in the small Ohio town thirty miles from Pittsburgh became examples of his dereliction of duty to the Ohio Steam Boat Company and his employer Robert Fulton. Eventually Latrobe decided that the city was "too distant from the Seaport towns to be an agreeable residence all the Year."[69] He considered moving to Clover Hill and living in his father-in-law's home until "an eligible arrangement" developed.

After the attack on Washington and the destruction of the US Capitol in the late summer of 1814, Latrobe solicited his friends in Washington. Unusually tentative, he offered his services to rebuild, having devoted, as he described in a letter to President Madison, "the best Years of my life to the public. . . . That I have shared the charge of extravagance with every Architect to whom the expenditure of money on public works has been committed, from the most ancient times and in every nation, I am very sensible." In the final version of this letter he struck out the subsequent exculpatory explanation, "but conscious that I should, on investigation, appear innocent." Latrobe pleaded on personal grounds: his wife was anxious to live near her father and brothers, and the children required a better education than that available in Pittsburgh. Latrobe did acknowledge an "excusable ambition . . . to restore the works which I have erected."[70]

To Thomas Munroe, who had earlier supervised the expenditures on the Capitol and who warned Latrobe of the opposition to his appointment, Latrobe responded:

> I am perfectly aware that the prejudice against me . . . does actually exist; nor can I altogether blame those in whose minds it has arisen. At my age, I cannot be ignorant of my own Character, or of the effect of my Manner. Whatever I do, or say, I do and say with energy. I find by experience that I am generally considered as imperious and haughty, until I am known intimately. For this Opinion of me, there must be a foundation in my Manner, tho there is none in my disposition.[71]

Anxious to avoid another humiliation, Latrobe understood that he was "personally obnoxious" to Madison and his cabinet. Still he admitted to a continuing ambition "to reclose my own works."[72] His wife was less apologetic. After Latrobe took to his bed with another episode of hemicrania, Mary Latrobe appealed to the president, several congressmen, and Secretary of the Treasury Alexander Dallas to reappoint her husband to the surveyorship. To her friend Ruth Barlow she described the family's financial circumstances. Barlow promptly responded with $200.

Then one day in March the family's future arrived in a large packet with the presidential seal, offering Latrobe reappointment as public surveyor of the US Capitol. As Mary Latrobe later described, her husband was sitting in one of the few remaining chairs in their rented Pittsburgh home: "I presented him the Packet. Behold, I said, what Providence has done for you! and what your poor weak wife has been the humble instrument of obtaining. He threw himself on my breast and wept like a child—so true it is that women can bear many trials better than Men."[73]

And so Latrobe left the place where he had moved with such anticipation eighteen months earlier to return to Washington. Again he mustered enthusiasm: he was leaving "this luxuriant country, over which Nature has wasted her exuberance . . . [to return] to the gravel and brick earth, and stunted vegetation of the Seaboard, as into my native element; for there I shall find literature, and science, taste, and some *taste* for honor, friendship, . . . and integrity, as well as for the arts that cheer and soften social intercourse. Here [in Pittsburgh] the only *taste* is for money."[74] As he had so many times in his life, Benjamin Latrobe was ready to put the disastrous episode behind him and undertake his next journey with optimism.

By the time Latrobe returned to Washington in April 1815 and developed a plan for restoring the Capitol, the war with Great Britain had ended. Weeks had passed between the British approving the peace treaty and the news arriving in the United States. The agreement still awaited Madison's signature and approval by the US Senate. The terms of the peace treaty negotiated in Ghent established the status quo before the war—without any reparations for human losses and property damage, an unsatisfying conclusion to a controversial war. Official Washington had hoped for some form of amends from the British. But with this treaty ending what critics labeled "Mr. Madison's War," nothing had been accomplished. President Madison was not the only resident of Washington who had observed the humiliating British invasion of the nation's capital and who hoped for some compensation from the British for the destruction of the US Capitol, the President's House, and the Treasury Building.

The previous summer in August 1814, a flotilla of British ships had moved up the Patuxent River, depositing 4,000 British troops near the tiny village of Benedict in southern Maryland. At first, Madison's cabinet believed Baltimore and Annapolis more likely targets than the capital, but Secretary of State James Monroe, who rode out to scout British movements, advised moving the government's archives. The enemy was clearly marching northward toward the nation's capital. A few days later most congressmen as well as the president, who had been present at the disastrous effort at Bladensburg to stop the invasion, fled the city. First Lady Dolley Madison and the White House enslaved loaded silver, official papers, the Latrobe-designed velvet curtains from the Blue Room, and the Gilbert Stuart portrait of George Washington onto wagons and fled across the Potomac into Virginia.

By dusk on August 24 a British brigade of 1,500 soldiers led by Major General Robert Ross and joined by Rear Admiral George Cockburn arrived on Capitol Hill. Perhaps—for their initial intention was never clear—the British commanders sought ransom money or a formal surrender from the now-departed officers of the US government. Perhaps they always planned some sort of retaliation for the burning of York (present-day Toronto). Most likely, the Capitol building of the United States was a target of opportunity. In any case, after shots rang out from private homes, several British soldiers were killed. The invaders demanded reprisals. And what would be more meaningful to destroy than the physical symbols of American sovereignty— the Capitol and the President's House?

At the Capitol, the British soldiers broke windows and gathered wooden sashes and frames, doors, tables, chairs, and the curtains that Latrobe had installed to improve the acoustics in the center of the assembly hall. Then they put rocket powder on the pile and fired iron cylinders filled with gunpowder, the much-feared Congreve rockets, into the flammable mass. In the north wing the books from the Library of Congress provided additional incendiary material. The resulting blaze was so intense that a giant plume of fire rose from the Capitol, blowing onto nearby homes and starting additional fires until, as one observer described, "The entire city was light and the heavens were reddened with the blaze."[75] Only a violent rainstorm later that night prevented the spread of the flames.

The British never intended to occupy Washington. Their strategy was to protect Canada and use their powerful navy to raid and retaliate against the Americans. After burning the Capitol, British soldiers left Washington and moved farther up the Chesapeake Bay to Baltimore, a haven for privateers considered by His Majesty's forces to deserve punishment. There, in September, after a twenty-four-hour bombardment, Baltimore was successfully defended on land at the Battle of North Point and by sea at Fort McHenry. The Baltimore lawyer Francis Scott Key described the British attack in what became the national anthem: "And the Rockets red glare, the Bombs bursting in air/ Gave proof through the night, That our flag was still there."

When Latrobe heard the war news in distant Pittsburgh, he expressed his surprise in a letter to the architect Maximilian Godefroy: "Is it not astonishing that Baltimore stands? That [the leaders of Baltimore's militia] should claim a Victory over General Ross's troops, over Wellington's troops and that appearances should be in their favor?"[76] During the fall, the war simmered on, continuing even after the peace negotiations were concluded. In January 1815 a final unnecessary battle took place in New Orleans, with Andrew Jackson leading American troops and Henry Latrobe serving as an engineer.

After the invasion of Washington, residents had clamored up the hill to observe the damage to the Capitol inflicted by those the *Niles Weekly Register* demeaned as "Goths."[77] As Latrobe described after his first viewing, the Capitol was "a melancholy spectacle. . . . They were the whole night about it, setting fire separately to every door and window, with the inflammatory composition of their rockets."[78] The exterior columns of the building had survived but cracked, frayed, and thinned, they appeared ready to collapse. Yet none of the arches on the interior had failed. The sheet iron roof over the south wing that Latrobe had insisted on had offered some protection. Parts of the interior of both wings including the vaulting remained. In the north wing William Thornton had used timber framing for the roof. Consequently, the damage was more extensive than that in the south wing. Overall the destruction to the entire building was obvious, even from the exterior. There the sooty stains from the fire had blackened the still standing, free stone walls.

Afterward, a British officer noted that the Capitol was the only building worth any attention in what he dismissed as this "infant town. . . . These modern republicans are led to flatter themselves, that the days are coming when it will rival in power and grandeur the senate-house of ancient Rome herself. . . . [The Capitol] however is or rather was an edifice of great beauty."[79] John Latrobe later spread the story of the British officer in charge of the destruction who hesitated to destroy such a noble edifice.

Returning in the fall for the third session of the 13th Congress, members debated whether the federal government should remain in Washington. The House considered a bill authorizing the removal of the seat of the federal government, at least until peace came and then perhaps permanently. Lancaster, Philadelphia, and Baltimore had their advocates, as the uncertainty of remaining in war-scarred Washington continued until the defeat of a bill moving the capital to Philadelphia finally settled the matter.

The ruins of the Capitol and the President's House also stimulated local proposals—to move the President's House to Capitol Hill, to make the Post Office building (formerly Blodgett's Hotel at Eighth and E streets) into a permanent site for Congress, and, most drastically, to move all government buildings to Georgetown. A Louisiana senator urged his colleagues to authorize the construction of a "large, convenient and unadorned house near Georgetown to serve as the new Capitol. . . . Our laws to be wholesome need not be enacted in a palace." Latrobe archly responded that it was possible "as good Laws may be made in a wigwam, as in the Capitol, and that all

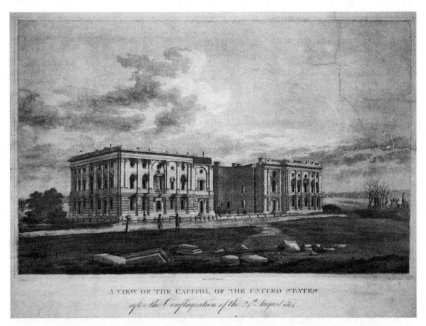

A VIEW OF THE CAPITOL OF THE UNITED STATES
after the Conflagration of the 2.º August 1814

FIG. 5.3 Capitol in Ruins. George Munger's painting shows the devastation to the Capitol by British troops in August 1814. Note the incomplete center. Latrobe returned to Washington in 1815 to begin the building's restoration and completion. Library of Congress, LC-USZC4-408.

decoration is useless, and all history mere idle amusement."[80] Rarely has the established location of a nation's capital in peacetime seemed so uncertain and the rapid restoration of its public buildings so important for continuity.

Only when these alternatives were defeated did Congress appropriate the vast, optimistically comprehensive amount of $500,000 for the restoration of the public buildings, $300,000 for the Capitol, borrowed from local banks at 6 percent interest and available without the uncertainty of annual appropriations that had so tortured Latrobe in his first Capitol campaign. However, 63 of 141 congressmen voted against the final appropriation bill, and in fact when the building was completed in the 1820s, it was well over budget. Madison, acting on his own authority, appointed three commissioners to supervise the work. After considering the applications of several other architects including Robert Mills, they made the decision to invite Latrobe to rebuild the Capitol.

Reappointed the surveyor of the Capitol, but notably not the President's House, Latrobe accepted a salary of $2,500 and, immediately after his arrival in Washington, began his careful assessment. To his wife, who was still

in Pittsburgh, he was optimistic: "Many important parts are wholly unin-
jured and what is particularly gratifying to me, the picturesque entrance of
the House of Representatives with its handsome columns, the Corn Capitals
of the Senate Vestibule, the Great staircase and all the Vaults of the Senate
chamber are entirely free from any injury which cannot be easily repaired."[81]

In many ways the burning of the Capitol validated his architecture
and made him, like the United States, more self-confident: his arches had
not collapsed, even with the intense heat that had melted the glass of the
skylights, cracked the marble floors, and turned the columns into lime dust.
His staircase in the north wing needed only repairs. Despite the sustained
gunpowder attacks of British soldiers and the grievous injuries it had sustained, the Capitol stood, a testament to its principal architect and the design
and materials he had insisted on employing.

With his customary energy Latrobe began immediately. He never had
difficulty creating designs; they came, as he had explained years earlier, un-
bidden, like mystical revelations, "unasked in multitudes," and in his earlier
description of genius, "without fatigue of mind or fingers or . . . painful
labor."[82] Within weeks he had reconfigured both the Senate and House assembly rooms as half-circles, a change from their previous oval shape and an
improvement in acoustics and ventilation. The lighting would be better after
his changes in the domes over both chambers where he would place lanterns,
as there was no Thomas Jefferson to disapprove.

In an acknowledgment of the imperfections in the Capitol that previously
had put him at odds with members of Congress, Latrobe reported to the
commissioners that while previous gratification had flattered "the vanity of
the Architect . . . [n]o part of the room had the simplicity and gravity which
large Masses impart to buildings." Even if just practical repairs were made, "it
[the assembly room of the House] would always have had an air of magnificence bordering on ostentation and levity."[83] Instead he intended transforma-
tive improvements. In the enlarged Senate assembly hall in the north wing an
upper gallery with tobacco capitals over the columns at the western entrance
would be an additional enhancement. He included galleries for the people to
observe their legislators, a feature that had always been an important component of Latrobe's understanding of a republic's architectural requirements.

Latrobe's new vision responded to changes in the political culture of the
republic. The United States had survived two wars with the leading power in
the Western world. It no longer had to exhibit defensive grandiosity. Instead,
Latrobe believed, the United States could rely on the more practical, efficient designs of a half circle for its assembly rooms—a hemicycle—familiar

to ancient theatergoers who expected to hear the words of the play. Latrobe's revisions also reflected his maturity as an architect. Middle-aged and economically battered, he was more willing to correct the practical deficiencies of his previous design and less inclined to provide the magnificent, showy space that had reflected the exuberance of his youth.

The commissioners, whom Latrobe found useless nuisances ignorant of design, approved his new concept. So too did President Madison whose primary concern was how quickly Congress could return from their crowded quarters. Immediately after his return to Washington in the spring of 1815, Latrobe had been hired to expand a former tavern on Capitol Hill that became known as the Brick Capitol, today the site of the Supreme Court building. He had hastily constructed a large side wing notable for its stylish grand Palladian windows over the two doorways with large meeting rooms for the House and Senate on the first and second floors, a temporary arrangement but one that lasted for nearly four years.

In the US Capitol, Latrobe insisted on a temporary roof over the north wing so that the building could dry out and plastering could begin, a feature that the commissioners considered unnecessary. To impatient congressmen and watchful local residents, for months it appeared that no progress was occurring. But Latrobe reminded his critics of one of his guiding principles: "*rapid* building is *bad* building."[84]

Habitually over-optimistic, Latrobe hazarded a possible completion date of December 1816 for the House, both wings to be finished in 1817. Yet it was late 1818 before the Capitol was ready for legislators, and even then the rotunda was not complete. Latrobe had underestimated the amount of time necessary to raze parts of the building as well as the difficulty in getting materials and unskilled workers, along with the well-trained sculptors who would shape the decoration of the new columns. "At all events no exertions will be wanted on my part to effect it," he promised the commissioners.[85]

Latrobe immediately began to hire workers, many of whom had left Washington during the war for better wages in nearby Baltimore. Eventually there were over 200 men on his labor force, many of them enslaved, whose competencies included carpentry, masonry, and stone cutting. During the first winter it was necessary to put up a temporary roof over the Senate wing and to take down both columns and vaults, dangerous endeavors carried out by hesitant, disgruntled workers. A few months later the stonemasons walked off the job, demanding higher wages during a period of postwar inflation. Latrobe, supportive of republican ideals and the rights of the sovereign people, was unsympathetic. Within weeks the impoverished strikers were back at work at their prewar pay rates. Still, the work stoppage temporarily slowed the restoration, as did recurring problems of men and materials for this complex project.

Throughout the Capitol's reconstruction there were labor controversies between Latrobe and the commissioners and between Latrobe and the workers until these matters became a serious jurisdictional matter. In 1816, the commissioners limited the working hours of all workers on the Capitol to ten hours a day, except for the unskilled laborers who worked the traditional, shifting seasonal hours from dawn to dark. Latrobe also opposed what he viewed as the ambition-stifling payment of stonecutters by the day—usually $2.50 a day. He preferred payment by the piece, citing the example of one stonecutter. "By paying [such a man] $2 or 2.50 a day while by the piece he can earn $4, no money is saved and much time is lost."[86]

During another labor flareup, the commissioners ordered Latrobe to fire certain workers they considered guilty of negligence and abusive conduct. But in a sequence of escalating disagreements with his supervisors, he refused. Managing workers was his purview. With a touch of ironic accusation, he explained that "men will not obey a Man they think their inferior in talent or knowledge."[87]

Along with his labor difficulties, Latrobe faced daunting challenges in finding materials. Bricks and timber were easy, if expensive, to obtain. It was the stone and the carving of that stone into decorative capitals required by the neoclassical elements of his design that slowed construction. Latrobe had hoped to use the nearby quarries at Aquia, Virginia, as he had earlier, but the available freestone there was nearly exhausted. The quarries had been closed for years, and the remaining stone was too difficult to excavate in the large amounts needed for the Capitol. After a year the restoration still lacked half the number of freestone blocks required.

Latrobe offered a partial solution for the problem. In an inspired version of nineteenth-century transatlantic exchanges, he proposed, and the commissioners accepted, a plan whereby Giovanni Andrei, one of the Italians who for years had sculpted the exquisite Grecian Corinthian-order capitals for the Capitol, would travel from the United States to Italy to supervise the purchase of Carrara marble. Using Latrobe's drawings he would oversee Italian sculptors in the chiseling of the capitals needed for the restoration, which would then be shipped back to the United States.

Andrei had learned American tastes and, according to Latrobe, would resist any "roman finery." He now prefers, wrote Latrobe to the commissioners about Andrei, "the simplicity of the Grecian taste which I have labored to introduce into our country."[88] Even after the shipping costs, each capital would cost an estimated $400, cheaper by $200 and more artistic than if the process had been carried out in the United States. While in Italy, Andrei might be able to enlist Italians skilled in decorative sculpture to accompany him back to the United States where there were few such artists.

On an early trip after his arrival in Virginia in 1796 and then more recently when he traveled to Pittsburgh, Latrobe had discovered an extraordinary stone along both the Maryland and Virginia shores of the Potomac River. Ever the curious geologist, he was impressed with this marble composed of pebbles of different colors. Technically it was not a marble, but a form of sedimentary stone called breccia or puddling stone and known by various nicknames including "calico rock." At the time he had sent a sample to a chemist, and, nearly twenty years later, he brought a fragment of the stone for Congress to view.

Far more handsome than brown sandstone, especially when polished into a striking dark purplish gray, it was as beautiful as anything he had ever seen. Excited by the elegance of a native material to be used as a column topped by contrasting white sculpted marble entablature, Latrobe believed it would exceed even the marvels of the ancients' use of various colored stones. To his friend Robert Harper he boasted: "I may say cedite romani—yield to me Romans."[89] Available in large blocks for the many columns needed in the interior, it could easily be transported by barge down the Potomac River to the Capitol. "Imagine," he described to the editors of the *National Intelligencer*, "these pebbles [of lovely green and beautiful red] rounded and mingled by attrition for ages . . . and cemented into a solid mass." He then explained in detail the centuries-long process that had created a handsome stone for the columns that would enhance the interior of the Capitol, seen today in Statuary Hall and the old Senate Chamber.[90]

Latrobe made progress his first year. The exterior no longer bore the marks of the British invasion; the walls had been scrubbed and some blocks replaced. The rubbish from the fire and demolition had been removed. He had hoped to leave one fire-damaged room in the basement where Americans could view the damage inflicted by the British but was dissuaded. Andrei had left for Italy and had returned the next year bringing with him several skilled Italian sculptors. The temporary roof had been erected. Most critically, Latrobe had finished the working plans for both the House and Senate assembly halls, though after a reassessment by a Senate committee, he had to create a larger assembly hall to accommodate the forty-two senators of the Fifteenth Congress. In the House, he proudly noted, the space for representatives was

FIG. 5.4 Samuel Morse Painting of the House. In 1846 artist and inventor Samuel F. B. Morse completed this dramatic depiction of Latrobe's second version of the House assembly room at lamp-lighting time. Latrobe reconfigured the shape of the room and added the breccia columns. Morse provided a popular guide identifying the individual representatives. Corcoran Collection (Museum Purchase, Gallery Fund), 2014.79.27.

increased from a crowded 4,517 feet for chairs and desks to a more spacious 5,754 feet. Additionally, there would be improved acoustics.[91]

Sometime during these busy days, Latrobe found time to sit for his fourth portrait, on this occasion with Rembrandt Peale, his friend Charles Willson Peale's son. Born into America's first family of art, with brothers named Raphaelle, Reubens, Titian and Van Dyke, Rembrandt Peale had become a well-known American artist, dedicated to improving the fine arts in America and famous for his multiple depictions of George Washington. Although Latrobe had once disdained portrait painting as a trade, not an art, it emerged as the most popular art form in the early republic. In any case, portraits by any of the Peales conferred status and were a means for Latrobe to preserve himself for his family and posterity. Besides, the Peales did not charge their impoverished friend.

In this final portrait by Rembrandt Peale, Latrobe no longer has the mischievous ebullience of his youth displayed in Von Breda's 1794 portrait, nor the vulnerable expectant searching of Charles Willson Peale's 1804 portrait, nor the attention-claiming hair of Raphaelle Peale's porcelain image. In keeping with the architect's disdain for allegory, there is no background to distract. Nor were objects needed to give clues to the subject's interests, since Latrobe considered himself a sufficiently well-known architect.

As in his earlier portraits, the concentration is entirely on the subject's face. Latrobe wears the customary dress of upper-class men in the new republic: a waistcoat with a high collar, a cravat tied at the throat with a large, white linen bow. Rembrandt Peale, recently returned from France, intended his portraits to show character, and he achieved this in his painting of Latrobe. Now fifty-two, Latrobe's unruly, curly black hair is receding; no longer clean-shaven, his face is fuller. He looks away from, not at, the viewer with a hopeful and resolute, yet detached, gaze. Most notably, Latrobe chose to be painted wearing the eyeglasses that in previous portraits lay on a table or, as in the Charles Willson Peale portrait, on his head behind his ears. This departure from most subjects, who disdain such symbols of aging, reveals the importance of seeing in his professional life as an architect and engineer.

FIG. 5.5 Rembrandt Peale portrait of Benjamin Henry Latrobe. This fourth of the Latrobe portraits, three by members of the Peale family, shows a resolute Latrobe, looking to the future. At fifty-two, the myopic Latrobe wears his signature glasses. Courtesy of the Maryland Historical Society, 1981.15.

By the fall of 1816, Latrobe and the board of commissioners were at odds. This board was made up of Richard Bland Lee, a planter and former congressman from Virginia; Tench Ringgold, who owned a local rope walk (a covered pathway where long strands of material were twisted into rope); and John Van Ness, a prominent banker for whom Latrobe was designing a house. All lacked building experience but complained about the lack of progress. Like some of Latrobe's previous employers, they attributed the delays to the architect's absences. When they stopped by his office in the basement of the Capitol, Latrobe was frequently absent, despite his arrangement with the commissioners that he must be on location every day but Sunday from ten until three. Latrobe was required to get special permission to take on extra projects or leave the city, but he often traveled to Baltimore without it.

As complaints deepened into disagreements, both sides made their case. The commissioners insisted that they had been fair and helpful to the architect. They had provided extra money for a draftsman; they had supported his examination of the quarries along the Potomac River. The commissioners also reminded Latrobe that they had the sole power to direct the repairs and rebuilding of the Capitol and that during the spring of 1816 there had been delays. When Latrobe complained of his treatment, the commissioners denied any effort to "wound your feelings." They were not aware of any conduct toward Latrobe that was "inconsistent with that delicacy which is due from one Gentleman to another." In any case Latrobe should confine himself to "subjects connected with the public work."[92]

Latrobe did have private projects—among them, the Van Ness and Decatur homes and St. John's Church in Washington and the Merchants Exchange in Baltimore. He had also accepted the position of surveyor of the city of Washington, which entailed overseeing various city building regulations. The position came with a salary of $1,500 but brought with it more suspicions about his commitment to rebuilding the Capitol. On the other hand, he considered these buildings—the private homes, St. John's Church, even a design for a national university that was never built, along with his most significant work, the restoration of the Capitol—his contributions to the capital's renaissance. More than anyone else, Latrobe was responsible for the creativity and elegance of this generation's architecture in Washington.

Even before he began the restoration of the Capitol, Latrobe had been hired by John Van Ness, Washington's mayor in addition to being a prominent banker. After his marriage to the heiress Marcia Burnes, Van Ness owned 600 acres in the District. He was rich enough to afford a showplace and hired Latrobe to provide one. The project proceeded in fits and starts after Latrobe's

return to the city, with Marcia Van Ness taking an active role in decisions
about the interior. But her husband proved to be another difficult client who
insisted on providing the building materials and who also happened to be one
of Latrobe's supervisors. Over the five-year period in which the house was
being designed and constructed, the two men argued about Latrobe's fees,
with the architect insisting that he "would never betray the interests of my
profession so far as to charge *less* than five percent."[93]

They also exchanged personal insults: Latrobe claimed that he was treated
"illiberally," by which he meant not as a gentleman should be. "I am utterly at
a Loss to conceive in what society you can have acquired the extreme facility
with which you treat a Man of equal education, connections and standing in
society with yourself in a manner in which I find it contrary to my feelings
and habits to treat those who in every respect are my inferior." Privately he
called Van Ness "an insolent brute." Despite the bad feelings, the Van Ness
home was a triumph.[94]

FIG. 5.6 Van Ness House, Washington, DC. The Van Ness House, completed in 1817
and demolished in 1908 to make way for the Pan American Union building, was an outstanding success and at the time the city's most monumental private residence. Library of
Congress, LC-DIG-npcc-00075.

On a six-acre lot along what is today 17th and C streets, Latrobe created a solid yet graceful domestic structure that incorporated three large rectangular rooms divided by shallow vaults, with the internal scenery that had become one of his specialties. The dining room, the largest in the city and embellished by revolving doors into the pantry, became the talk of the town. The entire structure demonstrated permanence to residents of an uncertain capital. Latrobe had intuited as much, recognizing that the house "would be pretty well exhibited at Washington."[95] Given its external dimensions of seventy-by-forty-five feet, he claimed it as the largest as well as the best private house he had ever designed, larger than his English villas—Ashdown and Hammerwood—and better than the Waln house in Philadelphia or Adena in Chillicothe, Ohio. On the outside, Latrobe installed an artificial hill leading up to a portico that, as in his earlier design for the White House, served as a porte cochere. His tripartite windows, narrow-belted separations of floors, and hipped roof were examples of his mature domestic style.

So too was the Decatur House built for the national naval hero Stephen Decatur who used his prize money from captured vessels to fund his new home. Notable for its niches, pilasters, and unifying moldings in the front hall and varied window treatments on the exterior, the Decatur House established the significance of what was then an empty area filled with apple trees. Today the space is known as Lafayette Square. In a letter to Secretary of the Treasury Alexander Dallas, Latrobe anticipated its future: the house was "a means of making an exhibition."[96] Its location near the White House assured its later use for social functions and guaranteed that unlike some of his other houses, it would survive, into the twenty-first century, with few structural changes.

Across the park from the Decatur House, Latrobe designed St. John's Church as an unassuming Greek cross with a glazed cupola in the center to light the interior and, on the exterior, simple arched windows. In keeping with his high-minded standards, Latrobe did not charge for his work: "a church or litterary institution manufactures only Christians and philosophers and their wealth is not of this world."[97] To his son Henry he described St. John's as "a pretty thing and has a celebrity beyond all bounds. . . . It has made people religious who were never before at church."[98] For the church's dedication, Latrobe, the self-proclaimed "indifferentist" about religious denominations, played on the organ the celebratory hymn that he had composed. The Episcopal clergy found it "too *deistical* and too *liberal . . . not peculiarly* Christian," though it was sung with gusto by the congregation. The third verse paid homage to his profession and to his contributions to America and the nation's capital: "Once oe'r this favor'd land/ Savage wilds and darkness spread/ Fostered now by thy kind hand/ Cheerful dwellings rear their head."[99]

These years were fertile, active ones in his private architectural practice, and they required his attention to multiple projects, leading to continual arguments with the commissioners. The differences over his availability went deeper than whether he needed to be present at the Capitol six days a week. For Latrobe the issue was how the commissioners treated him and whether they had the authority to control his time, as a foreman did a laborer's. Thus the conflict went to the heart of who he was and architecture's development as a profession.

From Latrobe's perspective the commissioners were uninformed "villains" who made contracts without informing him, dictated orders to him, and interfered with his plans. They were "little men" who "have no right of ordering me on an expedition fit rather for a Marble mason than an architect."[100] He had promised to work with "zeal and ability" and was doing so, but they had not treated him with the "liberality which every Man in a liberal profession has a right to demand."[101] Besides, he had an agreement with them; they could not replace him.

After threatening him, they humiliated him, informing him that there were plenty of architects who could take his place and that he had only been appointed "from motives of charity" to his family. As he complained to President Madison, "If I meant to continue in their Service, I must obey their orders implicitly, even when contrary to those given to me by the Committee of the Senate."[102]

At stake was the denial of his professional authority, the insult to his social standing so important to him that he still claimed a fictional descent from French aristocrats, and his acknowledged "morbid sensitivity." Latrobe's sense of personal humiliation also arose from differing expectations of behavior between émigrés and natives. Latrobe was a new American, an outsider whose early roots were in royal England with its impermeable social hierarchies and in the Moravian church which, for all its communal practices, was led by aristocrats. His understanding of both his personal status and his profession clashed with the sentiments of native-born Americans whose sense of equality made them insensitive to his pride in the profession that he was intent on establishing in the United States.

In an appeal to President Madison written a year after his return from Pittsburgh, Latrobe explained the specifics of his debasement. The commissioners did not recognize his experience, his knowledge of the arts, and his days and nights spent working on the plans for the restoration of the Capitol. The commissioners treated him in "a manner more coarse and offensive than I ever permitted to myself, or felt myself capable of using to my poorest mechanics."[103] He reminded Madison that for ten years he had the sole management of *all* the public buildings in Washington. He also reminded the president of his status: he was educated; he had "unsought honors . . . bestowed upon me by societies of letters and of arts"; he had "highly respectable family connections"; and he had been on friendly terms with all the presidents of the United States. But now, he was treated with an incivility that not only threatened his personal integrity but also the profession of architecture. Yet with his experience in Pittsburgh in mind, the only choice he had was "to consume my life in the chagrin of professional degradation or to escape it by the sacrifice of my principal means of support."[104] The latter he could not afford.

Despite the humiliations, he stayed, until an anticipated welcomed relief came in the late spring of 1816 when Congress eliminated the costly board of commissioners and appointed a single commissioner, Samuel Lane, a former army colonel and a friend of incoming president James Monroe. Latrobe had unsuccessfully lobbied for the same kind of arrangement he had established with Thomas Jefferson, to whom he reported without any other intervening officers except Thomas Munroe who oversaw the accounts. But Monroe was no Jefferson; he had no interest in Latrobe's gifts. He wanted the Capitol completed quickly.

At first a hopeful Latrobe described his new supervisor as "a Gentlemen of honor and feeling," "a disbanded officer with one arm useless and a ball in his thigh," who had been wounded in the War of 1812.[105] But it did not take long for his relationship with Samuel Lane to sour. Rather than distinguished wartime service, Lane had been no more than a commissioner of dead horses, according to Latrobe in his revised estimation.

In his annual report at the end of 1816, Latrobe catalogued his progress on the Capitol: the south wing remained internally as it had been at the end of 1815. It awaited the necessary material for the columns and the construction of a semi-dome topped by a cupola. It was in the north wing that many of his improvements were apparent. He had effected "the boldest vaulting I ever heard or saw" in the enlarged Supreme Court Room where the vaults cleverly reinforced walls rather than bore weight on them. Workmen were erecting a masonry, ninety-foot in diameter, double-shell dome carrying a cupola that would produce what Latrobe always intended—the entrancing, mysterious daily play of light and dark in an interior.

In addition to his corn capitals that had survived the attack on the Capitol, Latrobe saluted American agriculture in the new tobacco capitals he designed to decorate the columns in the vestibule to the Senate Chamber. He anticipated further decoration in the Senate where he proposed marble caryatids representing each state, in keeping with his theory that allegorical decoration must be grounded in meaningful identifiable symbols. But for reasons of economy they were never built. To decorate the south wing assembly room he sketched images of what he called the "Car of History," later exquisitely carved by Carlo Franzoni. Clio, the muse of history, watched over the legislators, tablet in her hand, her billowy robes suggesting the passage of time, atop a chariot with a clock's dial set in its wheel. It was a clever representation of the historic nature of the legislature's work as time moved from past to present and future. [106]

Most fulfilling, as Jefferson had always hoped, Latrobe was working on the grand rotunda—the awkwardly named Grand Vestibule, Hall of Inauguration, Impeachment, and of all Public Occasions, referred to by Latrobe simply as the Hall of the People. There, in a temple celebrating the nation's struggle for sovereignty, Latrobe planned for America's premier artist John Trumble to install four giant paintings commemorating the American Revolution and the signing of the Declaration of Independence. When completed, these vast spaces—the senate and house assembly rooms, the supreme court, and the rotunda—comprising the most important public rooms in America, would furnish an impressive sequence of neoclassical interiors and would become Latrobe's legacy.

Challenges to the completion of this ambitious agenda haunted Latrobe throughout 1817, the worst year of his life in "this world of care."[107] First he had to persuade his critics that breccia, the material in which he saw such beauty, was appropriate and could support the vaults in the House. He had to convince workers that his bold, umbrella-like vaulting in both wings would not give way, as it had nine years before. He had to win over the new president James Monroe, who had insisted that timber be used on the roof of the north wing as a cost-saving measure. Latrobe, who favored more permanent masonry, argued that wood was unworthy of columns; besides "suppose it to last a century, what is a century in the life of nations?"[108] Most critically, he had to deal with Colonel Lane who, in the hierarchical style of military men, sent interrogatories that Latrobe was required to answer, ordered materials without advising the architect, and, like so many others, humiliated him with such treatment.

Almost immediately a controversy emerged over Latrobe's absences while he was supervising the building of Baltimore's ambitious Merchants Exchange. Lane charged that during a period when crucial arches were being erected in the south wing of the Capitol, Latrobe had left a novice bricklayer in charge while he was away. Complaining about Lane's abusive letters, Latrobe replied that his presence was not constantly required.

Then Lane fired Shadrach Davis, Latrobe's clerk of the works and second in command, without any discussion with the architect. The two men's relationship further deteriorated, as the restoration of the building continued, until everyone in Washington knew that either the architect or the commissioner must go. Latrobe complained to his father-in-law that the commissioner was "weak and ignorant . . . zealous in performing what he conceives his duty. . . . [H]e rises before the sun & watches among the bushes to see whether the laborers & mechanics attend bell-ringing"—and of course, whether the architect was in his office in the ground floor of the Capitol.[109]

In 1817, William Lee, a Washington merchant, former diplomat, and man about town who had hired Latrobe to do some renovations on his home, wrote Charles Bulfinch, a prominent Boston architect, to see if he would be available to replace Latrobe. Lee pitied Latrobe—"an amiable man who possesses genius and has a large family but who has many enemies; his great fault is being poor." Sympathetic, yet anxious that the Capitol be completed as soon as possible, Lee believed that there was "unfair prejudice against Latrobe who has many enemies in Congress. . . . Every carpenter and mason thinks he knows more than Latrobe."[110]

In another blow to Latrobe's credibility, local residents had begun comparing the progress at the President's House, where the postwar restoration had mostly involved simple lathing and plastering, to that at the unfinished, but far more complex restoration of the Capitol. (Latrobe continued to denigrate the President's House as a building where nothing more was attempted than simply sheltering the president from the weather.) Meanwhile Samuel Lane had James Monroe's ear, often dining and even staying overnight with the Monroes, who had moved into the restored President's House.

Then, in the fall of 1817, Latrobe suffered the greatest blow imaginable. He had heard from his son Henry during the summer and had responded in a long letter that discussed their mutual New Orleans waterworks project and included family news: fourteen-year-old John, "a giant in bodily strength and courage" had translated a French novel and climbed a rope to the top of the Capitol, Julia, amiable and wise, and Ben, "deficient in nothing. Your mother as affectionate and warmhearted as ever and your father laboring, not unsuccessfully, from dawn till Dark to reestablish his affairs." Latrobe closed the letter as he always did, "your affectionate father."[111] But his son never read this letter.

Twenty-four-year-old Henry died of yellow fever in early September, though the news did not reach his family for weeks. A constant affliction in New Orleans, yellow fever had been of special concern during an outbreak in 1817. After a rainy summer the aggressive *aedes aegypti* mosquitoes that carried the virus and fed on multiple victims had exploded in numbers, festering in water barrels and puddles, biting the infected and carrying the lethal germ to other humans. In an August letter, Henry had assured his family that he was well. His father had always been confident that Henry's "temperance and activity" protected his son, although Henry worked in the most dangerous conditions—out-of-doors and near water as he completed the construction of a lighthouse near the Mississippi River and surveys for the municipal waterworks that would make the family fortune.

By 1817, Henry had been living in New Orleans for six years. Folklore and observation held that the prime targets of yellow fever were young male newcomers; today outdoor activities and lack of immunity would be blamed for their unique exposure. In Latrobe's day the causes of yellow fever were unknown and subject to disagreement. Latrobe was not the only American convinced that contaminated water caused the disease and that alcohol somehow increased susceptibility.

Through the fog of his grief, Latrobe managed a loving remembrance to his son in an obituary published in the *National Intelligencer.* Henry, he wrote, had promise of "eminent usefulness"; he had the "brilliance of genius and a presence of mind, a civil courage and discretion beyond his years." Latrobe recalled his son's many attributes: his saving another child from drowning in the Schuylkill River, his much-applauded valedictory oration at St. Mary's College on education as a civic necessity, his work on the Capitol and the New Orleans waterworks, his service as an engineer in the Battle of New Orleans that had been complimented by General Andrew Jackson. Of course, it was his family who knew his character best: for his twenty-four years they, especially his stepmother, had been "enlivened by his cheerfulness, his wit and the eloquence of his affection." Now they could only be comforted by "some higher power."[112]

There were practical ramifications to Henry's death, mostly involving his supervision of his father's last best chance—the New Orleans Waterworks. Latrobe was forced to ask for another extension from the City Council, which was granted after he noted the effect of Henry's death as well as the $43,000 of their own money that the Latrobes—father and son—had already spent on the project. With his habitual optimism, Latrobe predicted the waterworks would result in an immense fortune when the municipal supply was finished in a few years. To council members, he promised his own presence "to see that the works are completed."[113]

Additionally, there were claims on Henry's personal estate. His creditors received permission to sell a slave belonging to the estate. At the time the enslaved in the city's active markets could bring as much as $1,400. Latrobe's letters to Henry's lawyer do not mention Henry's other family—his paramour, whose color prevented any legalization of their status, and his three children, on whom his son had earlier settled an annuity. Perhaps Latrobe never knew of them; perhaps he avoided mention of them. In any case Latrobe insisted to Henry's lawyer that his son's brothers and sisters were his legal heirs and that as his father he hoped to obtain the books, drawings, papers, and "such other remembrances of him as a father naturally desires to possess."[114]

Depressed and dispirited, Latrobe continued his work on the Capitol. By the fall, twenty-three stonecutters, twenty marble cutters, nine polishers, twelve sculptors and carvers, eighteen bricklayers, and forty carpenters, along with 135 laborers, many of them enslaved, were working on the Capitol—in all, 257 men. Those judged skilled earned $2.50 in winter, $2.75 during the longer hours of summer and fall; laborers were paid $1.00 a day no matter what the season.[115] But their progress was not fast enough to satisfy an angry president who after returning from an extended northern trip had expected the Capitol to be finished. Every day Latrobe dealt with Lane, who insultingly demanded an accounting of his absences, which Latrobe calculated in his detailed, purposely satiric "Latrobe's Account of His Absences from Washington." By the architect's accounting he had been absent a minuscule thirty-seven and a half out of 432 days.[116]

Six weeks after he heard about his son's death, Latrobe met with President Monroe and Commissioner Lane in a tumultuous encounter. Assailed for his absences, the slow delivery of materials, and his angry reaction to the replacement of his clerk, Latrobe had tried to avoid Lane, who, according to Latrobe's account, had demanded that Latrobe apologize for angering him. Then Lane had rushed to Monroe to state his case. Called to the President's House for a meeting with the president and Lane, Latrobe erupted. As described in Mary Elizabeth Latrobe's memoir, he lunged at Lane,

> seized him by the collar and exclaimed, "Were you not a cripple I would shake you to atoms, you poor contemptible wretch. Am I to be dictated to by you? [After the president intervened] Latrobe went on . . . "I ask your pardon, but when I consider my birth, my family, my

education, my talents, I am excusable for any outrage after the provoca-
tion I have received from that contemptible character.[117]

Latrobe returned home and drafted a letter of resignation to the president.
He wrote that he was left "no choice but between resignation and the sacrifice of all self-respect." As for his work on the Capitol, neither the delay nor
the expense of the restoration were "chargeable" to him. Latrobe addressed
his letter to the president, but in a final act of humiliation it was Lane who
accepted it. To a friend Latrobe described insults "no schoolboy could have
borne patiently."[118] Yet his disappointment was profound, as he would not
complete the building that for so long had been the object of his architectural
attention.

Latrobe had left Washington by the time his successor arrived. Charles
Bulfinch, well-born and politic, the latter a talent learned as a Boston city
alderman and essential in his new position, had hesitated to accept the

FIG. 5.7 "Capitol in the 1840s from the West Side." This view shows the completed
work of Latrobe and his successor Charles Bulfinch on the US Capitol. Note the low
saucer dome and cupolas, soon to give way to the huge dome of Thomas Walter. Library
of Congress, LC-DIG-pga-03496.

position: the Capitol was well known for its mistreatment of architects. When Bulfinch did come, he was initially awed by the beauty of his predecessor's three-dimensional elevations as well as his bold designs: "My courage almost failed me." But like most architects surveying a contemporary's work, he soon found flaws that he believed justified Latrobe's critics. He also found areas for improvement: Latrobe's staircases were crowded; his passages were dark. "The whole interior, except for the two great rooms, has a somber appearance." Latrobe reciprocated his criticism: Bulfinch, he wrote, "is destroying all hopes of a Capitol that will not disgrace us."[119]

What Bulfinch accomplished in his eleven years working on the Capitol was to alter Latrobe's western colonnade, to design a new Library of Congress in the north wing, and to substitute a higher hemispheric dome for Latrobe's saucer dome over the Rotunda. Yet by any measure the central portions of the Capitol, except for the later extensions of the southern and northern wings, remain Latrobe's creation, as do several interiors, including the Rotunda. When he resigned in November 1817, Latrobe feared that all "my exertion for the public is of no avail."[120] The history of the Capitol suggests otherwise.

In fact, Bulfinch modified rather than altered Latrobe's work, acknowledging that he had mostly followed Latrobe's "prescribed path." It is Latrobe's Capitol that, save for the details, survived until the late 1850s when the extensions of the north and south wings required a higher, more imposing dome over the Rotunda.[121]

In 1857, Thomas Walter, an architect trained by one of Latrobe's students, provided it. Rising 288 feet from ground level to the Statue of Freedom and 180 feet from the floor of the Rotunda, the Capitol dome remains a construction miracle of cast iron metal with rows of surrounding columns—what architects call peristyle—painted white, a structure that has become a shining representation of the United States. No doubt it would have horrified Latrobe, an architect accustomed to using natural material—stone, not glossy painted metal—and committed to simple classic designs that gained their predominance by their unity, not by such a single, eye-catching, flamboyant feature.

But domes had always been popular with congressmen and presidents, the higher, the more prestigious. Latrobe's critics had complained that his saucer domes were too low, not monumental enough. Bulfinch also heard complaints that his was not high enough, and by the 1850s some congressmen hoped that the entire Capitol could be enclosed by a dome supported by some sort of gigantic columns.

Two weeks after he resigned his position as architect of the Capitol, Latrobe declared bankruptcy, an important matter in a capital-short nation with unregulated credit arrangements but boundless speculative opportunities. Without his salary of $200.83 a month and with mounting claims—there were forty-three claimants from Washington, Baltimore, Philadelphia, and Pittsburgh—he petitioned the courts to enter a judgment of insolvency. Congress, given authority in the US Constitution, had attempted to establish a uniform system of dealing with unpaid debts in the Insolvency Act of 1800. But the legislation tipped the balance to debtors over creditors, had limited application, lacked enforcement, was considered an improper extension of unwanted federal authority, and so was repealed. As a result, state governments and, in the case of the District of Columbia, Congress established the arrangements regulating the critical elements of debtor-creditor relations: how debtors could discharge their debt and what property they could protect, which creditors were to be reimbursed in what order and whether, as would be the case in the District of Columbia into the 1830s, debtors who could not provide bonds went to prison.

Latrobe was familiar with monetary failure, having left England bankrupt. In America insolvency seemed even more pervasive—America's greedy tolerance. In Philadelphia he had observed Robert Morris, the richest man in town one decade, go to debtor's prison the next decade, as had the Washington developer James Greenleaf. His father-in-law Isaac Hazlehurst's firm twice had been forced into insolvency. After Andrew Hazlehurst's mercantile house in Baltimore had failed, his brother-in-law was "so shaken by the event that the family is broken up."[122] Latrobe's successor at the Capitol, Charles Bulfinch, had twice declared bankruptcy after the failure of his building projects in Boston. In the financially free-wheeling United States, debt was viewed less as a moral failure than a temporary condition. Latrobe even argued that insolvency was often "outdone in criminality by actions that receive applause among us."[123]

Still, in 1817 Latrobe had mixed feelings about the process. It would cure what he called "this cancer of my peace and of my talents." His debt absolved, he would no longer be hounded by creditors as he had been throughout his life. He could start again, as he often had, but this time free in mind and body. He still held to the fiction that, given time, he could "more than pay every body," if they would just wait for those who owed him to cancel their debt.[124] In the United States, while not routine, insolvency was common enough to diminish the humiliation of having to give up all his possessions save for his family's mattresses and clothes and whatever else the court decided was essential to his livelihood. Latrobe never lived extravagantly; it was his optimism about his projects and, when they were underfunded, his use of his personal funds to buy materials and sometimes pay workers that caused his financial problems. Yet given his debts from speculations and his rash decisions to use his own money, even his combined public salaries of $4,000 from the city and federal government had not been sufficient to prevent his insolvency.

In December Latrobe sent a letter full of magical thinking to his local creditors, asking them to meet with him. He explained that his "unfortunate connexion with Mr. Fulton at Pittsburgh and his subsequent death has involved me in great pecuniary embarrassments. But by my great industry, a total seclusion from General society and its expenses and much self-denial, I hoped to have extricated myself in a few years and to have given no one to whom I am indebted reason to complain of me." Then, he continued, Henry had died and the prospects for the New Orleans water system had become more remote. And so he had decided to take "the benefit" of the Insolvent Act in order to "regain the activity and peace necessary to the support of my family."[125]

There is no report of this meeting. In his petition to the court, Latrobe claimed, as he had so often in the past, that debts owed to him far exceeded his commitments to others. Included was $4,226.96 due from Robert Fulton and $1,380 from John Van Ness for his architectural services. Some money owed to him he considered uncollectable, including a mysterious loan of $1,133 to Henry Short of Washington as bond for the latter's bail. Short had absconded and joined the British during the War of 1812, leaving Latrobe responsible for the debt. The largest of Latrobe's paper assets was his "privilege" to supply New Orleans with water. In fact, without the Fulton debt, he calculated that he owed "on my own account say 8 or 900 dollars," a manageable liability.[126]

His personal property, including furniture, horses, carriage, and polygraph, netted $943.76, to be distributed among his creditors. He also claimed a farm in New Castle County, Delaware, that "might become very valuable." Latrobe protested the court's appropriation of his books and instruments, arguing successfully to the judge that they were the tools of his trade, as much as any mechanic's hammer or awl.[127]

Inflating prospective assets protected Latrobe's equanimity during the legal process of insolvency. He wrote his friend and benefactor Robert Harper that because his own debts were "so trifling [when] detached from the Pittsburgh incumbrance," he was "not at all depressed in mind." But that was before he went to jail—"my detention" he called it—for no one posted the necessary bond to keep him out of debtor's prison.[128] For a man raised to consider debts affairs of honor among gentlemen, the intervention of the courts and his incarceration added to his misery. And the public announcement of insolvency did not help his professional reputation.

Latrobe spent Christmas and New Year's in a tavern room the District of Columbia set aside for debtors. After his release from his nightly incarceration in early January, the family was on the move again—this time to Baltimore where Latrobe was designing several buildings and where his friend Robert Harper lived. As always, he was optimistic, especially since his agreement with the New Orleans City Council had been renewed.

6

Final Beginnings

*A few hundred Years hence some historian may notice
the labor of Yourself and perhaps mine, with a skim of
praise . . . for us.*

BENJAMIN HENRY LATROBE TO WILLIAM TATHAM,
February 5, 1810

IN JANUARY 1818, the Latrobes prepared for their move to Baltimore. This
time there was no fancy coach, only a cart to take their few possessions—
the mattresses and clothes allowed by the court and the books and tools
considered by the insolvency judge to be "instruments of trade" necessary
for Latrobe's architectural and engineering work. There was no housekeeper
to prepare their new living quarters after Kitty McCausland had died in a
kitchen fire two years earlier. They had no money to hire a replacement. No
longer owning either a horse or a carriage, Latrobe sold his coachman David.
Even the polygraph he relied upon to record copies of his letters was gone,
another result of his bankruptcy. Consequently, Latrobe's thoughts on this
family move, unlike those of his other residential changes, are unknown.

Latrobe did comment on his bankruptcy, expressing neither remorse nor
culpability. Rather, he judged his circumstances the fault of Robert Fulton
who had refused to pay his expenses for the steamship *Buffalo*. As Latrobe
did in money matters, he exaggerated and thereby protected himself with the
deceptions about money that he employed throughout his life. Debts he calculated at $800 were closer to $3,000.[1] In any case, the family had barely arrived
to set up housekeeping in their small rented house on Baltimore's Lexington
Street when Latrobe collapsed from "my old complaint, the Hemicrania."[2]
For three weeks he languished in his room, dizzy, nauseated, and tormented
by light and sound.

But as in the past, Benjamin Latrobe was resilient. As he recovered, he had
time to consider what several publishers in Britain were encouraging him to

do: write a book on architecture. Latrobe had earlier resisted the editor of the *Edinburgh Encyclopedia* Joseph Delaplaine's solicitation for a treatise, article, or even the presentation plans of one of his major buildings from which an engraving could be made.

Instead Latrobe completed a short technical essay on acoustics, a practical matter he had studied after congressmen complained they could not hear each other's speeches in their imposing hall. (Latrobe responded that the clerk heard them well enough for the accurate transcriptions published in the *Congressional Globe* and besides, many speeches were a waste of everyone's time.) Latrobe's reluctance to publish a theoretical study such as those by Jacques-Francois Blondel in his *Cours d'Architecture* and Sir John Soane's *Lectures in Architecture* went to the heart of his understanding of his profession, his place in it, and his use of his time.

Latrobe informed Delaplaine that he had already earned his professional reputation from his work in Philadelphia and Washington. "Unless therefore I write myself down, I am sure of *some* degree of applause from posterity. When I therefore take up the pen, it must be with a certainty that I shall have leisure to write a book that will be worth reprinting and rereading." He had no time for such a project and refused to produce any slapdash effort to create a manual for carpenters and millwrights. When Delaplaine replied that books survive longer than buildings, Latrobe responded that he would rather be forgotten by all the world than be remembered for some inferior explanation of his work. In fact, even without such a practical guide, carpenters and millwrights copied his work. "I have changed the whole taste of the city. My very follies and faults have been mimicked. . . . I cannot write a book for mean capacities. . . . My own deficiencies are the strongest proof to me that the talents required for my profession are very rare."

Boastful of his own architectural strengths in comparison to those of his American contemporaries, Latrobe remained humbled by the intellectual challenges of his profession. He continually acknowledged "how much I had still to learn and how much I shall leave unlearned when I die." In any case, if he wrote at all, it must be "for men of sense, and of some science."[3]

Despite his refusal he continued to think about two types of architectural publications aimed at the educated: first, a technical description "of all my great works, expressly calculated for the use of professional Men, as well as adapted to the taste of those who collect books as they do furniture, or who have a taste for the Arts without practicing them; the other, a collection of Essays in a convenient form on the principles on which public as well as private buildings ought to be constructed." But neither, he feared, would sell.

And so Latrobe delayed. Despite the continuing interest of publishers, he closed off one opportunity for what he called "the applause of posterity."[4]

But Latrobe continued to ponder an issue necessarily considered in any treatise on architecture: to what extent should Americans rely on European precedents? Granted that the all-encompassing story of the United States was its successful rejection of political systems based on the authority of hereditary monarchs, still there were useful precedents from past European practices in engineering and architecture. Instead, many Americans, accustomed to thinking of themselves as self-made and oriented toward the future rather than the past, dismissed European ways as inappropriate, expensive, and unpatriotic. In other fields, especially literature, this tension between using English precedents and achieving an American style also existed.

Latrobe made clear his position. As he explained to Thomas Moore, a self-trained American engineer who had been critical of his work on the Washington Canal: "We err on [the] side of paying dear for our own experience, instead of buying cheap that of Europe. . . . We place a mark of disgrace on all foreigners whether pretenders or not. In our haste to be the most enlightened (*wisest*) nation in the world we forget that our very existence is of recent importation from Europe."[5] Americans imported blankets, scissors, wine, and a thousand other cheap things from Europe, so why not knowledge?

In any case, opportunities for contemplation and writing disappeared in Baltimore. The Latrobes had moved to the city because of Latrobe's architectural prospects in a community that he already knew. He also discovered opportunities in his capacity as an engineer. Earlier he had been hired to solve the problem of silting in the Baltimore harbor and the more immediate threat of the flooding of the Jones Falls, a small river that bisected the city. Latrobe now revisited his detailed, expensive plan that involved diverting the waterway into a canal. The city council tabled his idea, and as a result the Jones Falls continued to flood the city's streets and homes until the twentieth century.

By April Latrobe was working on two major architectural projects and sharing the local gossip with Robert Harper. The two men had been friends since Latrobe's early days in Washington when Harper, representing South Carolina in the US Senate from 1795 to 1801, had recognized Latrobe's talent and recommended him for a number of projects. Harper married into Maryland's first family of Carrolls, moved to Baltimore, and substituted civic leadership for his previous service to the national government. Latrobe often stayed with the Harpers during his commuting days to the city, and when he corresponded with Harper, his letters conveyed the two men's intimacy: "I write as I talk; too much; but I am talking to You."[6] In a similar vein, after a loan of $100 from Harper came due, with "unvaried attraction to you," Latrobe assured his friend that he would soon pay and now close by, recounted his "pleasure and honor to be on your list of friends."[7]

Organized in 1729, long after most East Coast port cities, Baltimore had developed quickly, as a result of its privileged location on the upper Chesapeake Bay, with an excellent harbor on a branch of the Patapsco River that flowed into the bay. As late as 1765 the community was no more than a small village with fifty houses and one ship in the harbor. Thirty-five years later, while traveling from Washington to Philadelphia, Latrobe encountered a city of 26,000 with a busy harbor. In subsequent trips he traveled by stage coach to Baltimore, then boarded one of the sloops that offered smooth and, if the wind was right, fast transportation down the Patapsco into the Chesapeake Bay, then northward to the north side of the Susquehanna River, where he took a coach to Philadelphia.

By 1800 Baltimore was a commercial center favorably situated to carry on trade with the Caribbean sugar islands as well as the Middle Atlantic interior. From the fertile soil of Pennsylvania and Maryland, grain, carried down the Susquehanna River on flat-bottomed arks, encouraged ambitious entrepreneurs like the Ellicott and Worthington families to develop mills, some employing the new invention of a steam-powered engine. Just outside the city, these mills processed a raw agricultural product into flour for shipment to Europe and the West Indies. In 1811 Latrobe did not exaggerate when he described Baltimore as "thriving."[8]

Hired earlier to survey the route to the Susquehanna River that would enable Philadelphia to compete with Baltimore's natural water route, Latrobe knew the city as a rival when he was employed by the Chesapeake and Delaware Canal Company. That company's intention was to place Philadelphia merchants closer to the Susquehanna and thereby divert trade from Baltimore. In 1801 Latrobe had surveyed the river and, subsequently in his capacity as an engineer, he had located the best pathway for a canal across the neck of land in Delaware and Maryland that would connect the Delaware River and the Chesapeake Bay. Such activities made him well aware of the possibilities for Baltimore's development.

Despite efforts by rivals, increasing amounts of whiskey, wheat, and iron arrived in the harbor of Baltimore, whose boosters proclaimed it "nearest to the north, nearest to the south and nearest to the west—so central on the seaboard as to be nearest all classes of industry and produce."[9] In the early years of the republic when raiding privateers and warring Europeans threatened

FIG. 6.1 William Bennett Baltimore Landscape. This view of Baltimore shows the city in the 1840s from the south side of the harbor. Note that two of the most prominent landmarks are Latrobe's Basilica and his Merchants Exchange. Enoch Pratt Library, Maryland State Library Resource Center.

American commerce, Baltimore held an advantage over other coastal cities with its protected harbor and improved roads into the interior. Agricultural goods from the west and tobacco from Maryland's southern counties made their way to the city wharves, to be exported throughout the world by fast sailing ships. In the kind of commercial exchange that established the fortunes of several merchants and bankers in the city, everything from Peruvian guano to finished goods from Europe was transshipped to the interior from the harbor.

By 1820 Baltimore's population had grown to 62,000, a population as diverse as any in the United States. Significant numbers of the enslaved, free blacks, immigrants from Germany, Scots-Irish émigrés, and refugees from revolutionary France and St. Domingue, as well as a ruling class of elite, white, mostly Protestant and some Catholic males, created a hyper-partisan political culture. It was politics that led to violence in the Great Baltimore Riot of 1812. In this first of the many nineteenth-century riots that earned the city the nickname Mobtown, a crowd of partisans had attacked a Federalist newspaper that opposed the war. A few weeks later a mob attempted to destroy the home of the paper's editor, Alexander Contee Hanson, in the center of the city. Latrobe was in Baltimore during the riot and described the casualties—a boy shot dead, twelve wounded, a lost eye, broken limbs. It was, he wrote, a blight on the city and a "dreadful transaction."[10]

Latrobe was in Pittsburgh when the city redeemed itself. After the British attacked Washington in the summer of 1814, local militia in Baltimore had stopped the British invaders on land and sea. It was cause for celebration as a postwar exuberance swept over residents. A public event held at the city's Fountain Inn included toasts to the citizens of Baltimore whose "patriotism and valor defeated the veteran forces of the enemy who came, saw and fled."[11] Baltimore's boosters predicted that their community would soon overtake Philadelphia as the second largest city in the United States.

It was the harbor that made Baltimore and brought prosperity to its leaders, but it was the optimism after the War of 1812 that created a climate of civic energy. The city grew physically as it annexed more land in a sur-prisingly informal process.[12] Local leaders—merchants like Robert Gilmor, William Patterson, and Latrobe's brother-in law Andrew Hazlehurst, lawyers like Robert Harper, and political leaders like the Smith family whom Latrobe called the thinking men of the town—organized associations and underwrote the cost of libraries, monuments, and, most ambitiously, a merchants exchange. In 1814, local booster and Latrobe portraitist Rembrandt Peale opened his gallery of fine arts on Holliday Street in the first structure in the United States designed and built as a museum. There, Baltimoreans could view portraits of famous revolutionary figures, listen to lectures and concerts, watch scientific experiments, and observe a collection of "naked beauties" in a nearby rival exhibit. New debating societies and men's groups such as the Delphian Club were organized; a savings bank was incorporated, along with a society to pro-mote science; a medical school was started. Most needed meeting places and anticipated raising the necessary funds through subscriptions and lotteries. So began a brief period in the city's architectural history that transformed a previously brick-and-wooden environment into a community with several monumental masonry structures.[13]

Latrobe had spent more time in Baltimore after he became the architect of the Roman Catholic Cathedral, a vast, often-delayed project begun in 1806 and completed fifteen years later. Aware that the cathedral presented a prestigious opportunity, Latrobe promised and delivered a landmark struc-ture that created a dramatic cityscape symbolizing the community's and the church's ambitions. "I have studied to give the Church the effect of being on the summit of a hill," he remarked.[14] Eventually Latrobe provided seven sets

FIG. 6.2 This digital map of Baltimore in 1814 shows the city's development during the time Latrobe lived in the city. Note the Basilica under construction and the Peale Museum. Imaging Research Center, University of Maryland Baltimore County.

of plans for the building and, as was his custom with churches and schools, he charged nothing, only reimbursement for his expenses. It was, he said, ample compensation to have the confidence of the trustees and "to contribute to the religion which is the mother of all others."[15] Twice he resigned, indignantly asking for the return of his drawings. Several times he complained about changes demanded by Archbishop John Carroll and an interfering building committee.

For example, the archbishop wanted more pews as they were money-makers that, sold to prominent families, provided financial support for the church. Latrobe believed they ruined the design of the interior. Later the committee insisted on wider aisles that significantly altered the interior. But he admired Carroll, and both men understood the significance of their endeavor. Compromise reigned, and immediately after his return to Baltimore in 1818, Latrobe began overseeing the final phase of the church's construction.

Archbishop John Carroll—still "Jackie" to his family and friends—was a member of the influential Carroll family whose members had long promoted their local community. Educated abroad, conversant with European cathedrals, and especially fond of the domed Lulworth chapel in Dorset, England, where he had been consecrated a bishop, Carroll was among a special group of insightful Americans who recognized Latrobe's genius as well as his perilous financial circumstances. On at least one occasion the archbishop lent the architect $100.[16] Given the choice of a Gothic design or a neoclassical one, he chose Latrobe's specialty, anticipating the construction of an awe-inspiring temple in a nation where the First Amendment to the US Constitution guaranteed that Catholics would never be spiritual exiles. Still, "Catholics," Carroll complained, "have free exercise of their worship but no temple where they can assemble with becoming decency."[17] He was determined to create one.

With an instinct for monumentality, Carroll moved the proposed location of the cathedral to the most commanding hill in the city, paying for the land the vast sum of $20,000 to John Eager Howard, a prominent officer in George Washington's cabinet. Though the project stalled, a casualty of financing as much as shifting plans, after the War of 1812 building resumed. Carroll had organized another lottery to raise funds and in a serendipitous marvel—surely an example of divine intervention--the archbishop won the lottery and devoted his winnings to the project. But he died in 1815 before its completion.

In 1815, returned to the east from Pittsburgh, Latrobe supervised the final stages of the construction of his masterpiece that became the city's most important work of architecture and remains so, two centuries later. Earlier his attention to the cathedral had required guilty but necessary absences from his work on the US Capitol, since he was uncertain of the competence of the workers and their often drunk supervisor who on one occasion read the plans upside down. For the exterior, Latrobe had chosen, rather than bricks, mottled gray stone from nearby Ellicott City that could be transported by oxcarts into the city. "Bricks externally," he explained in one of his persistent efforts to educate uninformed Americans, "I hope the Committee will reject altogether. Bricks can never produce an effect beyond *neatness*; they are the dress of all our private buildings down to the meanest of them. With a stone building the idea of strength and permanence is always connected."[18]

Once settled in Baltimore, he lived only blocks from the cathedral. Every day, often four times a day given other demands on his time, he walked uphill to the structure to oversee the crucial final stages of its construction, "climbing these steep hills," and sometimes suffering leg cramps.[19] Finally in early October 1818 he could report to his son John, "This day we close the Dome of the Cathedral." A few days later, he described the ritual driving of the final bricks into the cornerstone, after which "with some ceremony and a great deal of punch . . . about 60 persons were collected on the top of the building and 3 Cheers given, which resounded half over the city."[20]

In fact, the dome, the hallmark of the building, was a double shell with an upper timber dome containing twenty-four skylights, each ten feet long, that brought light through an oculus in the coffered internal masonry dome, thereby producing in the church's interior the kind of mysterious lighting Latrobe achieved in his principal buildings. A technical marvel of its time, it remains the most glorious feature of the basilica. Sixty-eight feet in diameter, rising to the height of a seven-story building, the dome climaxed an awe-inspiring setting. It arose, in an unusual feature, without the clutter or visual interference of weight-bearing piers or pendentives (that is, curved triangular masonry elements that make a transition between a square space and a circular dome). Latrobe's cathedral needed and received little of the meddlesome interior ornament from which many churches suffer.

Worshippers moved from the shaded exterior portico (which was not finished until the 1840s) into an open, naturally lighted, barrel-vaulted space. As architectural historian Charles Brownell has written, "The center and side aisles and transept flow into the domed center like rivers of space pouring into an inland sea."[21] Despite its size there is a sense of intimacy, in part because of the four Ionic columns on the side screening the narthex.[22] There were obvious influences on this building including Christopher Wren's St. Paul's Cathedral, Sir John Soane's Bank of England, and, much earlier, Hadrian's Pantheon dome in Rome, all admired by Latrobe. But through Latrobe's

FIG. 6.3 Cross Section of the Baltimore Basilica. This cross-section elevation of the Basilica is an example of Latrobe's sophistication as a designer as well as an artist. His excellent drawings set a new standard for the profession he was trying to establish in the United States. Archives of the Archdiocese of Baltimore, Associated Archives at St. Mary's Seminary & University, Baltimore, MD.

genius, the cathedral was its own design and, for those who followed his architectural development, it established his maturity as an architect.

The cathedral was especially noteworthy for the vaulting, deployed by most builders only on bridges. Here, as much as in any of his major structures, the architect adhered to his ruling notion that his buildings were stand-alone sculptures and needed no other decoration. In the undercroft that had so often been a source of contention with the building committee, transverse walls topped by brick barrel vaults supported the floor above. Four inverted cradle arches held up the main piers and ultimately the weight of the dome. It was a brilliantly engineered support system and a tribute to Latrobe's development as an architect and his skill as an engineer. Its innovative features explain why a member of the building committee turned the plans upside down. As a justly proud Latrobe said of the first all-masonry church in the United States, "It bids fair to vie in permanence with the proudest edifices of Europe."[23]

The light that shone through the dome represented for Latrobe and Baltimore's Protestants, who also took pride in the city's greatest ornament, the illumination of religious freedom in the republic. For Catholics, the future basilica was what Carroll intended: a proper place of worship and a statement of power. Only an earthquake could destroy it, the architect predicted. In 2011 there was such an earthquake, an unusual occurrence in the Middle Atlantic region, requiring a major restoration. And after this most recent, painstaking restoration, the building shines with the majesty that Latrobe and the church fathers intended. Today's basilica has the kind of inspirational quality that inheres to certain structures and conveys a sense of eternity.[24]

A religious temple on a hill, the building became the most notable feature of Baltimore's cityscape. For all its monumentality it was smaller than the cathedrals of Europe; yet its mass, the clear geometry, the daring scale of its dome, and the overall spiritual quality spoke to the ambitions of an international religion, an aspiring nation and city, and of course, a proud, talented architect. Throughout the nineteenth century, before the age of tall obscuring structures, Baltimoreans could see the building from almost anywhere and it became a recognizable feature in representations of the city.

The cathedral cost $225,000 (approximately $5 million today), but its trustees judged it well worth its cost as "the most splendid temple on this side of the Atlantic." In a gracious letter written to the architect in 1820, they noted that the cathedral would stand for the ages as "a monument not only to the piety of those who have contributed to its construction but likewise of your genius and Architectural skill and taste." And they prayed that Latrobe's abilities would meet with further encouragement and that "the Almighty Being would take you and your amiable family under his special protection."[25] After the War of 1812, during the postwar euphoria that led to so many projects for the city's development, a group of Baltimore merchants began planning an exchange. For years they had accomplished their essential tasks face-to-face in a small room near the harbor; now they hoped for a vast building that would incorporate both private and public functions and that would be, as the cathedral to Catholicism, an architectural temple to the city's commerce. The concept was not new; exchanges were well known in Europe, with Venice's Fondaco dei Turchi and nearby Rialto Bridge early examples of meeting places where merchants did business. "What's new on the Rialto?" became an international query for business news.

In an increasingly complex economic environment—a time that historians have labeled the beginning of a market revolution in the United States—the word "exchange" came to signify a physical setting for the business functions of buying, selling, and transporting goods, depositing and withdrawing funds from banks, obtaining insurance, dealing with US Customs, and using the US Postal Service—all involving the reciprocal giving and receiving tasks of early nineteenth-century mercantilism. Even before Baltimore's ambitious undertaking there were coffee exchanges in Charleston. For years there had been talk of similar buildings in Boston and New York. Latrobe had designed such a building in Philadelphia, though the project never received sufficient funding.

To fund their building, Baltimore merchants established a subscription system, issuing stock up to $200,000, later increased to $500,000. A share in the Baltimore Exchange Company cost $200, payable in installments over two years. In the days before a central stock exchange this was a familiar way to raise capital, and Baltimoreans responded enthusiastically. So too did Latrobe who bought a share for his daughter Julia. The company purchased a prime site a block from the harbor, near the city's main market, bounded by Gay, Water (now Lombard), Second Streets, and an alley. The building would be oblong, 240 feet by 140 feet, with space for a variety of functions. Robert Harper, the head of the company's building committee, suggested that his friend Benjamin Latrobe be hired as the architect.

Busy in Washington with the reconstruction of the Capitol, Latrobe proposed a partnership to his friend Maximilian Godefroy, a refugee from the French Revolution, professor at St. Mary's College, and architect of its much-admired chapel. The classically educated Godefroy had led the kind of dramatic life that appealed to Latrobe's Francophile romanticism. And

Latrobe was grateful for Godefroy's recommendation to President Madison that he be retained as the architect for the Capitol after its burning. Latrobe was also aware, after he stayed in Godefroy's home in Baltimore, of the French émigré's "frustrated ambitions, disappearing hopes and desperate poverty."[26] He also knew that Godefroy dismissed his elegant presentation drawings as pretentious advertisements. Godefroy believed that by using them to attract clients, Latrobe was behaving as no more than a professional charlatan.

Born in Paris, Godefroy had been educated in the world's premier schools of civil and military engineering. Serving as an officer in the French army, he had been arrested and briefly imprisoned during Napoleon's regime. Exiled from France, he arrived in Baltimore in 1805, where he had been hired at St. Mary's College to teach architectural drawing and drafting, as well as for-tification; his students included young Henry Latrobe. Within months of his arrival in the United States, Godefroy had become a fixture in the city's French-speaking community. In 1808 he married Eliza Crawford Anderson, who edited the *Companion and Weekly Miscellany,* a short-lived publication for which Latrobe wrote two essays on the encouragement of the fine arts in America.

In correspondence begun in 1805 with Godefroy, Latrobe complained about "the insolent ignorance of those who have acquired a little power within the *equality* of our republican *fraternity,* and who use it with a fury and a grossness that are unknown to the enlightened *tyrants* of a monarchical government. And nothing is more tiresome and humiliating than the inso-lence of ignorance."[27] Such was the shared lament of two émigrés who were never completely at home in the United States. Latrobe despised "committee men, Boards of Directors, members of Congress and legislative bodies—the ignorant crowd. . . . Let them talk but don't believe anything they say."[28] He railed to Godefroy, as he could not to his native-born friends, about the "mushrooms of fortune whose vile patronage" he must submit to in order "to get employment at all and bread for our families."[29] He shared with his French-born friend his view that men of the arts fared poorly in America, corrupting a couplet from Horace into an assertion in Latin that "Now we must go hungry, now with free foot we must kick all."[30]

To Godefroy, Latrobe complained that "it was a great misfortune to be born and educated a *Gentleman*: at least on this side of the Atlantic."[31] Certain of a sympathetic audience, he shared multiple versions of his self-defined quandary: "My habits were formed on the dilemma of honor & virtue & how then can I make money, the only substitute for both, unless I had the necessary habits & were without the unnecessary, & incompatible feelings. So we must drudge on." And it was to Godefroy that Latrobe exposed his views on the importance of educated elites establishing public taste, even if those elites contradicted the national vision of equality: "You and I must carry on the war against the Goths and Vandals with perseverance."[32]

In 1815, the Latrobe-Godefroy collaboration produced an initial presentation drawing for the Merchants Exchange. "It is evident," wrote Latrobe with his habitual optimism, "that we *two* are *one* in the great principles of our conceptions," though he acknowledged that they differed in both training and their understanding of design.[33] Despite their inside track, by the fall the Merchants Exchange Building Committee had adopted another course and advertised a competition for the building in the Baltimore newspapers, just the kind of process that Latrobe despised for its politics, disregard of his commanding expertise, and favoritism by ignorant judges. His point was reinforced when one judge wanted "only *lines* without elevations or Sections or the *trouble of fine drawings.*"[34] There were warnings that the Latrobe-Godefroy partnership would not be chosen after one judge informed Latrobe that he was known to be extravagant. He might have warm friends, advised the merchant William Patterson, but he also had warm enemies. There were rumors if French expatriate architect Joseph Jacques Ramee was chosen, one committee member would contribute $40,000 to the venture.[35]

Among Latrobe's competitors was Robert Mills, his former student. Latrobe had always had mixed feelings about Mills, believing him a hard worker but no genius, "a wretched designer," "an enthusiastic methodist" devoted to prayer and the singing of hymns," but with a bad temper—"a very useful citizen but never a very amiable Man."[36] Yet it was by comparing his own ways of proceeding to those of Mills that Latrobe arrived at an understanding of the character of genius so necessary for architects but "as troublesome as it is absolutely necessary to the projects of a great work. By genius, I mean that power of seizing accurately, combining, and applying all the *facts* belonging to the nature of the country and of, as it were, intuitively fixing upon the governing principles on which the work must proceed as to unite oeconomy with efficiency. A Man possessed of this faculty makes no experiments and corrects no blunders at the public expense while another is groping his way gravely and silently, depending upon correcting."[37]

Earlier he had explained to Jefferson that just as a poet did not first determine his meter and then settle on the grammar and eventually the content and words of his poem, so an architect must not "make two separate labors of the arrangement, and construction of his work. . . . The operation of the brain which produces a design, is a simultaneous consideration of the *purpose, the connection and the construction* of his work."[38]

Of course Latrobe did modify and redesign: he had developed seven separate plans for the cathedral. And in his later work he developed programs and the articulated design explanations that became standard operating procedures in twenty-first-century architectural offices. But never did he proceed without a governing principle, and rarely did he experiment and subsequently correct.

In a letter still quoted in texts on American architecture, Latrobe described to Mills the perilous status of architects in the new republic and the necessary standards they must follow in their dealings with clients. Architects in the United States were threatened on two fronts, advised Latrobe: on the one hand, by gentlemen architects who did not know how to build (his arch-enemy William Thornton was the prime example) and, on the other, by carpenters, mechanics, and millwrights who knew nothing about design and merely copied from pattern books. To establish architecture, Mills must follow certain principles: to do nothing gratuitously, to understand the client's intentions before the work began, to work out a payment plan, to control the employment of workers, to design with the site in mind, and to never leave drawings in the hands of the client or the public. At one time or another Latrobe violated all these principles. His letter was as much a caution to himself as to Mills.[39]

By 1816, Mills, having followed some of his mentor's advice, was the most successful of Latrobe's students, most of whom had apprenticed with Latrobe in Philadelphia. Mills had been awarded commissions in two competitions in which Latrobe was at least preliminarily involved. By not withdrawing immediately Mills violated Latrobe's rule that as a member of a profession, architects must never compete against friends or needy colleagues, and certainly not against their mentors. An unsustainable matter of honor in a competitive environment, Latrobe's view represented his continuing commitment to establishing not just the economics of architecture but the ethics of its practice, in this case his imagined view of a collegial professional community bound by certain standards of etiquette and honor.

He was not jealous of the preference given to Mills for a monument in Richmond. But, as he wrote, he was "most sensibly hurt that you should not have become aware of the indelicacy." After all, Latrobe had trained Mills; to continue in a competition against him was a mistake "of which no inducement of profit could have made me guilty towards you" and which in "service of sentiment only ought to have been impossible." Besides, Mills had copied the way in which Latrobe inserted marble panels into freestone. Surely, he chastised Mills, his student should not have "waged war against me in my own armor."[40]

Recently Mills had captured the commission for Baltimore's monument to George Washington, with a design that Latrobe, who had not competed, believed "wretched," no more than a mundane column copied from that in London to honor Vice-Admiral Horatio Nelson, hero of Britain's recent war against the French. By this time Mills was well known among the men of the exchange who considered him dependable. Latrobe worried that his former student might also receive the exchange commission. While the architects waited, Latrobe in a fit of pique demanded that Mills return all the drawings that, as a student living in Latrobe's home, he had kept of Latrobe's earlier designs for the Bank of Pennsylvania and the Markoe house in Philadelphia.

After months of uncertainty, in February 1816, Latrobe and Godefroy learned that they had received the commission for the Baltimore Merchants Exchange with five votes. Mills had received one vote and the other contenders none. And so, during the winter and spring of 1816, the hard work began on a final design for a mammoth, multipurpose building, along with the increasingly difficult task of maintaining a collaboration with Godefroy.

At first there were disagreements about stylistic issues between the two men. Godefroy favored a colonnade along the entire Gay Street front; Latrobe believed such a colonnade impossible given the proposed length of the structure and the slope of the land. Godefroy disliked Latrobe's arched windows. Godefroy believed Latrobe's plan lacked dignity, wasted space, and was, in the gendered complaint of French architects, "too feminine," by which he meant it lacked character and firmness.[41]

Meanwhile, Latrobe believed that Godefroy's French manners and broken English limited his usefulness in discussions with the committee and the supervision of workers: "I speak *English*; carpenters, bricklayers and Blacksmith's English. I know their tricks, their practices of Work, their modes of measurement, and *am up to all the Slang of the Shop.*"[42] Certainly in the subsequent dealings with the building committee Latrobe was the leader, the one who answered the committee's questions, ordered the materials, and spoke ever more possessively of *his* design and *his* plan. By the spring Latrobe believed, as he had not originally, that "one or the other must do the whole." And that one, of course, was Benjamin Latrobe.[43]

Beneath these differences rested a precarious arrangement between two architects with sharp tongues, prickly tempers, and differing understandings of their mutual roles. Godefroy, proud and talented, intended a partnership in which he would contribute as a principal; Latrobe, like most lone star architects then and now, found equality impossible and considered Godefroy a junior associate who might supervise construction while Latrobe remained in Washington. Latrobe considered architecture, like most mental endeavors, an enterprise of solitary individualism: "*design* is by nature a *monopoly*."[44] And he had contributed most of that design, "the details of which were the result of *mine* and not of *your* studies . . . [all] in the Character of my habitual manner, now Spread throughout the United States."[45] Latrobe's was an early manifestation of a profession that has become an avatar of individualism.[46]

The professional union that Latrobe had glibly promoted as "we are one" foundered in what he now admitted were "differences of education, of habits, of the countries and schools in which we have studied."[47] By May, Godefroy, stung by his treatment, criticized Latrobe's conceptualization and the predominance of Latrobe's style in the drawings. He offered a rival design, and even shared a private letter from Latrobe with the committee, an indefensible violation of their friendship in Latrobe's code of behavior. "Notions of honour," the benighted Latrobe lamented, "are said in the Books, to be such phantoms, and are known to change with Circumstances so very frequently, that I begin to imagine, that those I was taught in my boyhood, and which I have carefully nursed ever since, had better be discarded as soon as possible as totally unfashionable and inapplicable to the relations which surround me now-a-days."[48] Meanwhile, Godefroy continued to challenge Latrobe's design as too English: "In Europe we do not accept modern English architecture as either masculine or pure."[49]

Less than six months after they had received the commission and together had signed a presentation drawing of the Gay Street entrance, the partnership of Latrobe and Godefroy exploded with bitter feelings on both sides. To Latrobe's irritation, Godefroy subsequently received the commission for the US Bank to be built in the southwest corner of the Exchange Building, a commission that he had anticipated receiving. Godefroy never forgave Latrobe for his supposed treachery over the exchange commission. Years later after he had returned to Europe, he still considered Latrobe's actions a betrayal that had ruined his life. Godefroy did endow Baltimore with three surviving examples of his talent—the Unitarian Church a block away from Latrobe's cathedral, the chapel at St. Mary's, and the obelisk commemorating the Battle of Baltimore in 1814.

As the Merchants Exchange evolved in 1816–17, the building became Latrobe's—his design, his striking interior, his details, and particularly, his solid masonry construction. The structure, which was completed in stages and survived for nearly a century, testified to the idea that merchant princes deserved their own palaces. Only the long prosaic entrance on Gay Street with twenty-five rectangular bays remained of the collaboration with Godefroy, though Latrobe admitted he could have made it more "dashing."[50] Still, its rows of uniform windows spoke to the orderly, utilitarian practices required of nineteenth-century merchants. Its size recognized Baltimore's expanding commerce.

On the interior the Merchants Exchange had character, vitality, and consistency, all elements of Latrobe's architectural style. Fifty-three-feet square with entrances from three sides and flanked by interior colonnades of Ionic capitals carrying balconies, the central hall featured a spectacular dome that rose 115 feet above the floor and was internally secured by iron chains and frames of oak. Four large windows flooded the interior with light on sunny days when the merchants and shipowners gathered at noon. All three floors held counting rooms as well as offices for the emerging occupation of insurance that opened onto the hall. Those who walked up to an inner circular gallery were rewarded with commanding views of the city and its busy harbor. Soon the Exchange Building, with its huge weather vane on top connected to a compass in the hall below, was the talk of the town. Even the wind's direction could be read by merchants below in an example of how information—that is, the time a ship would arrive in the port—improved commerce by accelerating the planning for transportation on land.

In the exchange, Latrobe showcased the masonry construction that was his hallmark. He intended his buildings to be free-standing sculpture; they needed no decoration. He linked the austere simplicity of the design to the virtues of the republic—frugality, efficiency, and unpretentiousness. Yet utility did not mean stale normality. As architectural historian Talbot Hamlin has written, "The way in which the weights [of the dome and roof] were carried down by heavy piers at the end of the colonnaded passages on each side, the use of the weight of the drum and the upper dome to help buttress the thrusts of the lower pendentive dome, the lightening of the total weights by the large windows and panels of the drum and the deep coffering of the inner surfaces of the dome—these were all brilliantly original."[51]

Latrobe had no difficulty collecting his fee of $4,000 from the committee, though only the central portion of the Merchants Exchange was completed while he lived in Baltimore. Part of the money was immediately invested in his future—specifically, the steam engine required for his New Orleans waterworks. Despite his solidly middle-class income, he worried about the economy, advising his son John, at the time a cadet at West Point, to

FIG. 6.4 Elevation of the Gay Street Front of the Baltimore Merchants Exchange. Largely completed before his death, the Exchange was Latrobe's largest commission with the exception of the US Capitol. Its prominent features were the dome and the fifty-three-foot square exchange hall where Baltimore's merchants met. It was demolished in 1901. The John Work Garrett Library, Sheraton Libraries, Johns Hopkins University, Baltimore, MD.

economize. "Times are very hard with us here."[52] Still, he had hopes for other public work in the city and for a few private homes.

Latrobe did design outbuildings and a barn for Robert Harper's estate Oakland, acknowledging the structure's low roof. "If you want a Dutch barn," he advised his client, "you must overrule [my] prejudices."[53] A library committee headed by his friend Harper had chosen him to design a city library, and he complied with preliminary drawings. But the company was unable to raise the necessary funds. And as public opportunities disappeared, so too did private commissions.

Though this aspect of Latrobe's professional contributions to the building of America is often neglected, he frequently served as a consultant on architectural and engineering projects.[54] Sometimes he was paid, sometimes not. In 1817, Thomas Jefferson had written "as a friendly beggar," asking his friend's ideas about his design for the University of Virginia. Jefferson, retired from the partisan politics that he disdained, had worked for years to create a university that would be the culmination of Virginia's public educational system.[55] In 1816, the state legislature finally supported the project with funds. A site was located and purchased near Charlottesville, and Jefferson reached out to Latrobe for his thoughts on the "academical village" he had in mind. Jefferson's plans featured two-story pavilions. These differing units would house professors and students and would include classrooms. Attractive enough to lure European professors from more established universities, they would be arranged in a U-shaped plan with a lawn between. They would be united by a classical colonnade running along their fronts.

Latrobe responded promptly with the kind of self-effacing compliments he lavished on Jefferson and few others. Happy that "I still retain your esteem and friendship," he complimented the former president on his "novel" plan that avoided "the usual *barrack* arrangement" used for colleges and universities, even though earlier he had submitted a similar plan for a national university on the mall. Latrobe sketched two pavilions that Jefferson adopted and that are today Pavilions VIII and IX.[56]

Latrobe's most critical contribution resulted from his visual talents: he imagined the village not just as a series of buildings but as a whole. In the process, he saw that it needed a dominating structure. Stubborn about such issues but ever receptive to good ideas, the former president immediately accepted Latrobe's advice for a "Center building which ought to exhibit in Mass and details as perfect a specimen of good Architectural taste as can be devised." The architect included a sketch of such a Pantheon-like temple and so today, in another benefit from the Jefferson-Latrobe partnership that so enriched early America, Jefferson's brick cylindrical library with its Corinthian portico presides over the country's most distinguished and most often copied college campus space.[57]

As the building of the pavilions proceeded in fits and starts, Latrobe reassured Jefferson of his pleasure in helping a man for whom he held enduring respect. His pro bono work on the village was no trouble and never interfered with business. Rather, it gave satisfaction: "In truth," he assured Jefferson, he prided himself much more "on the power which my profession gives to me to be useful to the public and to my friends than any wealth which I might acquire in practising it." Still, as a result he had neither money nor time to accept Jefferson's long-standing invitation to visit Monticello.[58]

Meanwhile Jefferson, whose arthritis made writing difficult, shared with Latrobe the slow progress of the university. He wrote as well of his "great grief" that Latrobe was no longer working on the US Capitol. He had hopes that "under your direction, that noble building would have been restored and become a monument of national taste and spirit. I fear much for it now."[59]

At the time, Latrobe anticipated that he would receive the commission for the Second Bank of the United States, politically one of the most controversial institutions in the early republic. The charter for the first bank had expired in 1811 amid continuing opposition by Jefferson, Madison, and leading party members who argued that the federal government lacked constitutional authority to create a national bank. But financial difficulties during the War of 1812 and the obvious need for a uniform currency in an expanding nation overcame objections by supporters of state banks and opponents of the exclusive privileges granted to bank directors. In April 1816 Congress passed legislation chartering the Second Bank of the United States for twenty years. Capitalized at $35 million, the national bank would be the custodian of public funds and the much-needed regulator of the currency. Its central office was to be located in Philadelphia, with branches in other states.

Latrobe wanted this commission as much as any in his career, and his solicitations, embarrassing for America's premier architect, reveal just how much it meant to him. Despite his frequent repudiation of public work, to build a second bank in Philadelphia would be the climax of his architectural career. He had always thought the design of his Bank of Pennsylvania, pronounced so simple and beautiful by visitors, one of his best. But the new bank would be "*the ne plus ultra,* of American Architecture." Twenty years' experience had sharpened his ability: "I should even succeed better than I did at that time."[60]

For years, even when he lived in Washington, he had considered Philadelphia his future home and had said so in the closing remarks of his lengthy oration delivered to the Society of American Artists in the spring of 1811: "Although the course of my business has for some years separated me from you for the greatest part of every year, I feel that my home is here."[61] Latrobe appreciated the city's intellectual offerings of societies, libraries, book stores, and erudite citizens. Besides, Philadelphia was the place where he had courted and married his beloved wife and become part of an American family. His seventy-five-year-old father-in-law Isaac Hazlehurst whom he considered as a blood father missed his only daughter and hoped that she might live nearby.

Just months after official legislation rechartering the Bank, Latrobe began his solicitations with letters to his friend, the retiring secretary of the treasury, Alexander Dallas. He also wrote William Jones, a Philadelphia merchant, fellow member of the American Philosophical Society, and former secretary of the navy and the treasury, who became the first president of the Second Bank of the United States. In this and other appeals to prominent Philadelphians, Latrobe noted that he had never before "made any interest for professional employment," that he rarely entered competitions, and that his "professional skill and integrity" were well known. To Pennsylvanians like William Jones he described his local spirit: "I am a Pennsylvanian, and all my friends of long standing, and relations reside there. I think I should prefer closing my career among the many friends who would there surround me. . . . Will you therefore not forget me, for you will be president of the institution."[62]

Unable to expand the building of the First Bank of the United States—it had been sold to Stephen Girard—and unwilling to offer Latrobe the commission without some deliberation, the directors purchased a lot on Chestnut Street and advertised what Latrobe disliked: a competition for architects of "science and experience" for a marble-faced banking house of 10,000 to 11,000 square feet with a portico on each front. "In this edifice, the Directors are desirous of exhibiting a chaste imitation of Grecian Architecture, in its simplest and least expensive form."[63] The description was itself a stunning acknowledgment of how Latrobe's architecture had molded American taste.

One director informed Latrobe that he could not win the competition, while another encouraged him. The conflicting judgments were based on just the kind of insider gossip that made Latrobe reluctant to enter architectural competitions, despite their attraction in a democracy. But the lure of Philadelphia, the need for employment after the completion of the Merchants Exchange, and the directors' specifications that intended what he had already done so successfully in the Bank of Pennsylvania prompted his entering the competition. Several others entered too, including two of his former students—Robert Mills and William Strickland.

For the competition, Latrobe completed drawings of a proposed building. He explained his design to the committee, along with comments about his previous experience in constructing banks: it would be "in its principal construction and general mass that of a Grecian Doric temple."[64] His son John helped with the early studies. The final design, subject to modification in terms of its size, was clearly an enlargement of Latrobe's earlier bank—a tripartite arrangement with a cubed block in the center containing the fifty-eight- by eighty-foot domed banking hall, rooms for the officers of the bank in the front and back, and columned porticos that were standard features of Greek temples.

As Latrobe recognized, the modern functions of a bank were different from those of ancient temples: more light was required so that windows on the sides and front sacrificed some of the serene beauty of unbroken marble facades in classical buildings. The need for office space for clerks and directors required careful attention to the interior spaces unknown in ancient Greece. Besides these necessary departures there were Latrobe's improvements, his unique contributions to his time and place: "For every part of the Exterior I have therefore, I believe, the authority of the best edifices of the best Aera of Grecian art. The interior being vaulted has no example in ancient Grecian Architecture."[65]

Latrobe estimated the cost at an eye-popping $433,440, which he justified, in Latrobean fashion, by pointing out to the committee the advantage of building for the ages. He warned against shortsighted budgeting, declaring that future expansion required such spending on an important institution, "the growth of which in importance and dignity must necessarily keep pace with the inconceivably rapid strides which our whole Country is making to wealth and power."[66] To design otherwise was to compromise not only his personal standards but also the development of American architecture and, through the physical presence of superb buildings, the nation's taste.

Latrobe was stubbornly consistent in these commitments. During the summer of 1817, he had been commissioned to design St. Paul's, an Episcopal church in Alexandria, and had complied with one of his rare Gothic plans. The design came with a warning to Rector William Holland Wilmer: once adopted, "you will not permit yourself *even to think of alterations.*" In Latin he advised that each man must be trusted with his own art or skill: "*Cuique in sua arte credendum.*"[67] But as often happened in the perpetual tug-of-war among a client's desires, monetary constraints, and an architect's control, the rector and the vestry sought cost-saving changes, especially on the sides and in the back. Latrobe erupted: "What a confession of ostentatious poverty! The congregation are proud enough to build a handsome front to show to passengers but too poor to be consistent in the flanks, and too inconsistent in their opinion of their Architect, (whether of his honesty or skill I will not pretend to say), to believe that he is capable of judging as correctly respecting the body of a Church as of its front."[68]

A year later, in September 1818, Latrobe received the bad news. William Strickland had won first prize and the commission to build the Second Bank of the United States. Latrobe had to settle for a second prize premium of $200 and the prospect of no future in Philadelphia. Latrobe had known Strickland for years; his father John worked as a carpenter and bricklayer on the Bank of Pennsylvania, often bringing his son to play at the site. Later Latrobe accepted Strickland as one of his apprentices, and for a brief period the arrangement had been mutually satisfactory. "I have nothing to say about him [William] that it would not be a pleasure to say of my own son."[69] But the next year a rebellious Strickland disobeyed his mentor's directions to rub the mold off Latrobe's Iron Hill log cabin and instead went fishing with friends.

Latrobe sent him home with instructions that he be severely dealt with. Two years later when John Strickland tried to get some money for his son's work, Latrobe replied that young William had left before he could be of any use.[70]

Over time, the Stricklands had become a respected middle-class family in Philadelphia, and, as such, examples of the nation's exalted mobility. With his father's help William set up an architectural and engineering practice in the city. An excellent draftsman, he designed and oversaw several local projects, including the Masonic Hall, a Gothic structure on Chestnut Street. Strickland was no fan of Latrobe's, even criticizing his former mentor's famous corn cob capitals: "The Architect flattered himself that he had made a new order of columns. But [they are] a novelty that flattered the eye, but not so the mind. What idea of strength and support can we have from a bundle of corn stalks?"[71] Strickland was best known for locating and overseeing the city's fortifications during the War of 1812 when every community along the East Coast feared an invasion by the British. Philadelphia was never attacked, but his patriotic endeavors brought Strickland the gratitude of city fathers, some of whom were judges of the competition for the Second Bank.

For the competition, Strickland entered a design. Then, after the extension of the contest and after all the plans were publicly shown, he withdrew it, offering a new one that was so similar to Latrobe's as to amount to architectural plagiarism, or at least Latrobe and his friends thought so. According to Latrobe, he was not the only one to observe that his former apprentice's second presentation "is said to be very similar to that presented by me"—a building of a Greek Doric temple, while Strickland's first design featured an Ionic temple on a tall base.[72] Although Strickland's first design has been lost, several observers agreed with Latrobe that it was ugly and failed to reconcile the interior and exterior. But Strickland's second version was a dignified Greek temple. And this new design did more than simply ape Latrobe's: it was, except for the shape of the banking hall and its interior divisions, a direct copy. Other observers, then and now, disagree, finding both designs the architectural offspring of Latrobe's earlier Bank of Pennsylvania and the Greek Revival style of public buildings that he had introduced to the United States and that had become the favored style for important civic structures.[73]

Latrobe did not file a formal complaint. As the foremost architect in the United States, he disapproved of the idea that designs must be publicly shared. But his failure to obtain this commission was a devastating blow. To take second place to a former student who had won by copying *his* ideas was humiliating. The loss also meant that there would be no chance of moving his family to congenial Philadelphia.

For the rest of his life Latrobe assailed Strickland as a copyist, and his obituary in *Ackermann's Repository*, based on an abbreviated memoir, included comments that the Second Bank of the United States "now building by one of my pupils is my design."[74] Later architects accepted his claim that the building followed Latrobe's design of 1818. But charges of plagiarism did not solve the problem of his future. There were few commissions in economically depressed Baltimore; he could never return to Washington after his confrontation with President Monroe, and he had just declined a possible position in North Carolina that would have placed him in charge of its canals and paid $4,000 a year. There was only one place to go.

In November 1818, Benjamin Latrobe boarded the brig *Clio* bound for New Orleans and his future as the principal investor and chief engineer of that city's waterworks.[75] For years the city had been a part of his pursuit of financial security as well as the focus of his restless imagination. Latrobe had moved to Pittsburgh in order to design a steamboat that would make him rich carrying commerce and passengers to New Orleans. He had completed an elevation and initial plans for a lighthouse authorized by Congress in 1804 at the mouth of the Mississippi River. Typical of Latrobe's architectural ambitiousness, the final design for the lighthouse was more than a directional system for navigation. Rather, the proposed eighty-foot-high, cylindrical tower with a colonnade around the base symbolized the importance of New Orleans and the United States to newcomers. Much delayed, the lighthouse was finally completed under Henry's supervision.

At the request of Treasury Secretary Albert Gallatin, Latrobe also designed the city's custom house, a critical building for cities that relied on foreign trade. The Latrobe version, completed in 1816 also under his son Henry's direction, introduced New Orleans to his elegant classical architecture. And, of course, for years Latrobe had been involved in municipal efforts to obtain a convenient, safe water supply that Henry had been overseeing. He had dispatched his son to the city to persuade the mayor and city council that he should be given an exclusive contract. When Henry succeeded with his charm, fluent French, and knowledge of engineering learned at home, his father exulted to a potential investor that "this grant is considered an immense fortune to those that hold it."[76] The exclusive contract was first awarded in 1811, the works to be completed in an optimistic three years.

After Henry's death and many delays, the city council considered granting the contract to someone else. Latrobe now understood that he must personally oversee its completion. "I shall have the honor," he advised the council in the late spring of 1818, "to wait upon You in person . . . in order to evince to You in person . . . my sense of Your indulgence in the execution of a work which, without it, must have utterly ruined me."[77] He signed himself, in a flourish intended to impress the French-speaking members of the council, B. Henry Boneval Latrobe.

Meanwhile all the necessary material for the waterworks—the parts for the boring machine, the iron fixtures, the special bricks to encase the steam engine, everything but the steam engine—had arrived in the city. What remained was supervision and labor. To allay the council's impatience, Latrobe assured its members, "Your city is destined to be one of the flourishing sentinels of the globe and these works will yield a revenue proportionate to the incalculable benefit they will dispense."[78]

During his three-and-a-half-week journey down the southern coast of the United States, into the Caribbean, then westward through the Gulf of Mexico, and finally up the Mississippi River 100 miles to New Orleans, Latrobe had no demands on his time. No carpenters and bricklayers asked for directions, no clients altered his designs, and no creditors hounded him. He missed his family but had always enjoyed traveling. Journeys had been an essential feature of a life spent in motion. And without his family he had time to keep a journal, as he had twenty-two years earlier when he had traveled across the Atlantic to the United States.

The *Clio* provided a more congenial captain and passengers as well as calmer seas than the *Eliza,* the sloop that had brought him to the United States. He captured the one storm—a gale off the North Carolina coast— in a dramatic pencil sketch. Throughout the trip he enjoyed the company of men who represented the accelerated movement of Americans southwestward. Among the "good-humored company" was a doctor taking ten enslaved individuals to set up a cotton plantation on the Red River, a young man leaving the East to make his fortune in New Orleans, a shipbuilder, an English merchant, and Baltimorean Elias McMillan, whom Latrobe had hired to take charge of the engine at the waterworks.

One of the enslaved kept in steerage died, a "light mulatto," owned by a slave dealer and expected to be sold in the notorious New Orleans slave markets for over $1,000. Latrobe read the Episcopal services before the body was committed to the sea. Subsequently he remarked how difficult it would be to suppress the internal slave trade, which he abhorred, as long as slaves were considered private property and as long as a complicit government aided the trade by permitting the use of public jails as holding cells for the trading of human property. Throughout his life Latrobe deplored the institution of slavery but feared it was so embedded that "it must long, perhaps forever, prevail in this state."[79]

Once in New Orleans, Latrobe kept his journal throughout the spring of 1819 and intermittently in 1820. Written in notebooks roughly seven-by-eight inches with covers of marbled paper, their pages were filled with Latrobe's careful handwriting, sketches, and soliloquies on everything from vice and virtue to growing old. He wrote for his family, and this family, mindful of their heritage, understood the significance of this inheritance, enjoying the journals privately for generations and then placing them in the public domain. Subsequently Latrobe's journals have become an essential repository of information about New Orleans in the early years of the republic.

As part of Latrobe's immense paper trail they reveal his thoughts on everything from the French statesman Count Richelieu's promiscuity and its effects on the French nation to religion and its practice, especially among the city's Roman Catholics and African Americans. They illuminate the personal migration of a young, brash English émigré in 1796 to a seasoned, sometimes sardonic American, a man who, now middle-aged and weathered by disappointments, maintained his observational powers and his ability to express ideas with flashing insights. Latrobe had a taste for the absurdity of human behavior and a special eye for individual stories—the Creole women who looked so delicate but who beat their slaves mercilessly with cowhide whips; the American woman who showed off her French in New York, but fearing condescension, refused to speak the language in New Orleans; the Catholic priest Father Anthony who declined to recognize the authority of the new Bishop of New Orleans; the merchant Dominique Rouquette who lost a fortune at the city's ubiquitous gambling tables and committed suicide by drowning himself.

Sensitive to his status as a stranger, Latrobe declined to observe New Orleans through the lens of habits acquired elsewhere, though in some instances this proved impossible. He was determined not to judge, he wrote, as some English "Smellfungi" did, by critically measuring different cultures by their own customs. (Latrobe's reference was to Smellfungi, a traveler in a Laurence Sterne novel who found fault with almost everything in the places he visited.) Instead, Latrobe acknowledged the superficiality of his impressions.

Some observers of the city's peculiar culture, incorrectly in his view, insisted they had discovered the "actual state of things."[80] Culture, as he viewed it, was a matter of habit and modes of living that only slowly changed. Such insights coincided with his opinions about professions: there were no instant experts in architecture or engineering, nor could there be on the state of society in New Orleans.

Like many visitors Latrobe found New Orleans unlike any place he, an experienced traveler in the Western world who had seen more of the United States than nearly all of his fellow citizens, had ever been. He accurately perceived himself as a man who had seen the world "on more sides than one."[81] As the *Clio* made its way around English Bend into the city's harbor, he first heard the city before he saw it. There was a "strange and loud noise . . . from the voices of the Market people." And then as the fog cleared, he observed a strange city where "everything had an *odd* look." It was impossible not to stare as he walked to his boarding house off the main square and observed the famed market place, where the articles to be sold were as various as "the 500 sellers and buyers, all of whom appeared to strain their voices to exceed each other in loudness. . . . White men and women, and of all hues of brown and of all classes of faces, from round Yankees, to grisly and lean Spaniards, black Negroes and negresses, filthy Indians half naked, Mulattoes, curly and straight haired, Quateroons of all shades long haired and frizzled, the women dressed in the most flaring yellow, and scarlet gowns, the men capped and hatted."[82]

On sale were the unique and the familiar—oysters and sugar cane, as well as the oranges and bananas rare in the Middle Atlantic and New England states. There was "wretched beef, but some excellent large fish." And to his delight there was a well-stocked book store with a collection of pamphlets on the American Revolution he considered buying for a friend. Latrobe admired the potential of the public square, the Place d'Armes, now Jackson Square, though not its principal buildings—the famous St. Louis Cathedral, the Presbyter, the parish house, and the Cabildo, where the city council met. Their handsome location along the river was framed by the city's protective earthen mounds, its levees. Yet the square was neglected, marred by trash and broken fences. "Thus a square, which might be the handsomest in America, is really rather a nuisance than otherwise."[83]

At first Latrobe boarded at Tremoulet's on the southwest side of the square, affording a view from its upper story of the Spanish tiled roofs that he disliked. He intended to improve his French, but finding the place filthy and horrified by the harsh treatment of Madame Tremoulet toward the enslaved, he moved. But before he did, Latrobe noted that Tremoulet had three times gone bankrupt, simply because he had written his name across a slip of paper endorsing a note that made him responsible for another's debts. Latrobe sympathized; such penalties were part of his own story.

Meanwhile in Baltimore his wife worried about his health and accommodations. "Your own" Latrobe responded in a letter to "my dearest

Mary" written a month after his arrival. He had seen few mosquitoes and there were no bedbugs. He had been free of his headaches. He was lodging in a room "about the size of our drawing room" at John Nolte's, the German-born cotton broker who later commissioned Latrobe to design a house for him. Latrobe enjoyed "the delicious and soft air" of the city as well as his lodgings with "a very good french bed of 3 or 4 Mattresses, a blanket, good sheets, a handsome quilt, 6 painted chairs, a drawing table which I have made, a small mahogany Pembroke table and a small Chest of drawers which I have bought and charged to the Company." He knew his wife, living in a rented house in Baltimore, craved these domestic details. He closed with what had long been a personal commitment: "All I want to be happy is You, and my dear Children. . . . Heaven bless and protect You my own Mary."[84] With his habitual optimism he assured his wife that "we are now, my own love, above want for the rest of our lives. The price we have paid for it has been too long an absence."[85]

In lonely moments Latrobe filled his journal with impressions about what he called "the state of Society in New Orleans."[86] When he had first arrived in the United States, he had tried to do the same thing in Virginia and eventually had found a central theme in the gentry's attachment to land. Now he posed a similar question about a complicated heterogeneous society, finding the answer "puzzling." Citing the exchange in Shakespeare's *Hamlet* between Hamlet and Polonius about the ever-changing shape of clouds, Latrobe described New Orleans as multifaceted. The city was made up of three *white* societies—the French, the American, and the mixed, by which he meant the Creoles, those residents of French and Spanish ancestry who were born in the Western Hemisphere.

The Americans, he concluded, had come to make money and they remained preoccupied with buying and selling tobacco and cotton. "Americans are pouring in daily. . . . In a few Years therefore, this will be an American town. What is good and bad in the French manners, and opinions must give way, and the American notions of right and wrong, of convenience and inconvenience will take their place."[87] What he judged "the flat, dull, dingy character of Market Street in Philadelphia or Baltimore street" was already replacing the "motley and picturesque effect of the Stuccoed french buildings of the city. We shall introduce many grave and profitable improvements, but they will take the place of much elegance, ease, and some convenience."[88]

An assimilationist intellectually, he remained a cultural pluralist in his personal behavior, never abandoning his manufactured family inheritance of class superiority nor his authentic English training. He might hope that "a *mean* or *average* character" would emerge from the city's heterogeneous population. In the meantime, he enjoyed the high society of expensive, specialized taste: the city's elaborate dinners, where the women did not retire after dinner; the celebration of George Washington's birthday, where a seated dinner for 100 was served; and the famous masked balls, where American gentlemen who might have other qualities were, according to Latrobe, hopelessly "deficient" in dancing.[89]

Slavery, simultaneously abominated and utilized by Latrobe, was an unavoidable subject. According to the New Orleans *City Directory*, in 1822 there were 13,908 whites in the city, 6,237 free Negroes, and 7,355 enslaved. Concerned that a day of rest on Sunday was not observed by most slave owners, Latrobe with his habitual thoroughness consulted the state's Black Code for the official regulations governing the treatment of the enslaved. He found leniency in the section that dictated, if the enslaved were employed on Sundays, they must be paid. He found abominably harsh the section that a white person might deliver twenty lashes to a slave found off his owner's property, in addition to the unregulated number of lashes expected from the owner. Latrobe considered the criminal part of the code more humane than he had anticipated. Still, the enslaved knew little of their rights and rarely had the ability to invoke them. The legal system for the enslaved in Louisiana was only another example, albeit far harsher, of what was true for white citizens as well. To make his point, he cited a favorite verse from Oliver Goldsmith: "Of all the evils mortal men endure/ How small the number Laws can Cause or Cure."[90]

On one of his frequent walks around town Latrobe heard an extraordinary noise and stumbled upon "an Assembly of Negroes" who met Sundays in the colloquially named Congo Square, a former military parade ground, at Rampart and Orleans Streets (today Louis Armstrong Park). In an indelible portrait, Latrobe described a crowd of 500–600 blacks dancing and singing. Because color was important in multi-hued New Orleans, he specified that there were "no yellow faces" present; all were black. Arranged in circles, the women were dancing "a miserably dull and slow figure," accompanied by drums and curious instruments of strings and calabashes that Latrobe, with his background in precise European harmonies, single rhythmic lines, and tuneful melodies delivered softly by violins and harpsichords, concluded must be imported from Africa. Overlooking any pretense of avoiding the judgments he declined to make in other areas, he described "an uncouth song" in some African language: "The Women screamed a detestable burden on a single note. I have never seen anything more brutally savage and at the same time dull and stupid." Still, in the white man's primal concern, "there was no disorder." Inquiring among his friends, he was assured that "these weekly meeting of negroes" never produced "any mischief."[91]

Missing from Latrobe's journals is any discussion of what made New Orleans a singular American community: the generally accepted, though unequal legally, interracial sexual relationships between white men and black or mixed-blood women that created a city of many colors, all measured by their distance from whiteness. His son Henry had adopted such a placage arrangement and had fathered three children, but Latrobe never commented on his son's death or family arrangements, only referring to his heroic service as an engineer in the battle of New Orleans. Perhaps Latrobe did not know of Henry's arrangement; perhaps writing about placage was too devastating and Latrobe wanted to shield his wife. Or perhaps he did write about it and then reconsidered. In any case, Latrobe's journal covering the period from January 26 to February 16, 1819, is mysteriously missing, though sections before and after have survived.

On Sundays Latrobe went to church, sometimes to the cathedral. By the spring his visits there were partly professional as he had been hired to redesign the central façade of its tower to hold a clock en route from Paris. He deemed his alterations "a trifling work," though they cost $13,250.[92] He also had been hired to redesign the grounds of the Place d'Armes and had responded with a plan centered on a pool and fountain. Latrobe disliked the cathedral architecturally, but in his journal it is the sociology of religion that attracted his comments and led him to a series of spiritual reflections.

Three times during Easter week he observed Mass, noting that the Catholics no longer paraded through the streets of New Orleans en route to the cathedral because, in gestures of inadvertent disrespect, so few men took off their hats to honor the presentation of the Host, the sacramental bread that represents the body of Christ. The Catholic congregation of the cathedral was overwhelmingly black and mostly female. He was surprised that worshippers brought their own chairs; he was astounded at both their fervor and their informality during Easter week's ceremony of the Adoration of the Cross when the faithful kissed a wax figure of Christ.

These practices were different from the simple prayers and excellent organ playing he enjoyed in nearby Christ's Church, the Episcopal church on the corner of Bourbon and Canal Streets. Such variations in the celebration of Christianity as that between Catholics and Protestants only deepened Latrobe's lifetime indifference to any specific denomination. He held no partiality to Moravianism or to Catholicism or to the Presbyterianism whose followers in New Orleans sought to prohibit recreation on Sundays.

(Eventually Latrobe decided that blue laws were justified to the extent that they gave workers, enslaved and free, a day off from their labor.) Investigating religion in New Orleans as a longtime critic of doctrines and creeds, he wondered whether "there [would] be a pious Christian in the world, if instead of the joys of heaven decreed from all eternity to the faithful their rewards were proclaimed to be only doubtful?"[93]

Like many travelers, Latrobe investigated the city's unusual cemeteries with their floating underground graves, crowded above-ground tombs, and catacombs two stories high. By this time Latrobe was something of an expert in monuments for the dead. In 1802 he had commemorated his deceased first-born daughter's grave with a simple marble marker. Several years later he had designed the sculpture carved by Giuseppi Franzoni and embedded as a panel in the monument for Governor William Claiborne's first wife and daughter, which he found less eroded by its outdoor exposure than he had expected. Earlier, Latrobe had explained to his friend Robert Harper that the purpose of monuments was the perpetual memory of the deceased. Although he favored cremation for practical and public health reasons, he feared that urns filled with the ashes of the deceased rarely survived a generation.

While working on the US Capitol, Latrobe designed 185 identical monuments in the Congressional Cemetery in southeast Washington. To commemorate the nation's congressmen and senators, Latrobe created a cubic block of sandstone, on a broad base six feet square and three feet high, topped by a cone over a short cylinder, with room for an inserted tablet with the name and dates of the deceased. The severity of these tombs and cenotaphs—for some congressmen were buried elsewhere—mystified later congressmen accustomed to the period's more flamboyant decorations of angels, cherubim, and flowers. One complained that burial under a Latrobe marker "brought new terror to death." Another found it difficult to conceive of "an uglier style."[94]

Latrobe's trips to the St. Louis Cemetery and the adjoining Protestant burial ground provided the occasion for his inquiries about various practices of disposing of dead bodies from Hindus to ancient Greeks to Catholics in New Orleans. Should the bodies be positioned toward the east in order to face the resurrected Jesus? Wasn't cremation better for the health of cities and the development of public areas than cemeteries? Did fishmongers actually gather crawfish and lobsters from the open graves in New Orleans where tombs regularly filled with water? The answers, according to Latrobe, depended on established practices. Certainly "if habit did not reconcile us to everything," how could a husband put the body of his wife and child "into a hole full of stagnant water about three feet deep, to be there devoured by crawfish, as is done, unavoidably in New Orleans; or to place it in a Catacomb, where the worms may dispose of it?"[95]

In his first months in New Orleans when he had time to walk around the city, dine at midday with friends, and fill his journals with random thoughts, Latrobe was also working to make certain that all was prepared for the completion of the waterworks. It lacked only the steam engine and the trenches for the pipes that would carry the water to holding ponds. During the winter, he set up the boring mill behind the engine house and surveyed the trench line for nearly 10,000 feet of pipes. He contracted for 35,000 feet of pine and cypress, found fire bricks for the boiler foundation, and even began a campaign for much-needed private investors. All was in place to supply water to a city with muddy wells and no municipal public water system. Despite its location along a mighty river and a large lake, the city could not deliver sufficient water for cleaning the streets and fighting fires, much less for private consumption.[96] And every year the urgency grew greater, given the popular suspicion that cleaner streets might stem the lethal annual epidemics of yellow fever.

Finally, in March, three months after his arrival, the last and most crucial component of his water project arrived. Latrobe had hoped to bring this used steam engine, which he judged very powerful, with him from Baltimore, but it was too heavy for the *Clio*. Even unassembled, it required a large workforce to unload it from the *Missouri* and carry it the seven blocks to the Engine House. Latrobe had earlier found the clanking of the ankle and waist chains of public slaves in the city jail "a distressing sound."[97] Now he successfully petitioned the city council for permission to use the city's chain gang to unload his engine. The work progressed rapidly, and he anticipated that 6,300 gallons of water an hour would soon be pumped from the engine house.[98]

But in the early summer, the annual curse of yellow fever arrived, some said on a ship from Havana. The passengers and crew were quarantined for twenty days and the ship, flying the ominous yellow jack, remained in the harbor. Two infected sailors jumped ship and died in the city, reportedly bringing yellow fever to residents. By August, rumors of an epidemic became more frequent, though to Latrobe's irritation the newspapers gave no notice, "thus sacrificing to commercial policy, the lives of all those who, believing from the silence of the public papers, that no danger existed, might come to the city."[99] For residents, it was comforting to believe that the invasive scourge came from the outside and therefore could be prevented by isolation. In fact, the ingredients for an epidemic existed within New Orleans where the mild climate assured the survival of the mosquitoes who fed off previously infected human survivors and then carried the virus to others. Between 1817 and 1860, New Orleans experienced twenty-seven yellow fever epidemics in which more than 100 people died. Three of those—in 1817, 1819, and 1820—came during Benjamin and Henry Latrobe's time in New Orleans.

By August, the city's doctors were carrying their ineffective treatments of emetics and bloodletting to sick patients, one-third to a half of whom died. Wealthy residents fled the city, but Latrobe, too busy to leave and within months of finishing the project, remained. With his characteristic precision he described four cases of yellow fever in his boarding house. All had survived, adding to Latrobe's sense that he was impervious to the disease. In the case of the merchant Mr. Ritchie, after seven days of fever, vomiting, and an irritable stomach, he was given a cold bath and improved.

But Latrobe's labor force of thirty-four had been decimated: five workers had fled the city because of the epidemic, ten had died of yellow fever, five had survived the disease but were still too weak to work, and one was currently ill. "The sober lived, the drunken died with few exceptions," he concluded.[100] The ancient cry "Bring out your dead" resounded in the streets of the city in the summer and fall as some 3,000 residents died of yellow fever. On just one day in September, fifty-three victims were buried. Latrobe had also been ill, though from boils, no doubt the consequence of his constant exposure to contaminated water and fungally infected soil.

By this time the waterworks project was tantalizingly close to completion. Latrobe informed the mayor and city council that "had the workmen remained together, the pipes necessary to throw the Water into all the Gutters perpendicular to the Levee would have been laid [before September]." But, unable to hire workers, he decided to return to Baltimore and "bring hither my family," leaving his competent engineer Andrew Coulter in charge. Of course, he would return, he assured the mayor, citing his partial payment on a house about a mile from the city, the first home he had not rented. Besides, he had invested his entire future in the waterworks and despite the difficulties "encountered and overcome," he expected to "derive from it a competency for my advanced Years and a provision for my family."[101]

Two days later Latrobe boarded the *Emma,* a two-masted brig of 235 tons en route to New York. The ship, piloted by a man Latrobe called "a dunce of a captain," ran aground off Balize, the small settlement at the mouth of the Mississippi. But the rest of the trip was uneventful. With time on his hands Latrobe filled his notebook with observations about what, after nine months in the city, he found the two most salient circumstances of life in New Orleans—"muskitoes" and yellow fever. Medical knowledge in the early nineteenth century obscured their lethal connection; yet Latrobe recognized their importance in the lives of the residents of New Orleans. He discussed the pests that were "so important *a body* of enemies, that they furnish a considerable part of the conversation of every day, and of every body; they regulate many family arrangements, they prescribe the employment and distribution of time, and most essentially affect the comfort and enjoyment of every individual."[102] He correctly noted that the number of mosquitoes increased after rainy weather and, with his Enlightenment instincts for classification, he described four distinct species that buzzed around his bedroom at night. He offered his insights as to the best defenses against them: a net in the bedroom and in the outdoors "light boots, loose pantaloons and thin gloves."[103]

A week later as the *Emma* approached the Virginia capes, Latrobe still had New Orleans on his mind. He pondered the disease that had killed Henry and delayed his waterworks. He noted the symptoms, the differences among physicians as to its cause and treatment, and the yearly variations in its severity. He had been told that 1817 was the year of a great devastation of yellow fever, but in his journal he made no mention of the fact that his own son had been one of its victims.

After arriving in New York in October, Latrobe had no time to write in his journal. He traveled to Baltimore to spend time with Mary, fifteen-year-old Julia, and twelve-year-old Ben. He was filled with optimism: "We are now above want for the rest of our lives."[104] As the family prepared to leave for New Orleans, Latrobe wound up his affairs in Baltimore, conscientiously providing drawings for the future needs of his two great masterpieces in that city—the Catholic Basilica and the Merchants Exchange.

Then he traveled northward with Ben, first visiting his father-in-law at Clover Hill and then going on to West Point where John was a cadet in his second year. Later John remembered how his father "with his wonderful conversational powers popularized himself with the Professors and those of my friends who were introduced to him."[105] On his return to Baltimore, Latrobe visited Lydia, his son-in-law Nicholas Roosevelt, and three grandchildren in New York and then saw friends in Philadelphia, the scene of his first engineering and architectural success. Perhaps he sensed these were final goodbyes, not just temporary farewells for the few more years he expected to live in New Orleans. In any case, his wife Mary, having lost three daughters and a stepson, was "miserable" at the great distance soon to separate her from her eldest son. Still, as she advised John: "You *must* be educated. . . . If I were to remain *here* I could not have you with me. . . . God in heaven bless and preserve you."[106]

In January, the little band of Latrobes, along with the enslaved, surnameless Johnson and Frank, the German cook Mrs. Grunevelt, and Mars, the family dog, set out in the "huge" wagon Latrobe had purchased in Baltimore. They started inauspiciously in cold winter weather. It took three days to reach Gettysburg where the snow was heavy, the wagon got stuck in a dung heap, and the inn was dirty. Here Latrobe hired a sleigh for the family, sent the wagon off with the servants, and enjoyed "a delightful and rapid ride" to Wheeling, then a town of 1,800. There, a month after the family had left Baltimore, they boarded the steamboat *Columbus,* traveling down the Ohio River to the Mississippi. It was Latrobe's first ride down the Mississippi, something he had hoped to do in the *Buffalo.* Everywhere they were delayed, finally arriving in New Orleans in April. At one point the Louisville sheriff, advised by a Pittsburgh claimant, boarded the *Columbus* and threatened to take Latrobe to debtor's prison.

As on most personal matters, his journal is silent on any regrets about leaving the East. Instead he offered vivid descriptions of the interesting city that New Orleans was, along with rosy projections of good times without financial worries. Later his daughter Julia recalled "Papa's" anxiety about reaching New Orleans as soon as possible and the excruciating hemicrania he suffered during the eleven-week journey.

Marooned by weather, delayed by the *Columbus*'s defective steam engine and by the captain's unexpected detour to take on freight, an anticipated eight-day trip down the Mississippi took five weeks after the boiler burst and the shafts of the waterwheels broke. During the ten-day delay in Louisville, Latrobe spent mornings teaching Julia and Ben Italian, Latin, and drawing. At night he had time to write detailed descriptions of what he had seen— the Indian mounds in Marietta, Ohio; the place where a battle during the French and Indian War had taken place near Bloody Run, Pennsylvania; and the bridges he observed along the way. With his lifelong interest in internal improvements, Latrobe paid special attention to the roads, observing that in some cases construction crews had applied the principles of his 1813 Report on Turnpikes. Others had made the mistake of placing large stones on the bottom and small ones on top and of failing to survey properly the contour of the roadway, resulting in rough roads full of holes as the large stones rose to the top.

After arriving in New Orleans in April, Julia sent her brother John a letter describing a journey of "so many chapters of accidents that this unlucky boat has met with. . . . It was a trial of patience. Job himself would have murmured. How then could we forebear." Her father added his characteristically positive thoughts: "We are in our own house. Your Mother over head & ears in bustle. . . . She has already made it very habitable. We are all perfectly well. Our Captain, a purse proud blockhead, rendered our journey or voyage very unpleasant, but the magnificent scenery about us, & the kindness of friends wherever we stopped compensated for his & his wife's brutality."[107]

On her first view of the city, Mary Latrobe was "*astonished* at the appearance of everything," from the old Spanish houses to the levee to the goods sold in the market. Just as her husband had been, she was surprised by the sounds of the city and the tangle of French, Spanish, English, African, and Choctaw Indian words: "A jargon assailed me equal to babel its-self." Ever the consummate, adaptable helpmate, she was delighted by her new home—a classic New Orleans cottage, a mile and a half south of the city, on the bluffs overlooking the river. It had a painted column, a piazza, and ample interior space, and was enhanced on the outside by the perfume of oleanders, rose bushes, and orange trees. Her husband anticipated that with her taste and domestic capabilities "it could be made a paradise like our humble dwelling at Iron Hill."[108]

Proud of her housekeeping, Mary Latrobe confessed to a friend in Baltimore that she was learning to keep house: "Everything is different from what I have been used to but [like the challenges to her husband] I can submit to little privations . . . if a kind Providence blesses us with health I shall be quite satisfied to remain here for a year or two."[109] Both Latrobes were pleased with their new home's healthy location; yellow fever had never appeared among their neighbors.

By the late spring, Latrobe had navigated challenges from the Water Board and some stockholders over his control of the waterworks contract. He was hard at work supervising the trenching for the wooden and iron pipes. Habitually overextended, he was also overseeing the construction of the Louisiana State Bank, a handsome building based on a plain cubic symmetrical exterior with a large domed banking room and dignified by an elegant treatment of windows. It survives in today's French Quarter, recycled as an antiques store. He had, as well, completed his plans for the grounds of the city's most important square, the Place D'Armes, rearranging walkways, installing a fountain of imported Italian marble, and constructing an iron fence and gates connected by arches, all improvements to the square he had earlier described as miserable. And he had developed a plan to improve the city's permeable levees.

As the city's wet spring turned into a dry summer, the level of the Mississippi dropped. Ominously as the water receded, the airtight iron suction pipe, designed to send water to the engine house and then to be pumped into holding ponds, had to reach a greater distance into the river to obtain water. It was necessary to stop the engine and carry the suction pipe further and deeper into the river. Again Latrobe petitioned the city council to use its prisoners. Again his request was granted, and he continued to direct the digging by the chain gang on a river bed that swarmed with mosquitoes, especially during the cooler working hours of early mornings and late afternoons. In opening passages through the levee, he often uncovered a moist, smelly concoction of old wood and vegetable matter, a haven for mosquitoes.

By August there were rumors of yellow fever in the city. Eternally optimistic, Latrobe wrote his friend Robert Harper that while disease existed in the city, "the cases however are comparatively with last Year few and scattered or *sporadic* as our medical pedants call it." Still, Latrobe had mortality on his mind, informing Harper that two of the city's "most valuable men" had died of the black vomit, the characteristic internal hemorrhaging marking the final stage of yellow fever.[110] In his journal Latrobe examined Catholic funeral practices and the revenue the cathedral received from burying the dead— the tolling of the bells cost $10, the burning of six large candles $15, and the placing of the coffin on the highest stage in the church another $10. Amazed at such practicalities, Latrobe noted that even the mention of the deceased's name during the funeral mass brought an additional charge. In all, a funeral might cost a rich man over $100. It went without saying that in Latrobe's deistic way of thinking such a system was an example of corruption.

During the last days of August, Latrobe fell ill, first with a headache, though a different kind from his hemicranias. Close to finishing his water project, he continued working, sending a note "to my dearest wife" that he would come "as soon as possible after our pipe is laid, this evening. God bless You and our Children. Yours forever."[111] The next day he was overtaken by a high fever and vomiting and hurried home. There, under a doctor's supervision, he was bled, blistered, and took the mercury compound, calomel. As he progressed through the cruel stages of yellow fever into the period of evident remission, in keeping with his nature he appeared, to his wife, "totally insensible of danger."[112]

Four days later on September 3, 1820, Benjamin Latrobe was dead, one more victim of the city's, and his family's, scourge. He had died three years after but on the same day and in the same city and of the same disease as his son, although the 1820 outbreak in terms of mortality was never considered an especially lethal one. The next day the *Louisiana Courier* announced the death of Mr. H. B. H. Latrobe; a week later his name was among those listed in the city papers as interred in the Protestant cemetery. While the grave may have been marked initially, today its location is unknown, something that Latrobe, with his sense of irony and knowledge of the city's floating graveyards, would understand. He had come to New Orleans to help defeat the yearly epidemics of yellow fever, only to become one of its casualties.

There was no funeral service. Most likely, Benjamin Latrobe would have disdained any formal religious ceremony, even if his wife had been able to organize one. In the weeks after his death, his widow was struggling to nurse Julia, who suffered from a milder case of yellow fever, and to comfort Ben, who had also contracted and survived the disease. Friends had removed the family from their home temporarily and, when they returned, as Mary Latrobe described, "I ran into our chamber and there beheld everything as it had been left when the body of my beloved husband had been removed. The very clothes, the blisters, laying on the floor. I had some nitric acid in the house which I burned as soon as possible—the bed laid on the ground and [I] gathered up all the clothes and sent them away. My poor children were panic strick. I must believe that the Almighty supported me. . . . We then knelt and pray'd that he would in his Mercy continue to give support."[113] Julia and Ben slowly recovered, but the family calamity forever shaped the future of Benjamin Latrobe's widow and children.

Besides the emotional shock, Mary Latrobe was destitute. In the perpetual widow's lament, she felt herself "so ignorant of business, so distract, and confused that I scarce know what I am about!"[114] With the risky behavior that marked so many of his financial dealings, her husband had put all of his resources into the waterworks—the several thousand dollars from his work on the cathedral tower and a similar amount from his commission for the Louisiana Bank. He had even turned over to a bank the deed for his half payment of $3,000 for his house in return for cash to pay the workers when investment money in the waterworks dried up. His thirty shares of stock remained unpaid as he had continued to use his personal resources to pay the expenses of a project that he gambled would bring financial security.

For years, his wife had heard about the probabilities of the waterworks. Now penniless, she expected that "the works *ought* to be a fortune to us."[115] Mary Latrobe soon learned otherwise: unfinished, they were worth nothing. She reached out to the members of the waterworks board, but most had fled the city. When Edward Livingston, the younger brother of Robert Fulton's partner John Livingston, came to call, he brought a threatening message. There were still claims on her husband that the insolvency had not erased, he informed Mary Latrobe. And the Waterworks Company was insisting that

Latrobe owed them money. "Mr. Livingston says there will be much litigation and he thinks that what property belonged to my husband will be liable to the old Steam Boat debts."[116] And after she investigated Henry's estate, Mary Latrobe had an additional shock: whatever her late stepson's assets, they now supported his widow and children.

There was nothing to do but take gifts from friends, sell their furniture, wait for a steamship, and retrace the family's steps north. But where to go? Mary Latrobe's father had no room or extra resources at Clover Hill now that one of her brothers lived there. Nor did her other brothers have the means to support her. In his final year at West Point, John, at eighteen the only Latrobe capable of earning any income, reluctantly resigned his cadetship. He stood first in his class but was well-schooled in his father's last admonitions to his son: "I was going to say, remember that you are now, or soon will be the head of a family and of a name which has not been hitherto disgraced by any individual belonging to it; but it is unnecessary."[117]

Conclusion

*Your mother and I live chiefly for our Children. We . . . shall
view the end of our lives with calmness and pleasure, if we
leave behind us those, whose conduct will reflect honor on
the parents, and procure happiness to themselves.*

BENJAMIN HENRY LATROBE TO JOHN H. B. LATROBE,
February 18, 1820

TWO YEARS AFTER Latrobe's death his family was living in Baltimore on
"scanty" means in a small rented house on Lexington Street. Mary Latrobe
had sold her furniture and her husband's library in New Orleans as well as
some inherited land in New Jersey, and these limited funds were the family's
only source of income. By this time she had practice in running what her husband called their humble dwellings. Nineteen-year-old John was studying law
in Robert Harper's office and Ben was a student at St. Mary's College. Julia
and her mother ran a home in which, according to John, "economy was the
order of the day. . . . [H]appily my mother had a prudence and judgement that
made money go a great way, while there was no appearance of niggardliness.
Still my father's death changed many of the habits of the family."[1]

The Latrobes—mother, two sons, and a daughter—remained in the city
for the rest of their lives, and as a result Baltimore became a principal site for
one branch of this internationally dispersed family. As it had been after their
father's bankruptcy, the city served as sanctuary and opportunity, offering education for both sons as well as professional advancement.

The family also settled in the city because their father's friend Robert
Harper advised Mary Latrobe of its practical advantages. In Baltimore he
could serve as a surrogate father, giving advice and financial support. Initially
Mary had considered living in Philadelphia, closer to her father and her childhood roots. But that city was more expensive, and with childhood friends
dead or living elsewhere and her father unable to help financially, she settled

on Baltimore. In time, both John and Benjamin married and raised their children in the city. Maintaining the vaunted fertility proudly acknowledged by their father, the Latrobe sons and their wives produced thirteen children. In turn, their male offspring served the community as lawyers, engineers, bankers, and, in the exceptional case of John's son Ferdinand, state delegate, Speaker of the Maryland House of Delegates and seven-term mayor of Baltimore. Their sister Julia, the traditional stay-at-home daughter, never married and lived with her mother until Mary died in 1842.

Like many women, Julia Latrobe disappears from historical sources, though not from family remembrances. She helped John when his first wife died in childbirth, leaving a son Henry. She nursed sick family members and was recognized by Ben, after he suffered an ear infection and an episode of pleurisy, as "a good sister."[2] Julia lived her father's insistence that "it is better to have an active nurse than a skillful doctor."[3] She also became the repository for information about their ancestors, including the fictive Bonevals. Her more accurate memories focused on her grandfather Isaac Hazlehurst and her mother Mary Latrobe.

Like many middle-class women in the mid-nineteenth century who had begun stepping out of their homes into public places, Julia became a member of an organization that represented her interests—the Indigent Sick and Protestant Society. She joined a group with officers designated as Christians that promised "to give support for the body and spiritual comfort for the mind." In an age before hospitals, she visited the "needy sick" of Baltimore in their homes, bringing food and the comfort of biblical readings. During the Civil War, Julia also served on the board of managers of the Union Protestant Infirmary, later Baltimore's Union Memorial Hospital.[4]

Harper, called the General by John for his service in the American Revolution, had an office on Gay Street, across from the Merchants Exchange. For two years John reported every morning "with military punctuality . . . and a volume of Blackstone [was] put in my hand."[5] He studied in the same room as the laconic Harper, surrounded by law books, while continuing to believe that he would have studied architecture if his father had not died. At first, John mourned the fate that had denied him graduation from West Point, first in his class. He worried that he might be considered a dropout—one of what were known at the time as "Uncle Sam's bad bargains"—until the Academy produced a certificate of his resignation.[6] In an acknowledgment of his prominence, John Latrobe was later appointed by President Zachary Taylor to West Point's prestigious Board of Visitors.

John's new situation—apprenticing with a lawyer—was a necessary process at a time when most legal training took place in lawyers' offices. Before the era of specialized graduate training in university settings, the law, like architecture, was considered a craft to be handed down from master to apprentice. After two years John was admitted to the Maryland Bar without the usual oral examination, an indication of his successful absorption of the principles of the law as well as the standing of his mentor. While Harper argued lofty appeals cases and charged hefty fees, his young apprentice began his practice with more mundane legal matters concerning property rights and estate issues, some clients paying no more than $1.00 for a consultation. His first fee came from a black woman accused of shoplifting; his next involved a counterfeiting case. After one year in practice he had earned over $100, and by the 1850s, as he ascended in the profession, he earned more than $6,000 a year.

For both sons, their father remained a constant presence, his advice followed (especially that of avoiding debt), his hard work replicated, and his family pride cherished. John took seriously his role as family patriarch and once warned Ben that he was in danger of sinking into what no Latrobe should be—a nobody in a country village.[7] Seven years after his father's death, Ben acknowledged that "there were few days in which my departed parent was not before my eyes, as my pattern, my model, which I strove to imitate however hopelessly."[8] Neither John nor Ben speculated; neither ever carried significant debt. They never found it necessary, as their father had so often, to "retrieve" their business affairs. They never forgot "old Daddie's preachings" about honor, integrity, and civic service.

"*Vitam impendere vero* [stake your life for the truth] be your motto, and you will seldom go wrong, and always do unto others as you would they should do unto you," Latrobe had advised his son John shortly before his death.[9] His sons carried with them another instruction: "I do not expect you to be more than man, but I expect you never to disgrace your name and throw a blot on a family that although partaking of the defects of human nature has never yet produced an individual of whom they had cause to be ashamed."[10]

Even before John was licensed to practice law, he searched for ways to increase the family income. He chose writing and soon was publishing children's stories. He also created a money-making calendar for young adults decorated with his watercolors. He authored a novel, submitted short pieces to magazines, and published a practical legal guide, *Latrobe's Justices' Practice under the Laws of Maryland on the Duties of Justices of the Peace.* Informative and useful, *Latrobe's Justices* was revised in seven editions. Another profitable pamphlet reflected his father's preoccupation with honor. Entitled *Practical Reading Lessons on the Duties that Man Owes to his God, to his Fellow Beings and to Humanity*, it earned its author $200. John's writing, like so much of his life, mirrored one of his father's many talents. Benjamin Latrobe had been a vivid writer, his expressive skill revealed in his letters, journals, and occasional papers.

John was a joiner, available for speeches and marching in parades with a drawn sword. He intended to keep the same social standards as his parents, and as something of an outsider in Baltimore he became adept at developing influential contacts. At first, he and his brother shared one set of the obligatory black stockings necessary for fancy dress parties, and when these became torn, they applied ink to their legs to disguise the holes. But after ten years in the city, Baltimore's best tailors outfitted John, and he was a fixture at the city's social events that served as platforms for professional advancement. He spoke as well on political occasions, once explaining that such speeches were "an honorable and sure way to become known," thereby "to further advance."[11] Somehow he also found time to design several monuments in Baltimore and to invent what became known as the "Latrobe stove."

In 1828, John Latrobe became the principal lawyer for the Baltimore & Ohio Railroad, a position he held until his death. His fees varied according to the economic condition of what he named "The Great Road." In the beginning, the concept of a steam-powered railroad was sufficiently novel that its detractors organized a famous race with a horse-drawn carriage which, to the delight of the antiquarians, the horse won. John had been one of the observers in the railroad car, the *Tom Thumb*. After a slow start, it overtook the horse amid great cheers. But in the thirteen-mile race from Ellicott City into Baltimore, the band that drove a pulley slipped off the engine. *Tom Thumb* collapsed in a giant sigh of steam. But the defeat was a last hurrah for those who distrusted engines driven by steam on wood and later iron tracks. Neither of Latrobe's sons ever hesitated in their commitment to the technological future represented by steam-powered locomotives.[12]

Trained as an engineer at West Point, John appreciated the possibilities of rail travel as well as its difficulties. Only slowly did the B&O overcome the challenges of laying track, first to Cumberland, Maryland, and then across the daunting topographical obstacles presented by 150 miles of wilderness, streams, and mountains that lay between the town of Cumberland and the railroad's intended destination of Wheeling on the Ohio River. As the company's lawyer, John Latrobe dealt with a range of issues, from obtaining

FIG. C.1 John H. B. Latrobe. This photograph of Latrobe's second surviving son shows the distinguished Baltimore lawyer in his sixties. At the time he was a civic leader and the Baltimore & Ohio Railroad's lawyer. Courtesy of the Maryland Historical Society, PVF.

rights of way from states and individuals and lobbying the legislatures of Maryland, Virginia, and Pennsylvania to negotiating conflicts with other railroads, dealing with an increasing number of labor issues, and on several occasions, settling with irate farmers whose cows had been killed by trains. He was present at the beginning of a railroad that expanded American markets and after the Civil War created new forms of business organization.

Believing "association the very essence of humanity," John became a Mason. His father had been a member of the fraternal organization but had paid it little attention. John rose to the 32nd degree and, admired by his fellows, delivered remarks at the laying of the cornerstone for the Masons' new building in Baltimore in 1866.[13] A member of the local militia, in time he became the most popular speaker in the city for the special civic occasions that required the combination of substance, rhetorical flourish, and a few appropriate anecdotes. Ben catalogued his brother's abilities as an orator, but as younger brothers often do, found some imperfections: "John delivered a beautiful address," he described in 1834. "He does well with the English language. His worst fault is that he makes his subordinate sentences too emphatic."[14]

John stood at the forefront of a group of young Baltimoreans with ideas for new civic institutions. In the 1830s, he and his friend, noted author John Pendleton Kennedy, decided that the city needed a historical society and he became a moving force behind the organization of the Maryland Historical Society. From 1871 to 1892, he was the president of the society, a position many believed "the most prestigious position in the city."[15] In the lecture hall of the Historical Society on Saturday afternoons he declaimed on subjects from the Napoleonic wars to the history of the Mason-Dixon Line. He was active in the founding of the Maryland Institute of Art and a leader in the creation of Druid Hill Park, Baltimore's first public park. A man of good humor, he insisted that the tender of the city's sheep in the park wear a shepherd's outfit for authenticity. Late in his life, sounding like his father, John Latrobe applauded the city's new, very grand city hall: "If our monuments redound to our patriotism, if our railroads demonstrate our enterprise, if our parks illustrate our approval of the beautiful in nature, then our public buildings should not disgrace us by their inconvenience and their insufficiency."[16]

John's most important association was with the Maryland Colonization Society, an organization that proposed to resettle the state's blacks in Africa, the latter continent ignominiously offered by white enthusiasts to blacks who had been in America for several generations as "their own native land." Today the ideals of colonization seem profoundly un-American and deeply racist, based as they were on the contention that the inferior race of blacks could not survive in a society with superior whites. Yet to those like John Latrobe in the period before the Civil War, living in the American city with the largest population of free blacks in the nation, colonization emerged as a solution to what these men considered the dual evils of the frightening extremism of abolitionism and the stagnating evils of slavery. Colonization was hardly a fringe movement. Some of the most respected leaders in antebellum America—Thomas Jefferson, Henry Clay, John Marshall, and Abraham Lincoln—supported it. In 1832, even the stingy Maryland legislature allocated $200,000 over ten years to oversee the "Removal of the Colored People."

John and his mentor Robert Harper agreed that you could free a slave, but you could not make him a white man. The assimilation of blacks, given their assigned inferiority, seemed impossible to this and subsequent generations. According to John Latrobe, "racial amalgamation" would destroy the republic because the two races could never "enjoy social and political equality

in the same land." The solution rested in removing blacks. This idea was especially important as emigrants from Europe were elbowing aside "the free
colored" in various trades. In Africa, according to John Latrobe, blacks would
have the opportunity for improvement and would develop "civilization and
Christianity." While colonization, as John Latrobe characterized it, was not
intended to abolish slavery in Maryland, it was a means of removing blacks
from the United States into a new environment where, given their capacity
for improvement, they could govern themselves.[17] So viewed, his support of
colonization demonstrated John Latrobe's inherited ethic of civic service.

One day, Robert Harper, the leader of Maryland's colonizers, proposed to
his young associate that they map, as best they could, the west coast of Africa.
In John Latrobe's retelling, they first determined that Liberia, a word drawn
from the Latin root for free, would be the appropriate name for the small
community near Cape Palmas on the west coast of Africa. Its capital would
be named Monrovia, for President Monroe, one of the society's sponsors. In
his small office in Baltimore, 3,000 miles away from Africa, John drew a map
naming places and even giving his surname to one small settlement. This was
only the beginning of his active support: John Latrobe raised money, wrote
a code of laws, bought supplies, handled the society's correspondence and
recruitment of settlers, and organized the ships, passengers, and provisions
that during his lifetime carried more than 1,000 settlers to the Las Palmas
settlement. In 1833, as the sloop *Ann* prepared for departure from Baltimore
with eighteen blacks aboard, John Latrobe joined them before they sailed,
raising the Liberian flag he had helped design for the occasion and wishing
the emigrants well.[18]

Four years younger than John, Benjamin Latrobe Jr. (Ben to family and
friends) took a different and slower route to prominence, financial success,
and service to the community. In 1824, Ben stood first in his class in mathematics and geometry and second in Spanish and literature when he graduated
from St. Mary's College, the institution his father called the "Alma-Mater of
the Latrobes."[19] His brother and fellow graduate John sat on the stage, while
in the audience his mother delighted in her youngest son's graceful bow as
he received his diploma. The family listened approvingly to his surpris-
ingly modern oration titled "The Influence of Climate on the Manners and
Customs of Nations." Mary Latrobe believed him "the best looking of the
graduates," but his physical resemblance—"how much he looks like my beloved"—moved her to tears.[20]

At first, Ben followed his brother into the law, studying in a local luminary's
office. Properly certified, he soon found that there was not enough work for

him in John's office. Even after moving to New Jersey, he attracted few clients. Ben spent more time selling the lumber from his mother's woodland property than in his office. He was developing a growing distaste for the law—"The law is a profession I was unfit for."[21] Nineteen-year-old Ben further upset the family with his engagement to his first cousin Ellen Hazlehurst. His mother and older brother were adamantly opposed, pointing out his youth as well as the incestuous possibilities for idiot children. The two sons quarreled; John warned that Ben's attachment to his cousin "went deep into Mama's heart."[22] In reply, Ben invoked family loyalty: "Dearest brother, we are the sole suppliers of our name in this country. We have every motive to keep us together."[23] Ben, a lion in youthful temperament according to his father, persisted.

Yet these were difficult years for a young man who had expected more rapid success. Ben located the problem with parenting that had left him unprepared for competition. In a letter to John, Ben explained that he had never been taught to believe "in the capacities of others," only in his own excellence, given the unflagging praise of his parents: "You know how enthusiastic a man our father was. He thought his children unequal to nothing, incomparable to any and his affectionate heart too often overflowed toward us to let us remain ignorant of the fancied qualities and endowments which he esteemed our gifts and mother was if possible less careful to conceal her pride and admiration of us." It had been a shock to his vanity and self-esteem to find others "superior or even equal."[24]

By 1826, Ben had abandoned the law and started a new career as a humble rod-man, surveying the line for the B&O Railroad and measuring broken stones for ballast on the track. Initially he earned $1.00 a day. Still, as his brother John reported, "he was as happy as a lord and as healthy as an Indian."[25] By the end of the year, Ben's confidence reasserted itself: "I have, I think, acquired a tolerable fund of experimental knowledge in relation to the creation of a road. . . . I think I could now lead a party to survey very well. My attachment to the profession increases and I daily congratulate myself upon the happy change effected."[26] By 1833, he earned $1,500, as much, he wrote in his diary, as a congressman and more than enough to take up boarding. That year, after a seven-year courtship, twenty-six-year-old Ben Latrobe married Ellen Hazlehurst.

Competent engineers were scarce, apart from West Point graduates, and Ben moved up quickly. Soon he was appointed "the engineer of location" for the B&O as well as the chief engineer for the Baltimore and Port Deposit Railroad, one of the many smaller lines that proliferated during the 1830s and '40s when steam-powered locomotives emerged as the future of American

FIG. C.2 Benjamin Latrobe. Benjamin Latrobe Jr. was Latrobe's third son. Described as a "lion" in his childhood by his father, he became a well-known railroad engineer. Maryland Historical Society.

transportation. By 1840, Ben earned $6,000, having learned mostly by doing. Occasionally, after consulting the topographical engineers trained at West Point, he studied the works of the eighteenth-century French engineer Jean Rodolph Perronet, famed for his stone-arched bridges. No doubt Ben had also absorbed a practical understanding of his craft from his father. Although it was not entirely accurate, John once joked, "It was a swap between us. I had been educated as an engineer and became a lawyer, and he, educated as a lawyer, became an engineer."[27]

As bold a builder of arches as his father, Ben designed and supervised the construction of the longest railroad bridge in the country which crossed the Patapsco River and valley outside of Baltimore. The span of granite blocks— 704 feet long, 26 feet wide, 66 feet above the water with a slight curve—was supported by eight massive arches and fifteen-foot thick piers. Finished in 1835, it consumed Ben Latrobe for two years as he rode out daily from Baltimore to oversee its progress. He recognized its monumentality, writing in his diary,

"What a stupendous work it will be." "The bridge will stand as long as the valley and its hemming hills remain in their places."[28] Officially known as the Thomas Viaduct after the president of the B&O, some Baltimoreans called it Latrobe's folly and believed it could not support a train, though it still carries CSX freight cars today.

For its decoration, Ben favored stone parapets, echoing his father in his disapproval of cheaper iron railings: "It is in matters of this kind that an architect has to bear so much wasting of his plans by the assuming interference of arrogant and tasteless ignorance."[29] The board of the railroad company finally approved funding for a stone obelisk but without the cornstalk capitals invented by his father that Ben had intended. When the bridge was finished, Ben gave credit to the workers, noting in his diary, "The public good in works of this kind is purchased by much individual suffering."[30]

While John traveled to distant places including New Orleans and Russia, Ben mimicked his father's existence of "unsettled wanderings."[31] As the engineer locating the line for the railroad, he traveled throughout western Maryland, southern Pennsylvania, and what is now West Virginia. He stayed in dirty taverns, shared beds and bedbugs with strangers, ate bad food, and

FIG. C.3 Thomas Viaduct. This 1858 photocopy of an engraving depicts one of Ben Latrobe's triumphs. The bridge still stands and carries railroad traffic. At the time it was considered unsafe and some called it Latrobe's Folly. Library of Congress, HAER MD,14-ELK,1-17.

suffered from wet feet as he tramped across streams and through forests. Like his father's generation, he depended on his theodolite, though by the 1840s he had replaced that clumsy angle-measuring instrument with the transit, a new kind of compass with a telescope attached. Despite the physical hardship and chronic illnesses he suffered, Ben carried out work of lasting value: the line he surveyed to the north from Baltimore to Wilmington and to the south from Baltimore to Washington is still used today.

By 1853 the B&O—the imagined great road of the 1830s—had reached Wheeling, 380 miles from Baltimore and its intended destination on the Ohio River. It was time for a celebration. Both John and Ben, along with the governors of Maryland and Virginia, legislators, and prominent guests, 500 in all, traveled on excursion trains from Baltimore to Wheeling. At a festive dinner in that city both sons were toasted for their contributions, and in turn both spoke. John emphasized the boldness of the project and its pioneering aspect as the first company to begin a railroad between the Atlantic and the Ohio.

Ben responded spontaneously; he had been too busy to prepare a speech: "I have been commended for the success of the grades, and for the tunnels and bridges of this road; but there is a source of pride more grateful to me just now in that I have been enabled to complete the line at the precise time I had promised." Still, he went on, referring to future plans for the B&O, "I have not a right to call it finished. No Rail Road, indeed, is finished while the trade for which it was constructed continues to grow; and progress is the genius of our people." After the usual toasts to the ladies, the crowd raised their glasses and toasted Benjamin Latrobe. The road might be unfinished but, as John had noted, in a certain sense, "The Work is done at last."[32]

Both John and Ben survived into the post–Civil War era, supporting the Union during the war, though several of their sons fought for the Confederacy. Ben became a popular consulting engineer; John continued his legal work for the railroad and his energetic efforts for the city's institutional improvement. In John's reminiscences he acknowledged what was true for both sons: "In fact I never had an idle hour, no, not an idle minute."[33] Ben died in 1878, John in 1891. Both had ably represented their father's ideals of working hard, avoiding debt, and serving the public. Respected civic leaders, both had become the kind of prosperous Americans that their father never was.

Besides the work of his two sons and through them a proliferating family of engaged citizens, Benjamin Latrobe left professional legacies, principally his architecture as represented by the US Capitol, the Bank of Pennsylvania, the Centre Engine House at his Philadelphia Waterworks, the Baltimore Basilica, and the Merchants Exchange. He also designed nearly seventy private homes that established a more rational model for American domestic arrangements. As an émigré, he had brought with him the classical style known in England and on the continent, but he had adapted it to the climate, habits, and political ideals of the new homeland that he both praised and denigrated. Latrobe had arrived in the United States at a time when architecture was central to the founders of the republic, and he applied their vision in his buildings. His architecture physically expressed the abstract political views of the early republic. The Latrobean approach was based on accessibility: his neoclassical expression featured balance and symmetry, careful proportions, porticos and columns, and dramatic open interiors set off by skillful, sometimes daring masonry vaults.

Given his broad practice, Latrobe's buildings and his engineering projects affected every aspect of life in the early republic—its worship, governance, communication, education, and domesticity. As the best architecture does, his designs conveyed an inspirational message to his new countrymen about the worthiness of their great experiment. Architectural styles express the age in which they flourish, and as times changed in the United States, so did building tastes and preferences. Latrobe's classicism became less popular, though it never died. His columned porticoes remain an almost universal feature of public buildings, even as modernized in the exterior of structures like New York's Lincoln Center and San Diego's Salk Institute designed by Louis Kahn.

Latrobe's students carried on his dedication to outstanding architecture with a direct line of succession that moved from William Strickland and Robert Mills to Thomas Walter, Richard Morris Hunt, Frank Furness, Louis Sullivan, and Frank Lloyd Wright. Even his sons contributed to this legacy: architect John Niernsee began his career as an engineer working under Ben Latrobe. In 1847, Niernsee, a leader in the American Institute of Architects, opened an architectural practice that produced distinguished structures in Baltimore.[34]

Equally influential were Benjamin Latrobe's contributions to internal improvements and to public hygiene. He supported state-financed canals and roads, and his contributions to the Gallatin Report were part of an ongoing political dialogue about government subsidies in the early republic. Latrobe's engineering projects, especially his waterworks in Philadelphia and New Orleans, demonstrated the importance of improving public health in nineteenth-century American cities.

Along with the physical expression of his ideas, Latrobe sought, not always successfully, to establish an American architectural practice. He insisted on professional norms relating to architects' control over their projects along with standard payments, even for designs that were not built. In time, his ideas became widely accepted, although a half-century elapsed after his death before the Massachusetts Institute of Technology offered the first advanced training in architecture. Latrobe was also a critical figure in establishing American highbrow culture and taste. Throughout his life he campaigned for the aesthetic value of good buildings as an imperative in the new republic. While today the temple form is a cliché, for Americans at the turn of the century, Latrobe's neoclassical buildings connected the nation with an admired former republic in ancient Greece. There, great buildings had inspired humanity; Benjamin Henry Latrobe intended nothing less for the United States.

Notes

ABBREVIATIONS
Latrobe Papers

BHL, *Architectural Drawings.* Cohen, Jeffrey and Charles Brownell, eds. *The Architectural Drawings of Benjamin Henry Latrobe.* New Haven, CT: Yale University Press, 1994.

BHL, *Engineering Drawings.* Stapleton, Darwin. *The Engineering Drawings of Benjamin Henry Latrobe.* New Haven, CT: Yale University Press, 1980.

BHL, *Journals, 1, 2.* Carter, Edward, ed. *The Virginia Journals of Benjamin Henry Latrobe, 1795–1798.* New Haven, CT: Yale University Press, 1980.

BHL, *Journals, 3.* Carter, Edward, ed. *The Journals of Benjamin Henry Latrobe, 1799–1820: From Philadelphia to New Orleans.* New Haven, CT: Yale University Press, 1977.

BHL, *Papers, 1,2,3.* Van Horne, John et al., eds. *The Correspondence and Miscellaneous Papers of Benjamin Henry Latrobe.* New Haven, CT: Yale University Press, 1984, 1986, 1988.

BHL, *Papers,* microfiche edition. Carter, Edward and Jeffrey Thomas, eds. *The Papers of Benjamin Henry Latrobe, Microfiche Edition, Guide and Index.* Clifton, NJ: James T. White, 1976.

BHL, *Watercolors and Sketches.* Carter, Edward, John Van Horne, and Charles Brownell, eds. *Latrobe's View of America, 1795–1820: Selections from the Watercolors and Sketches.* New Haven, CT: Yale University Press, 1985.

Other Sources and Collections

APS   American Philosophical Society
PMA   Philadelphia Museum of Art

LC   Library of Congress
MHS   Maryland Historical Society
NYHS   New York Historical Society

INTRODUCTION

1. BHL, *Papers*, 1: 72.
2. Ibid., 3: 769.

CHAPTER 1

1. Throughout this book I refer to Benjamin Latrobe, using his first name and omitting his middle name. He usually signed his letters B. Henry Latrobe or B. H. Latrobe, but sometimes B. Henry Latrobe of Bonneval. His friends universally referred to him as Benjamin.
2. The term "choir" used in the Greek sense of a band refers to the segregated age, gender, and marital status groups of the Moravians and has nothing to do with the modern usage. Choirs became the essential living structures of Moravian settlements.
3. Barbara Bulmore, "Education at Fulneck: Moravian Schools in the 18th and 19th Century" (PhD diss., University of Manchester, 1992), 401; Vernon Nelson, "An Admirable Draftsman: Benjamin Henry Latrobe's Moravian Background," *Unitas Fratrum Zeitschrift fur Geschichte* (2002), 115.
4. Geoffrey Stead, *The Moravian Settlement at Fulneck, 1742–1790* (Leeds: Thoresby Society, 1999), 37.
5. Bulmore, 48.
6. Ibid., 401.
7. Paul Peucker, "Inspired by Flames of Love: Homosexuality, Mysticism and the Moravian Brothers around 1750," *Journal of the History of Sexuality* 15 (2006), 30–64; Michele Gillespie and Robert Beachy, eds., *Pious Pursuits: German Moravians in the Atlantic World* (New York: Berghahn Books, 2007).
8. This quote is from a Diary of the Fulneck Congregation 1777–1787, entry for January 1777, R.13.D, Moravian Archives, Herrenhut, Germany. Professor Jenna Gibbs of Florida International University, who is working on a book entitled *Evangelism and Empire: The Global Latrobe Family*, kindly shared (and translated) her research in the Herrenhut Archives with me. BHL, *Papers*, 1: 547.
9. Stead, 33.
10. BHL, *Papers*, 1: 547.
11. Ibid., 1: 456.
12. Ibid., 2: 896.
13. John Hazlehurst Boneval Latrobe, *The Journal of Latrobe* (New York: D. Appleton, 1905), vii.
14. Stead, 33.

15. BHL, *Papers*, 1: 7; Translated notes from Herman Plitt, Box 1, English and German materials, Latrobe Collection, APS.

16. BHL, *Journals*, 2: 314–15.

17. Ibid., 315.

18. Material translated by Darwin Stapleton, Latrobe Collection, APS.

19. The Latin phrase was rendered in iron on the front gate at Fulneck "Vicit Agnus Noster Eum Sequamur."

20. BHL, *Papers*, 1: 8. Also Jonathan Yonan, "Evangelism and Enlightenment: Two Generations in the Okely Family," in Heikki Lempa and Paul Peucker, eds., *Self, Community and World: Moravian Education in a Transatlantic World* (Bethlehem, PA: Lehigh University Press, 2012), 136–8; unindexed material, Latrobe Collection, Subseries 2, Research Files, PMA.

21. Diary of Fulneck Congregation, January 1777, R 13. D. Moravian Archives, Herrenhut, Germany. Translation by Professor Jenna Gibbs.

22. Yonan, 130; Elisabeth Sommer, *Serving Two Masters: Moravian Brethren in Germany and North Carolina* (Lexington: University Press of Kentucky, 2000), 51–2, 118.

23. BHL, *Journals*, 3: 226–7.

24. Ibid.; Talbot Hamlin, *Benjamin Henry Latrobe* (New York: Oxford University Press, 1955), 516.

25. BHL, *Papers*, 1: 8–10. Also minutes of the Unity Elders Conference, August 6, 11, 1782, Moravian Archives, Herrenhut. For generations, family biographies of Latrobe included erroneous information that during this period he attended the University of Leipzig and served in the Prussian army.

26. BHL, *Papers*, 2: 608.

27. Ibid., 3: 608.

28. Victor Gatrell, *City of Laughter, Sex and Satire in Eighteenth Century London* (London: Atlantic Books, 2006), 7.

29. BHL, *Papers*, 1: 18. Some historians think that George suffered from the genetic disease of porphyria; others claim that he was bipolar.

30. Gatrell, 449.

31. Quoted in Michael Shinagel, *Daniel Defoe and Middle Class Gentility* (Cambridge, MA: Harvard University Press, 2013), 119.

32. BHL, *Papers*, 3:17.

33. Eva Schumann-Bacia, *John Soane and the Bank of England* (New York: Princeton Architectural Press, 1991), 75.

34. For further development of this point, see J. Mordaunt Crook, "The Pre-Victorian Architect: Professionalism and Patronage," *Architectural History* 12 (1969), 62–78.

35. Hamlin, 39.

36. Fanny Burney to Charlotte, December 7, 1784, *Early Diary of Frances Burney*, Anne Ellis, ed. (London: Bell Co., 1889), 2: 318. Quoted in Hamlin, 10.

37. BHL, *Papers*, 2: 149.

38. Ibid., 3: 991.

39. Ibid.,1: 82–3.

40. This abbreviated genealogy is based primarily on material in Latrobe International Symposium, *Les Latrobes dans le Monde* (Versailles, 1988).

41. BHL, *Journals*, 1: 53, 71; 3: 48–9.

42. Gillian Darley, "The Moravians: Building for a Higher Purpose," *Architectural Review* 177, no. 1058 (April 1993), 45.

43. BHL, *Papers*, 1: 11.

44. BHL, *Journals* 2: 309.

45. BHL, *Papers*, 1: 47.

46. Ibid., 1: 82. Habitually incorrect about dates including his own age, Latrobe mistakenly believed his father died in 1787.

47. Ibid., 2: 178.

48. BHL, *Journals*, 1: 55; BHL to Charlotte Burney Broome, August 13, 1816, 133/O/1, BHL, *Papers*, microfiche edition.

49. J. C. S. Mason, *The Moravian Church and the Missionary Awakening in England, 1760–1789* (Woodbridge, England: Boydell Press, 2011), 141.

50. *Early Diary of Frances Burney*, 2: 318.

51. Darwin Stapleton's Notes from Christian Ignatius Diary, March 4, 1789, in English and German Materials, Latrobe Collection, APS. Also Peter Latrobe's Notes on the Life of Benjamin Henry Latrobe, Series B, Fiske-Kimball Papers, PMA.

52. *Early Diary of Frances Burney*, 2:140.

53. BHL, *Journals*, 3: 50–1.

54. BHL, *Papers*, 2: 352.

55. BHL Notebook, Osmun Latrobe Papers, LC.

56. BHL, *Journals*, 1: 223.

57. Latrobe Collection, Subseries 2, Box 121, Fiske-Kimball Papers, PMA.

58. BHL, *Papers*, 2: 931.

59. *Characteristic Anecdotes to Illustrate the Character of Frederick the Great* (London: John Stockdale, 1788), viii.

60. *Scientific Elucidation of the History of Counts Struensee and Brandt and of the Revolution in Denmark in the Year 1772* (London: Stockdale, 1789), i–viii. (Copy in Peabody Library, Baltimore, MD.)

61. Michael Fazio and Patrick Snadon, *The Domestic Architecture of Benjamin Henry Latrobe* (Baltimore: Johns Hopkins University Press, 2006), 25. This book is a meticulous, deeply researched study of Latrobe's domestic architecture.

62. BHL, *Journals*, 1: 223.

63. Fazio and Snadon, 25.

64. BHL to Nathaniel Cutting, January 11, 1814, 114/E/8, BHL, *Papers*, microfiche edition.

65. BHL, *Papers*, 2: 231.

66. BHL, *Journals*, 1: 201–2.

67. Ibid., 1: 210–13.
68. Ibid., 1: 290.
69. Fazio and Snaden, 706, f.n.21
70. Obituary of BHL, Rudolph Ackermann, *Repository of Arts and Literature*, Series 11 (January 1821). Written by Latrobe shortly before his death, what was intended as a short biography in the *Repository* became his obituary.
71. BHL, *Architectural Drawings*, 2: 51.
72. Fazio and Snadon, 102.
73. Ibid., 154–5.
74. BHL, *Architectural Drawings*, 2: 54–5. Coade's stone was a light gray manufactured stone of quartz, crushed flint, and other ingredients that could easily be molded and was weather resistant.
75. BHL, *Journals*, 1: 204.
76. BHL, *Architectural Drawings*, 2: 55; Darwin Stapleton's Notes on Christian Ignatius Latrobe's Diary, Latrobe Collection, APS.
77. BHL to William Lovering, June 20, 1811, 85/G/11, BHL, *Papers*, microfiche edition.
78. Mary Elizabeth Latrobe, "Biography of My Husband," Family and Other Materials, Latrobe Collection, APS.
79. Fazio and Snaden, 12, 709, fn. 54.
80. Quoted in BHL, *Journals*, 1: xxii; poem in Hamlin, 33–4.
81. BHL, *Papers*, 1: 18.

CHAPTER 2

1. BHL, *Papers*, 1: 83.
2. BHL, *Papers*, 3: 238.
3. BHL, *Journals* (1905 ed.), foreword; BHL, *Journals*, 1: xlii–xliii.
4. BHL, *Journals*, 3: 7.
5. BHL, *Journals* (1905 ed.), xli.
6. BHL, *Journals*, 1: 15, 30, 48, 36, 5.
7. BHL, *Journals* (1905 ed.), 113.
8. BHL, *Journals*, 1: 163–9; *Papers*, 1: 38–9.
9. BHL, *Journals*, 1:43.
10. Steven Bullock, *Revolutionary Brotherhood and the Transformation of the American Social Order, 1730–1840* (Chapel Hill, NC: Institute of Early American History and Culture, 1996), 145–54; for Latrobe's membership, Charles Rady, *History of the Richmond Randolph Lodge*, no. 19 (Richmond, 1888), 16; Wayne Huss, *The Master Builders: A History of the Grand Lodge of Accepted Masons of Pennsylvania* (Philadelphia: The Grand Lodge, 1986), 1: 70, 408.
11. BHL, *Papers*, 3: 97.
12. BHL, *Journals*, 1: 75.

13. T. H. Breen, "Horses and Gentlemen: The Cultural Significance of Gambling among the Gentry of Virginia," *William and Mary Quarterly*, 3rd Series, 34 (1977), 239–57.

14. BHL, *Papers*, 1: 147–9.

15. Charles Royster, *The Fabulous History of the Dismal Swamp Company* (New York: Knopf, 1999), 393–7; BHL, *Journals*, 1: 235.

16. BHL, *Journals*, 1:142.

17. BHL, *Watercolors and Sketches*, 90–1.

18. BHL, "A Drawing and Description of the Bay Alewife and the Fish Louse," *Papers*, 1: 154–7. Latrobe's paper was the first technical description of the alewife, though Latrobe's name "tyrannus" is now applied to menhaden, not alewives.

19. BHL, *Watercolors and Sketches*, 116.

20. BHL, *Journals*, 2: 468.

21. Ibid., 2: 511, 499, 500.

22. Ibid., 2: 493, 491–8.

23. Ibid., 2: 341.

24. BHL, *Papers*, 1: 68.

25. Ibid., 2: 240.

26. Ibid., 1: 72.

27. Ibid., 1: 70.

28. Ibid., 1: 72.

29. In May 1797, Latrobe sent a long letter to a professor of mathematics at William and Mary in which he presented a new way in which Hadley's Quadrant might be used to measure distances. It was an example of his prowess in geometry, astronomy, and mathematics. BHL, *Journals*, 1: 213–20. "Cramped and local," in BHL, *Papers*, 1: 72.

30. BHL, Ibid, 1:85.

31. BHL, *Journals*, 1: 225.

32. Ibid., 1: 83.

33. Ibid., 3: 207–8.

34. BHL, *Papers*, 3: 496, 505–6; see also BHL Memorandum, 1/3 D/4; BHL to William Gadsby, September 13, 1816, 133/B/13; BHL to Dudley Digges, September 25, 1815, 127/D/4, BHL, *Papers*, microfiche edition. Gary Nash and Jean Soderland, *Freedom by Degrees: Emancipation in Pennsylvania and Its Aftermath* (New York: Oxford University Press, 1991).

35. BHL, *Papers*, 3: 17.

36. BHL, *Journals*, 2: 356, 1: 172.

37. BHL, *Papers*, 1: 162.

38. Ibid., 1: 160, 162.

39. Ibid., 2: 331.

40. Abe Wollock, "Benjamin Henry Latrobe: Activities in the American Theater" (PhD diss., University of Michigan, 1962); BHL, *Papers*, 1: 71–2; *Journals*, 2: 343–6.

41. BHL, *Papers*, 2: 288.

42. BHL, *Architectural Drawings*, 2: 98–107.

43. BHL, *Journals*, 2: 357–8.

44. BHL, *Papers*, 1: 77–8, 73.

45. Ibid., 1: 65.

46. Ibid., 2: 253.

47. Ibid., 3: 63.

48. BHL, *Architectural Drawings*, 1: 81.

49. BHL, *Papers*, 1: 73.

50. Ibid., 2: 28.

51. Quoted in Robert Oaks, "Seat of Empire, New York, Philadelphia and the Emergence of an American Metropolis, 1776–1837" (PhD diss., University of Southern California, 2006), 179.

52. Edward Carter, "A Wild Irishman under Every Federalist's Bed: Naturalization in Philadelphia, 1789–1806," *Pennsylvania Magazine of History and Biography* 94 (1970), 336–7.

53. BHL, *Journals*, 2: 424–5, fn. 62.

54. Ibid., 2: 376–8.

55. Ibid., 2: 357.

56. BHL, *Papers*, 3: 82.

57. BHL to James Todd, November 17, 1804, 36/C/9, BHL, *Papers*, microfiche edition.

58. BHL, *Journals*, 3: 48–9.

59. For an understanding of the changing meanings of the concept genius, Darrin McMahon, *Divine Fury: A History of Genius* (New York: Basic Books, 2008).

60. BHL, *Papers*, 2: 97–8.

61. Ibid., 2: 608.

62. Ibid., 3: 711.

63. BHL, *Architectural Drawings*, 2: 198–9; BHL, *Journals*, 3: 49–50.

64. BHL, *View of the Practicability and Means of Supplying the City of Philadelphia with Wholesome Water* (Philadelphia: Zachariah Paulson, 1799). See also BHL, *Papers*, 1: 111–22, especially 115.

65. BHL, *Papers*, 1: 142–3.

66. Ibid., 1: 145.

67. Ibid., 1: 146.; for a development of this point, see Mary Woods, *From Craft to Profession: The Practice of Architecture in 19th Century America* (Berkeley: University of California Press, 1999); BHL, *Papers*, 3: 579.

68. *Philadelphia Merchant, The Diary of Thomas P. Cope, 1800–1851*, Eliza Cope Harrison, ed. (South Bend, IN: Notre Dame Press, 1978), 57; also Eleanor Maass, "Thomas Cope and the Philadelphia Waterworks," *Proceedings of the American Philosophical Society* 125 (1981), 136–54.

69. Nelson Blake, *Water for the Cities: A History of the Urban Water Supply Problem in the United States* (Syracuse, NY: Syracuse University Press, 1956), 24–36.

70. BHL, *Papers*, 1: 496.

71. Ibid., 2: 779; 185–7; also Talbot Hamlin, *Benjamin Henry Latrobe* (New York: Oxford University Press, 1955), 171–80.

72. Ralph Gray, "The Early History of the Chesapeake and Delaware Canal," *Delaware History* 8 (March 1959); BHL, *Papers*, 2: 89.

73. BHL, *Papers*, 2: 942; 2: 89.

74. Ibid., 1: 300.

75. BHL, *Architectural Drawings*, 2: 291.

76. BHL, *Papers*, 1: 204, 563. Also Damie Stillman, "New York City Hall: Competition and Execution," *Journal of the Society of Architectural History* 23 (1964), 129–42.

77. BHL, *Papers*, 2: 368–9.

78. BHL to J. S. Wilcocks, March 12, 1805, 38/A/6, BHL, *Papers*, microfiche edition; BHL, *Papers*, 1: 368; 2: 35–41.

79. BHL, *Papers*, 2: 306.

80. Michael Fazio and Patrick Snadon, *The Domestic Architecture of Benjamin Henry Latrobe* (Baltimore: Johns Hopkins University Press, 2006), 185–92, quote on 544.

81. Frank Leach, "Old Philadelphia Families, Hazlehurst, No. 59," *North American*, July 19, 1908; Julia Latrobe, Comments on Grandfather Isaac Hazlehurst, Gamble-Latrobe papers, MHS.

82. BHL, *Papers*, 1: 185.

83. BHL to Miss M. Sellon, November 15, 1817, 234/C/1, BHL, *Papers*, microfiche edition.

84. BHL, *Papers*, 2: 403, 2: 156; 1: 369.

85. Ibid., 2: 353.

86. BHL, *Journals*, 3: 121–2.

87. Latrobe built a studio for Stuart in Washington in 1804. Stuart never paid any rent, and Latrobe hoped for a free portrait. The two men remained on friendly terms until Stuart declined into dementia and alcoholism. Latrobe came to believe Stuart "the greatest of our Artists, and most unprincipled of our Citizens." BHL, *Papers*, 2: 105; also Charles Mount, *Gilbert Stuart: A Biography* (New York: W.W. Norton, 1964).

88. BHL, *Papers*, 1: 540. This portrait of Latrobe is in the White House collection and in 2008 hung in the room where it was necessary to "redo" the presidential oath of office botched by Chief Justice John Roberts and President Barack Obama.

89. Ibid., 1: 516.

90. Ibid., 1: 340.

91. There is some controversy about Latrobe's relationship with Smeaton. He is never mentioned in records from Smeaton's office, but Latrobe often referred to his work in the office. An example occurs in his *Papers*, 3: 939, where Latrobe describes "having studied my profession under Smeaton and Cockerell."

92. BHL, *Papers*, 1: 347, 434.

93. Ibid., 2: 163.

94. Ibid., 1: 185.
95. Ibid., 2: 153.
96. BHL, *Journals*, 3: 39; also Lucille Toro, "The Latrobe Survey of New Castle, 1804–1805" (MA thesis, University of Delaware, 1971).
97. BHL, *Papers*, 1: 539; 2: 251.
98. Ibid., 1: 66.

CHAPTER 3

1. Elaine Everly and Howard Wehman, "Then Let Us to the Woods Repair: Moving the Government and Its Records to Washington," in Kenneth Bowling and Donald Kennon, eds., *Establishing Congress* (Athens: Ohio University Press, 2005), 56.
2. BHL, *Papers*, 3: 313.
3. Ibid., 2:227–8.
4. *The Papers of Thomas Jefferson*, Julian Boyd, ed. (Princeton, NJ: Princeton University Press, 1950) 8: 534–5.
5. Quoted in William Allen, *History of the United States Capitol* (Washington, DC: United States Printing Office, 2001), 15-17.
6. Ibid., 17,18.
7. S. C. Busey, "The Centennial of thePermanent Seat of the Government," *Columbia Historical Society Records* 3 (1900), 326.
8. The US Constitution did not specify that electors distinguish between the president and vice president. Thus, the vote for Aaron Burr who was expected to be vice president and Thomas Jefferson ended in a tie that had to be resolved by Congress.
9. Quoted in Mario Campoli, "Building the Capitol," in Charles Peterson, ed., *Building Early America* (Radnor, PA: Chilton Books, 1976), 205.
10. James B. Osborne, "Removal of the Government," *Columbia Historical Society Records* 3 (1900), 136-60.
11. Constance McLaughlin Green, *Washington: Village and Capital* (Princeton, NJ: Princeton University Press, 1962).
12. Thomas Moore, *The Poetical Works of Thomas Moore*, "Odes and Epistles" (London: Carpenter, 1814), 2: 28.
13. Henry Adams, *The United States in 1800* (Ithaca, NY: Great Seal Books, 1955), 21.
14. BHL, *Papers*, 1: 224.
15. Ibid., 1: 225.
16. Ibid., 1: 96.
17. Buffon's criticism engendered the defensive American response that employed size as contrary evidence. Jefferson spent years trying to find the largest moose in the United States, while the "Ladies of Massachusetts" provided their example by sending to Jefferson a homemade 12,351 pound "mammoth" cheese, some of which ended up in the Potomac the following year.
18. BHL, *Papers*, 1: 232.

19. Ibid., 1: 563.
20. The phrase *"la difficulte vaincue"* occurs frequently in Latrobe's descriptions of his work on the Capitol. It is also the term he used in his brief autobiographical sketch published after his death in the *Repository of Arts*. See BHL, *Architectural Drawings*, 2: 344.
21. Ibid., 2: 314.
22. BHL, Papers, 2: 66, fn.1.
23. Ibid., 1: 263.
24. Ibid., 1: 495.
25. Ibid., 3: 482.
26. Ibid., 2: 262. Relevant letters from Jefferson to Latrobe are included in Latrobe's correspondence.
27. Ibid., 2: 340.
28. BHL, "Report on the US Capitol," *Papers*, 1: 268–83. For a thorough account of the Latrobe-Jefferson connection, see Paul Norton, *Latrobe, Jefferson, and the National Capitol* (New York: Garland, 1977).
29. BHL, *Papers*, 1: 548.
30. Ibid., 2: 428.
31. Ibid., 2: 66.
32. Ibid., 2: 464.
33. Latrobe to John Lenthall, September 7, 1807, 59/C/13, BHL *Papers*, microfiche edition.
34. Pamela Scott, *Temple of Liberty: Building the Capitol for a New Nation* (New York: Oxford University Press, 1995).
35. BHL, *Papers*, 1: 381.
36. The fourth-century B.C. Choragic of Lysicrates Monument in Athens was a hallmark of classical architecture and the first known use of Corinthian capitals. A drawing appeared in James Revett's *Antiquities of Athens*, which was published in 1762 and was well known to both Jefferson and Latrobe.
37. BHL, *Papers*, 2: 409.
38. Ibid., 2: 411.
39. Ibid., 2: 280–1. By determinate shadows and light Latrobe referred to the passage of light over time through a room.
40. Ibid., 2: 411.
41. Ibid., 2: 283.
42. Ibid., 2: 429, 494.
43. Ibid., 2: 283.
44. BHL, *Architectural Drawings*, 2: 382.
45. Felicia Bell, "'The Negroes Alone Work': The Building Trades and the Construction of the US Capitol, 1790–1800" (PhD diss., Howard University, 2009).
46. American and European students of geology disagreed about the explanations for the character of the American environment. Latrobe believed that the freestone

so abundant in northern Virginia was the result of wind deposition and a process of crystallization on the ancient seacoast such as that he had observed at Cape Henry. He also believed that the fall line marked the coast of an ancient ocean. See his paper titled "Freestone Quarries on the Potomac and Rappahannock Rivers," printed in the *Transactions of the American Philosophical Society* 6, 1809. Also *Papers* 2: 380–9.

47. BHL, *Journals*, 3: 80.

48. Ibid., 3: 47.

49. BHL, *Papers*, 2: 178–9; 2: 735.

50. Ibid., 2: 22.

51. Ibid., 2: 144.

52. Ibid., 2: 215. See also William Alderson, ed., *Mermaids, Mummies and Mastodons: The Emergence of the American Museum* (Washington, DC: American Association of Museums, 2005).

53. BHL, *Papers*, 2: 503.

54. Ibid., 2: 613.

55. Annual federal budgets during this period ranged from $8 million to $12 million, with over 60 percent spent on defense and another 30 percent on debt and interest payments.

56. The most accessible version of congressional criticism appears in *The Documentary History of the Construction of The United States Capitol Building and Grounds*, 58th Congress, 2nd Session, House of Representatives Report, 646, Washington, 1904. It is also available on a disk in the Office of the United States Capitol Historical Society. The pages cited here are 124–8. Also House Proceedings, *Annals of Congress*, 10th Congress, 1st Session, 2276.

57. BHL, *Papers*, 2: 305–6.

58. Ibid., 2: 296–316, especially 306.

59. Ibid., 1: 480.

60. Latrobe had never been an admirer of Hamilton. After Hamilton's death, Latrobe wrote that he "had not been able to work myself up into the fashionable pitch of grief for the death of Mr. Hamilton." He noted that, like him, others were "refractory" in their grief. BHL, *Papers*, 1: 525.

61. Thornton later fabricated a story that the "cowardly" Latrobe had not shown up for a planned duel.

62. BHL, *Papers*, 1: 523, 482.

63. *Washington Federalist*, April 26, 1808.

64. Ibid. See also BHL, *Papers*, 2: 600–5.

65. BHL, *Papers*, 3: 470.

66. Ibid., 2: 228.

67. Latrobe to John Lenthall, May 3, 1805, 178/G/6, BHL, *Papers*, microfiche edition.

68. BHL, *Papers*, 2: 41.

69. William Seale, *The President's House: A History* (Washington, DC: White House Historical Association, 1986), 1: 6–37; Margaret Klapthor, "Benjamin Henry Latrobe and Dolley Madison," *Contributions from the Museum of History and Technology* 49 (1965), 153–64; Alexandra A. Kirtley and Peggy Olley, *Classical Splendor: Painted Furniture for a Grand Philadelphia House* (Philadelphia: Philadelphia Museum of Art, 2016). Klismos refers to the Grecian style of chairs and sofas.

70. BHL, *Papers*, 2: 595.

71. Ibid., 2: 502.

72. A striking digital recreation of the room appears in Richard Chenoweth's "The Most Beautiful Room in the World? Latrobe, Jefferson and the First Capitol," *The Capitol Dome* 51 (Fall 2014), 31–6.

73. *National Intelligencer*, October 27, 1807.

74. BHL, *Papers*, 2: 464.

75. Ibid., 2: 777.

76. Ibid., 2: 834; Papers in Libel Suit, Benjamin Henry Latrobe v. William Thornton, 212/A/1/1808, Record Group 21, National Archives, Washington, DC.

77. BHL, *Papers*, 2: 489; *Documentary History of the Construction and Development of the Capitol Building and Grounds*.

78. BHL to Nicholas King, November 8, 1808, 67/A/4/BHL, *Papers*, microfiche edition.

79. BHL, *Papers*, 2: 663.

80. Ibid., 2: 665.

81. Ibid., 2: 667, fn. 1.

82. Jefferson to Madison, March 30, 1809, in *Republic of Letters: The Correspondence of Thomas Jefferson and James Madison* (New York: W. W. Norton, 1995), 1577–9.

83. Quoted in Allen, 94; "splendid misery," in Jon Meacham, *Thomas Jefferson: The Art of Power* (New York: Random House, 2012), 305.

84. *Republic of Letters*, 1565.

85. Jefferson to Latrobe, July 12, 1812, 209/E/10, BHL, *Papers*, microfiche edition.

86. BHL, *Papers*, 3: 828.

87. Jeffrey Cohen, "Forms into Architecture: Reform Ideals and the Gauntlets of the Real in Latrobe's Surveyorships at the US Capitol," in Donald Kennon, ed., *The United States Capitol: Designing and Decorating a National Icon* (Athens: Ohio University Press, 2000), 43–6.

88. BHL, *Papers*, 2: 749–50.

89. Ibid., 2: 751.

90. Ibid., 3: 437, 439.

91. Ibid., 3: 818; BHL to Richard Skinner, April 12, 1817, 135/G/8, BHL, *Papers*, microfiche edition.

92. BHL, *Papers*, 2: 228.

93. Ibid., 3: 17.

94. Ibid., 2: 867.

95. Ibid., 2: 545.

96. Ibid., 3: 67–84.

97. Ibid., 2: 401.

98. Ibid., 2: 827, 831.

99. *National Intelligencer*, May 15, 26, 1809. For the best discussion of Latrobe's ideas about and contributions to internal improvements, see Lee Formwalt, "Benjamin Henry Latrobe and the Development of Internal Improvements in the New Republic" (PhD diss., Catholic University, 1977).

100. James Richardson, ed., *A Compilation of the Messages and Papers of the Presidents, 1798–1908* (Washington, DC: Bureau of Literature and Art, 1908), 1: 379.

101. *Annals of Congress*, 9th Congress, 2nd Session, 77–8.

102. BHL, *Papers*, 2: 541–59; *National Intelligencer*, September 23, 1808.

103. BHL, *Papers*, 2: 836, 857.

104. Ibid., 2: 858.

105. Historians have credited Pope and Buel with writing the bill, but it is now clear that Latrobe, in the manner of modern lobbyists, actually did so. See Latrobe to Joshua Gilpin, December 23, 1809, *Papers*, 2: 806.

106. BHL, *Papers*, 2: 806.

107. *Annals of Congress*, 11th Congress, 2nd Session, 598–613.

CHAPTER 4

1. A quarter of all infants in this time and place died before their first birthday with differentials, as is the case today, according to economic circumstances. Studies in Philadelphia in 1800 reveal a death rate of 187 per 1,000 for all children, with Quaker children at 146 per 1,000 and the children of the poor at 254 per 1,000. Latrobe was especially unlucky to lose four of his nine. See Harvey Graff, *Conflicting Paths: Growing Up in America* (Cambridge, MA: Harvard University Press, 1983), 28. BHL, *Papers*, 2: 28. Mary Latrobe's childbearing is somewhat unusual. Instead of the traditional two-year intervals between pregnancies that were the result of the anti-ovulant process of nursing, her intervals were briefer on three occasions: between John and the second Juliana, fourteen months; between the second Juliana and Mary Agnes, sixteen months; and between Mary Agnes and Benjamin Henry, thirteen months. This pattern suggests either a very brief nursing period because of the death of the child or her unusual condition as a nursing mother who was fertile during the nursing period.

2. BHL, *Papers*, 2: 565.

3. Ibid., 1: 564.

4. Ibid., 2: 200.

5. Ibid., 2: 157.

6. Ibid., 2: 403.

7. Ibid., 3: 481; 1: 564.

8. BHL to Miss M. Sellon, November 15, 1817, 234/C/1, BHL, *Papers*, microfiche edition.

9. BHL, *Papers*, 3: 701–2.

10. Ibid., 1: 496.

11. Ibid., 2: 156.

12. Ibid., 2: 178.

13. Ibid., 2: 75.

14. Ibid., 1: 369.

15. BHL to Miss M. Sellon, November 15, 1817, 234/C/1, BHL, *Papers*, microfiche edition. For a discussion of stepmothering, see Lisa Wilson, *A History of Step Families in Early America* (Chapel Hill: University of North Carolina Press, 2014). Wilson calculates that anywhere between 20 percent and 40 percent of all marriages during this period were remarriages.

16. Mary Elizabeth Latrobe to Richard Hazlehurst, May 3, 1802, Gamble-Latrobe Papers, MHS.

17. BHL, *Papers*, 2: 708.

18. H. Pierce Gallagher, *Robert Mills: Architect of the Washington Monument* (New York: AMS Press, 1966), 15, n3.).

19. BHL, *Papers*, 3: 548.

20. Ibid., 3: 395.

21. BHL to Robert Harper, June 15, 1815, 216/B/1; BHL to Mr. Robertson, March 29, 1815; 125/ E/ 4, BHL *Papers*, microfiche edition.

22. BHL to Charles Watson, November 7, 1803; July 23, 1807, 27/B/3; 58/B/2/, BHL *Papers*, microfiche edition.

23. BHL to John DeLacy, December 14, 1814, 121/B/5, BHL, *Papers*, microfiche edition.

24. BHL, *Papers*, 3: 609.

25. Ibid., 2: 350.

26. Ibid., 3: 435–6, n.2.

27. BHL, *Journals*, 3: 108–112.

28. BHL, *Papers*, 3: 711.

29. Ibid., 3: 776.

30. Ibid., 2: 397; 1: 185; 3: 1026; BHL to MEL, August 2, 1808, Gamble-Latrobe Papers, MHS.

31. BHL, *Papers*, 2: 331.

32. Ibid., 2: 519–20.

33. Ibid., 2: 255.

34. Ibid., 2: 649–50. Latrobe used both one "n" and two "nns" in the spelling of Bonneval.

35. Ibid., 2: 731.

36. Ibid., 1: 462.

37. Ibid., 2: 507.

38. Christian Ignatius Latrobe to John Frederick Latrobe, October 26, 1816, English-German Materials, Box 4, Benjamin Latrobe Papers, APS.

39. BHL, *Papers* , 2:175.

40. Ibid., 2: 176.

41. Ibid., 2: 331.

42. Ibid., 3: 882.

43. For an excellent discussion of the issues defining citizenship and nationality that often played out at sea, Nathan Perl-Rosenthal, *Citizen Sailors: Becoming American in the Age of the Revolution* (Cambridge, MA: Harvard University Press, 2015).

44. BHL, *Papers*, 3: 161.

45. Ibid., 3: 159–60.

46. Ibid., 3: 162. In the 11th Congress of 175 congressmen and senators listed in *The Biographical Directory of the US Congress* ninety-seven were lawyers.

47. BHL to Robert Harper, June 17, 1812, 99/B/7, BHL, *Papers*, microfiche edition.

48. BHL, *Papers*, 3: 1045; 2: 178; 3: 156.

49. BHL, *Journals*, 3: 98.

50. Ibid., 3: 98.

51. BHL, *Papers*, 3: 473.

52. Julia Latrobe's Dancing Book, Vintner Papers, MHS.

53. BHL, *Papers*, 2: 89.

54. Ibid., 2: 18, 155.

55. Ibid., 2: 349, 649, 178, 872.

56. Ibid., 2: 584.

57. Ibid., 2: 76.

58. Ibid., 2: 76.

59. Ibid., 2: 155.

60. Ibid., 2: 943.

61. Ibid., 2: 226.

62. Ibid., 3: 804.

63. BHL, *Journals*, 2: 417–8.

64. Ibid., 2: 424.

65. Ibid., 2: 424

66. BHL, *Papers*, 1: 10.

67. James Richardson, ed., *A Compilation of the Messages and Papers of the Presidents of the United States* (Washington, DC: Bureau of Literature and Art, 1908), 1: 568.

68. BHL, *Papers*, 1: 547.

69. Ibid., 1: 547.

70. Ibid., 2: 528–9.

71. Ibid., 1: 479.

72. Ibid., 1: 456.

73. Ibid., 3: 40.
74. Bernard Steiner, *History of Education in Maryland* (Washington, DC: Government Printing Office, 1894).
75. BHL, *Papers*, 2: 182.
76. Ibid., 2: 447.
77. Ibid., 2: 447.
78. Ibid., 2: 704.
79. Ibid., 2: 693, 2: 802.
80. Ibid., 3: 115; 2: 803.
81. Daniel Rasmussen tells the story in his *American Odyssey: The Untold Story of America's Largest Slave Revolt* (New York: Harper's, 2011).
82. BHL, *Papers*, 2:249.
83. Ibid., 3: 565–6.
84. BHL to Jean Blanque, August 7, 1814, 119/ B/12, BHL, *Papers*, microfiche edition.
85. Patricia Brady, "Black Artists in New Orleans," *Louisiana History* 32 (1991), 19.
86. BHL, *Papers*, 3: 573.
87. Ibid., 3: 427, 478.
88. Ibid., 3: 311.
89. Ibid., 1: 362.
90. Ibid., 2: 890.
91. Ibid., 3: 524.
92. BHL to Henry, May 11, 1806, 130/C/9, BHL, *Papers*, microfiche edition.
93. BHL, *Papers*, 3: 864.
94. Ibid., 3: 41, 703.
95. BHL to Christian Latrobe, October 22, 1806, Gamble-Latrobe Papers, MHS.
96. Ibid.
97. BHL, *Journals*, 2: 27.
98. Latrobe's symptoms are unusual in that they include symptoms characteristic of both migraine and cluster headaches. He certainly had all the typical indications of severe migraine headaches—the pain in and around his eyes, the vomiting, the vasoconstriction and sometimes numbness of one side of his body, the disturbed effect on his mind. But he also had symptoms of cluster headaches given their frequency in bouts lasting about six weeks one or two times a year, the blockage of the nostrils, and other indicators. Cluster headaches seldom last for more than an hour but repeat themselves often.
99. BHL, *Journals*, 2: 137.
100. BHL, *Papers*, 2: 147, 846, 727.
101. BHL, *Journals*, 2: 97–8. Latrobe was quoting from the English poet Edward Young's poem, "The Complaint; Or Night-Thoughts on Life, Death and Immortality."

CHAPTER 5

1. BHL, *Papers*, 2: 882.
2. Ibid., 3: 470.
3. Ibid., 3: 243–4.
4. Ibid., 3: 295.
5. Ibid., 3: 421–2.
6. Latrobe insulted Evans with his analysis of steam engines, and the two men remained antagonists. BHL, *Engineering Drawings*, 66.
7. Carroll Pursell, *Early Stationary Steamboats in America* (Washington, DC: Smithsonian, 1969).
8. BHL, *Papers*, 1: 304.
9. BHL to Robert Smith, July 4, 1811, 87/A/14, BHL, *Papers*, microfiche edition.
10. BHL, *Papers*, 3: 500.
11. Kirkpatrick Sale, *The Fire of His Genius: Robert Fulton and the American Dream* (New York: Free Press, 2001).
12. BHL, *Papers*, 3: 278.
13. Robert Fulton to Benjamin Henry Latrobe, August 18, 1812, LeBoeuf Collection, NYHS.
14. BHL, *Papers*, 3: 348–9.
15. Ibid., 3: 110.
16. BHL to Robert Fulton, June 9, 1814, 118/A/8, BHL, *Papers*, microfiche edition.
17. BHL, *Papers*, 2: 128.
18. Ibid., 3: 421.
19. Ibid., 3: 474.
20. Ibid., 3: 480.
21. Ibid., 3: 457.
22. Ibid., 3: 640.
23. Ibid., 3: 640. From 1812 to 1820, Louisiana, Indiana, Alabama, Mississippi, Illinois, Maine, and Missouri had been admitted as states while several areas in the Louisiana Purchase of 1803 had been organized as territories in preparation for their admission as states.
24. BHL, *Papers*, 3: 487.
25. Ibid., 3: 498.
26. Ibid., 3: 378.
27. Ibid., 2: 223.
28. BHL to William Duane, April 3, 1813, 109/B/7, BHL, *Papers*, microfiche edition.
29. BHL, *Papers*, 3: 448.
30. *National Intelligencer*, May 2, 1814.
31. BHL, *Papers*, 3: 516–7.
32. Ibid., 3: 487.
33. Ibid., 3: 515–6.

34. Ibid., 3: 487.

35. Ibid., 3: 500.

36. Robert Fulton to John Livingston, July 2, 1813, LeBoeuf Collection, NYHS.

37. John Semmes, *John H.B. Latrobe and His Times* (Baltimore: Norman Remington, 1917), 50.

38. BHL, *Papers*, 3: 492.

39. Ibid., 3: 524.

40. Robert Fulton to Benjamin Latrobe, October 26, 1814, LeBoeuf Collection, NYHS.

41. BHL, *Papers*, 3: 532.

42. Ibid., 3: 542.

43. Ibid., 3: 541.

44. *National Intelligencer*, May 2, 1814.

45. BHL, *Papers*, / 3: 545.

46. Ibid., 3: 545.

47. Semmes, 52.

48. BHL to Nicholas Roosevelt, May 24, 1814, 117/C/3, BHL, *Papers*, microfiche edition.

49. BHL, *Papers*, 3: 590.

50. BHL to Robert Fulton, May 21, 1814, 117/A/10, BHL, *Papers*, microfiche edition.

51. Robert Fulton to BHL, October 26, 1814, LeBoeuf Collection, NYHS.

52. BHL, *Papers*, 3: 578, 607.

53. Ibid., 3: 600.

54. Ibid., 3: 602.

55. Ibid., 3: 619.

56. BHL to Nicholas Roosevelt, November 20, 1814, 121/B/3; BHL to Robert Fulton, December 5, 1814, 121/E/10, BHL, *Papers*, microfiche collection.

57. BHL, *Papers*, 3: 608.

58. Ibid., 3: 617.

59. Ibid., 3: 608.

60. Thomas Cox, *Gibbons v. Ogden: Law and Society in the Early Republic* (Athens: Ohio University Press, 2009).

61. BHL to Robert Fulton, November 22, 1811, 121/B/12, BHL, *Papers*, microfiche edition.

62. BHL to John DeLacy, December 13, 1814, 121/G/11, BHL, *Papers*, microfiche edition.

63. BHL, *Papers*, 3: 579.

64. Ibid., 3: 606.

65. Michael Fazio and Patrick Snadon, *The Domestic Architecture of Benjamin Henry Latrobe* (Baltimore: Johns Hopkins University Press, 2006), 447.

66. BHL to Nicholas Roosevelt, July 23, 1814, 118/G/12, BHL, *Papers*, microfiche edition.

67. BHL, *Papers*, 2: 711.

68. Ibid., 3: 632.

69. Ibid., 3: 631.

70. Records of the Office of Public Buildings and Grounds, 213/F/18, Record Group 42, National Archives, Washington, DC.

71. BHL, *Papers*, 3: 627; BHL to Thomas Munroe, March 1, 1815, 125/B/3, BHL, *Papers*, microfiche edition.

72. BHL to Thomas Munroe, February 16, 1815, 124/F/5/, BHL, *Papers*, microfiche edition.

73. Mary Elizabeth Latrobe Memoir, Latrobe Papers, APS.

74. BHL, *Papers*, 3: 665.

75. Margaret Bayard Smith, *The First Forty Years of Washington Society*, Gaillard Hunt, ed. (New York: Charles Scribner's, 1906), 112.

76. BHL, *Papers*, 3: 580. For an excellent study of the War of 1812 on the Chesapeake, see Ralph Eshelman and Burton Kummerow, *In Full Glory Reflected: Discovering the War of 1812 in the Chesapeake* (Baltimore: Maryland Historical Society Press, 2012).

77. *Niles Weekly Register*, December 31, 1814.

78. BHL, *Papers*, 3: 644.

79. Quoted in Eshelman and Kummerow, 96.

80. William Allen, *History of the United States Capitol* (Washington: Government Printing Office, 2001),100; BHL, *Papers*, 3: 828.

81. BHL, *Papers*, 3: 644.

82. BHL, *Journals*, 3: 48–9.

83. BHL, *Papers*, 3: 656.

84. Ibid., 3: 652.

85. Ibid., 3: 652.

86. Quoted in Allen, 107.

87. BHL to the Commissioners of the Public Buildings, March 9, 1816, 221/E/6, BHL, *Papers*, microfiche edition.

88. BHL, *Papers*, 3: 661.

89. BHL to Robert Goodloe Harper, August 3, 1815, 127/C/6, BHL, *Papers*, microfiche edition.

90. BHL, *Papers*, 3: 851–4.

91. Ibid., 3: 657.

92. Ibid., 3: 740.

93. Ibid., 3: 792.

94. Ibid., 3: 789, 768.

95. Ibid., 3: 485.

96. BHL to Alexander Dallas, July 19, 1815, 126/G/10, BHL, *Papers*, microfiche edition.

97. BHL, *Papers*, 3: 863.

98. Ibid., 3: 842.

99. BHL, *Journals*, 3: 227–8.

100. BHL to Henry Thompson, March 11, 129/F/4, BHL, *Papers*, microfiche edition.
101. BHL, *Papers*, 3: 739.
102. Ibid., 3: 765.
103. Ibid., 3: 765.
104. Ibid., 3: 767.
105. Ibid., 3: 768, 770.
106. At the inauguration of Donald Trump in January 2017, Nancy Pelosi pointed out the Car of History to the incoming president. The word "car" was used by Latrobe.
107. BHL to Charlotte Burney Broome, August 13, 1816, 132/E/9, BHL, *Papers*, microfiche edition.
108. BHL, *Papers* 3: 877.
109. BHL to Isaac Hazlehurst, July 27, 1816; 132/C/7, BHL, *Papers*, microfiche edition.
110. BHL, *Papers*, 3: 954–5.
111. Ibid., 3: 924–5.
112. *National Intelligencer*, October 1, 1817.
113. BHL to the New Orleans City Council, November 15, 1817, BHL Papers, Tulane University, New Orleans, LA.
114. BHL, *Papers*, 3: 949.
115. Allen, 122; *Documentary History of the Construction and Development of the U.S. Capitol Building and Grounds*, House Report 646, 58th Congress, 2nd Session, 190–3.
116. BHL, *Papers*, 3: 957–60.
117. Mary Elizabeth Latrobe Memoir, Latrobe Papers, APS.
118. BHL, *Papers*, 3: 968, 969.
119. Ellen Bulfinch, *The Life and Letters of Charles Bulfinch* (Boston: Houghton Mifflin, 1896), 203, 204, 223–5; BHL, *Papers*, 3: 982.
120. BHL, *Papers*, 3: 968.
121. *Documentary History*, 200–2.
122. BHL to Henry Latrobe, September 9, 1817, 138/B/3, BHL, *Papers*, microfiche edition.
123. BHL, *Papers*, 3: 863; for an examination of attitudes toward bankruptcy in the United States, Bruce Mann, *Republic of Debtors: Bankruptcy in the Age of American Independence* (Cambridge, MA: Harvard University Press, 2002); BHL, *Papers*, 2: 128.
124. BHL, *Papers*, 3: 965.
125. Material on the bankruptcy from Benjamin Henry Latrobe, Records of the District Court of the District of Columbia, Insolvent Case Papers, Box 4, 1817, Record Group 21, National Archives, Washington, DC.
126. BHL, *Papers*, 3: 970.
127. BHL's Insolvency Case; *Annals of Congress*, 7th Cong, 2nd Session, 1603–8; BHL, *Papers*; 3: 971.
128. BHL, *Papers*, 3: 974.

CHAPTER 6

1. Records of District Court of the Disrict of Columbia, Insolvent Case Papers, Benjamin Latrobe, Box 4, 1817, Record Group 21, National Archives, Washington, DC.
2. BHL, *Papers*, 3: 975.
3. Ibid., 3: 236–7, 3: 18.
4. Ibid., 3: 222.
5. Ibid., 3: 18.
6. Ibid., 3: 982.
7. BHL to Robert Harper, November 14, 1814, Gamble-Latrobe Papers, MHS.
8. BHL, *Papers*, 3: 159.
9. Quoted in James Livingood, *The Philadelphia-Baltimore Trade Rivalry* (Harrisburg: Pennsylvania Historical Commission, 1974), 12.
10. BHL, *Papers*, 3: 351. For an analysis of the riot, Frank Cassell, "The Great Baltimore Riot of 1812," *Maryland Historical Magazine* 70 (1975), 241–59.
11. Thomas Scharf, *Chronicles of Baltimore* (Baltimore: Turnbull Brothers, 1874), 1: 382.
12. Sherry Olsen, *Baltimore: The Building of an American City* (Baltimore: Johns Hopkins University Press, 1980), 54–5.
13. William Alderson, ed., *Mermaids, Mummies and Mastodons: The Emergence of the American Museum* (Washington: American Association of Museums, 1992), 51; Mary Ellen Hayward and Frank Shivers, *The Architecture of Baltimore* (Baltimore: Johns Hopkins University Press, 2004).
14. BHL to Francis Guy, December 27, 1812, 105/D/3, BHL, *Papers*, microfiche edition. Latrobe always referred to the building as a church or a cathedral. It was not designated a basilica until the 1840s and today is officially known as the Basilica of the National Shrine of the Assumption of the Blessed Virgin Mary.
15. John Waite Associates, "The Baltimore Basilica of the National Shrine, Historic Structure Report," June 2007, 14, Archives of the Archdiocese of Baltimore, St. Mary's Seminary, Baltimore, MD.
16. BHL to George Murphy, April 24, 1813, cited in Waite, 17.
17. *Catholic Records* (Baltimore: Catholic Mirror Publishing, 1906), 22, Archives of the Archdiocese of Baltimore, St. Mary's Seminary, Baltimore, MD.
18. BHL, *Papers*, 2: 60.
19. Ibid., 3: 1000.
20. Ibid., 3: 1006; BHL to John, photograph of letter, 237/5/3/, Archives of the Archdiocese of Baltimore, St. Mary's Seminary, Baltimore, MD.
21. Charles Brownell, "Introduction," Waite, 8.
22. BHL, *Papers*, 3: 1006. The construction of the dome was accomplished by the erection of special scaffolding consisting of a circular working platform from which workers used the DeLorme method of framing with heavy timbers and connected timbers and bricks supported by lagging, that is, short pieces of wood that spanned the spaces between the ribs. Each course of masonry in a dome became

self-supporting when the last brick or stone in the ring was placed. For a further description, see James Dilts, "Basilica of the Assumption," unpublished paper in the possession of Jean H. Baker. Also BHL, *Architectural Drawings*, 2: 431–90.

23. Waite, 77–8.

24. Ibid. These towers have a Byzantine flavor and perhaps represent Latrobe's homage to his imagined ancestor, the Sascha of Bonneval. On the earthquake and subsequent restoration, *Baltimore Sun*, March 31, 2013. Among other discoveries during the restoration was that of a slave gallery.

25. BHL, *Papers*, 3: 1040.

26. Ibid.; BHL to MEL, January 5, 207/B/3, BHL, *Papers*, microfiche edition.

27. BHL, *Papers*, 2: 268.

28. Ibid., 2: 268.

29. Ibid., 3: 674.

30. Latrobe wrote "Nunc est bibendum/Pulsanda tellus"; in English, "Now we must go hungry, now with the free foot we must kick all." Horace, *Odes*, 1. 37. 1. BHL, *Papers*, 2: 268.

31. HL, *Papers*, 3: 579.

32. BHL to Maximilian Godefroy, October 23, 1808, 66/F/10, BHL, *Papers*, microfiche edition.

33. BHL, *Papers*, 3: 675.

34. Ibid.

35. Mark Reinberger, "The Baltimore Exchange and Its Place in the Career of Benjamin Henry Latrobe" (PhD diss., Cornell University, 1988), 33.

36. BHL, *Papers*, 3: 580; 1: 330.

37. BHL to James Madison, April 8, 1816, draft version, 221/ G/13, BHL, *Papers*, microfiche edition.

38. BHL, *Papers*, 1: 472.

39. Ibid., 2: 239–42.

40. Ibid., 3: 303.

41. Gilbert Chinard, "Maximilian Godefroy," *Maryland Historical Magazine* 39 (1934), 182–3.

42. BHL, *Papers*, 3: 675.

43. Ibid., 3: 781.

44. Ibid., 3: 781.

45. Ibid., 3: 783.

46. Architects provide novelists with examples of solitary heroes who march to their own reality. The most obvious example is the depiction of the architect Howard Roark as an avatar for unfettered capitalism and the pursuit of free and independent action in Ayn Rand's *The Fountainhead*. But there are other novels such as Peter Ackroyd's *Hawksmoor* that employ fictional architects as lone hero geniuses, unique masters working alone. On the other hand, most modern architects, led by Walter Gropius, have asserted that architecture is a collective enterprise.

47. BHL, *Papers*, 3: 675.

48. Ibid., 3: 782.

49. Quoted in Robert Alexander, *Maximilian Godefroy* (Baltimore: Johns Hopkins University Press, 1974), 213. This anthropomorphizing and gendering of architecture reflected the views of the leading French theorists of the day, Jacques Blondel and J. N. L. Durand.

50. BHL to Robert Harper, January 12, 1815[6], Gamble-Latrobe Papers, MHS.

51. Talbot Hamlin, *Benjamin Henry Latrobe* (New York: Oxford University Press, 1955), 495.

52. BHL, *Papers*, 3: 1020.

53. BHL to Harper, May 1, 1812, 97/G/2; 208/E/2, BHL, *Papers*, microfiche edition. Michael Fazio and Patrick Snaden, *The Domestic Architecture of Benjamin Henry Latrobe* (Baltimore: Johns Hopkins University Press), 652–3. Today there is a reconstruction of the dairy, sometimes called, though not by its creator, a spring house, on the grounds of the Baltimore Art Museum. Latrobe referred to it as a barn. In designing this elegant temple Latrobe was recreating the ornamental dairies constructed in English gardens as decoration. Thanks to Jonathan Herman, who worked on its reconstruction from original material, for explaining the building and suggesting that it originally had a second floor.

54. Lee Formwalt draws attention to this aspect of Latrobe's career. See Lee Formwalt, "Benjamin Henry Latrobe and the Development of Internal Improvements in the New Republic" (PhD diss., Catholic University, 1977), 242–65.

55. BHL, *Papers*, 3: 901.

56. Ibid., 3: 903–4; Susan Reddick, "The Influence of Benjamin Latrobe on Jefferson's Design for the University of Virginia" (Master's thesis, University of Virginia, 1988).

57. BHL, *Papers*, 3: 916; drawing on 3: 915.

58. BHL, *Papers*, 3: 916.

59. Ibid., 3: 988.

60. BHL, *Architectural Drawings*, 2: 708; BHL to John Markoe, September 7, 1817, 138/A/6/, BHL, *Papers*, microfiche edition.

61. BHL, *Papers*, 3: 84.

62. Ibid., 3: 806; also to George Harrison and Jonathan Smith, 132/G/11; 134/A/14; 138/A/14, BHL, *Papers*, microfiche edition.

63. BHL, *Architectural Drawings*, 2: 708.

64. BHL, *Papers*, 3: 996.

65. Ibid., 3: 997.

66. BHL, *Architectural Drawings*, 2: 710.

67. BHL, *Papers*, 3: 928; also BHL to Rev. William Holland Wilmer, 136/E/4; 136/G/137, BHL, *Papers*, microfiche edition.

68. BHL, *Papers*, 3: 927.

69. BHL to John Strickland, March 10, 1804, 30/A/7, BHL, *Papers*, microfiche edition.

70. Agnes Gilchrist, *William Strickland: Architect and Engineer, 1788–1854* (Philadelphia: University of Pennsylvania Press, 1950), 1–2.

71. Gilchrist, 38.

72. BHL, *Papers*, 3: 1002.

73. For more information on the controversy, Fiske Kimball, "The Second Bank of the US," *Architectural Record* 58 (December, 1925), 581–94; Agnes Addison, "Latrobe v. Strickland, *Journal of Architectural Historians* 2 (July 1942), 26–9. Memoir of Benjamin Henry Latrobe, *Literary Gazette* 1 (April 21, 1821), 253–4.

74. "Memoir of Benjamin Henry Latrobe," *Ackermann's Repository of Arts, Literature and Fashion* (January 1, 1821), 11, 29–31.

75. Latrobe noted the "curious town it is." BHL, *Journals*, 3: 192.

76. BHL, *Papers*, 3: 114; Gary Donaldson, "Bringing Water to the Crescent City: Benjamin Latrobe and the New Orleans Waterworks," *Louisiana History* 28 (Autumn 1987), 381–96.

77. BHL, *Papers*, 3: 986.

78. BHL to the Mayor and City Council, April, 23, 1813, BHL Papers, Tulane University Library, New Orleans, LA.

79. BHL, *Journals*, 3: 155–6; xiii.

80. Ibid., 3: 183, 186.

81. Ibid., 3: 185.

82. Ibid., 3: 171, 2.

83. Ibid., 3: 173.

84. BHL, *Papers*, 3: 1025–6.

85. BHL to Dearest Mary, May 8, 1819, Gamble-Latrobe Papers, MHS.

86. BHL, *Journals*, 3: 182.

87. Ibid., 3: 185.

88. Ibid., 3: 194–5.

89. Ibid., 3: 185.

90. BHL, *Journals*, 3: 212. The actual quotation from Goldsmith is "That part that laws or kings can cause or cure." Arthur Friedman, *Collected Works of Oliver Goldsmith* (Oxford: Clarendon Press, 1966), 4: 269. On the complex society of New Orleans, Eberhard Faber, *Building the Land of Dreams: New Orleans and The Transformation of Early America* (Princeton, NJ: Princeton University Press, 2016).

91. BHL, *Journals*, 3: 203–4.

92. BHL, *Papers*, 3: 1051.

93. BHL, *Journals*, 3: 177.

94. "History of the Congressional Cemetery," 59th Congress, 2nd Session, *Senate Document*, no. 72, 1906, 35.

95. BHL, *Journals*, 3: 246.

96. BHL to Mayor Macarty and Council of City of New Orleans, March 20, 1819, Louisiana Division, New Orleans Public Library, New Orleans, LA; "State of the Water Works," June 16, 1819, BHL Papers, Tulane University, New Orleans, LA.

97. BHL, *Journals*, 3: 212.

98. BHL to Mayor Augustin Macarty and Council of the City of New Orleans, September 17, 1819, BHL Papers, Tulane University, New Orleans, LA.

99. BHL, *Journals*, 3: 312. Unlike other types of mosquitoes, the *aedes aegypti* mosquito takes multiple blood-sucking nips from humans, hence its ability to spread the disease.

100. Ibid., 3: 314.

101. BHL, *Papers*, 3: 1036.

102. BHL, *Journals*, 3: 305.

103. Ibid., 3: 307.

104. BHL to Robert Harper, May 8, 1819, BHL, *Papers*, microfiche edition.

105. John Semmes, *John H.B. Latrobe and His Times* (Baltimore: Norman Remington, 1917), 83.

106. BHL, *Papers*, 3: 1038–9.

107. Benjamin Henry Boneval Latrobe, *Impressions Respecting New Orleans*, Samuel Wilson, ed. (New York: Columbia University Press, 1951), 174, 177.

108. BHL to my dearest wife, April 17, 1819, Gamble-Latrobe Papers, MHS.

109. Mary Latrobe to Mrs. Catherine Smith, April 18, 1820, Gamble-Latrobe Papers, MHS.

110. BHL, *Papers*, 3: 1061; Jo Ann Carrigan, "The Saffron Scourge: A History of Yellow Fever in Louisiana, 1796–1808" (PhD diss., Louisiana State University, 1961).

111. BHL, *Papers*, 3: 1063.

112. Memoir of Mary Elizabeth Latrobe, Gamble-Latrobe Papers, MHS.

113. BHL, *Papers*, 3: 1066.

114. Mary Latrobe to Robert Harper, September 23, 1820, Gamble-Latrobe Papers, MHS.

115. Ibid.

116. BHL, *Papers*, 3: 1067; Mary Latrobe to Robert Harper, September 23, November 4, 1820, Gamble-Latrobe Papers, MHS.

117. BHL, *Papers*, 1031.

CONCLUSION

1. John Semmes, *John H.B. Latrobe and His Times, 1803–1891* (Baltimore: Norman Remington, 1917), 85. Semmes's biography is based on John Latrobe's diary and letters.

2. Benjamin Henry Boneval Latrobe Diary, April 8, 1834, MHS.

3. BHL to Christian Ignatius Latrobe, October 22, 1806, Gamble-Latrobe Papers, MHS.

4. *Charity Organizations of Baltimore*, Listing for Indigent Sick Society, 62; "Society for the Relief of the Indigent Sick Annual Report," MHS.

5. Semmes, 100.

6. Ibid., 91.

7. John to Ben, October 13, 1827, Gamble-Latrobe Papers, MHS.

8. Benjamin Latrobe Diary, October 27, 1827, MHS.

9. BHL, *Papers*, 3: 1032.

10. BHL to Henry Latrobe, October 20, 1815, 127/F/13, BHL, *Papers*, microfiche edition.

11. John Latrobe Diary, October 20, 1824, MHS.

12. John Latrobe, "Recollections: A Lecture Delivered Before the Maryland Institute" (Baltimore: Sun Book and Job Printing Establishment, 1868). Latrobe's account created the story of this iconic event in American railroad history.

13. John H. B. Latrobe, *Address Delivered at the Laying of the Cornerstone of the New Masonic Temple* (Baltimore: Huber, 1866).

14. Benjamin Latrobe Diary, May 15, 1834, MHS.

15. Patricia Dockman Anderson, "A Most Remarkable Group, Gallery of Presidents," *Maryland Historical Magazine*, Special Issue (Winter 2006), 502.

16. John H. B. Latrobe, "Address at the Laying of the Cornerstone of City Hall in the City of Baltimore," October 18, 1867, LC.

17. John H. B. Latrobe, "African Colonization: Colonization and Abolition," Addresses Delivered by John Latrobe, LC.

18. The Maryland Colonization Society supported by John Latrobe had broken off from the American Colonization Society because of the latter's inactivity. For years the Maryland group sustained a colony near Las Palmas called Maryland in Liberia. The story is well told in Richard Hall, *On Afric's Shore: A History of Maryland in Liberia, 1834–1857* (Baltimore: Maryland Historical Society, 2003).

19. BHL, *Papers*, 3: 1024.

20. Mary Elizabeth Latrobe to Juliana Miller, July 21, 1824, Gamble-Latrobe Papers, MHS.

21. Ben to John, May 31, 1834, Gamble- Latrobe Papers, MHS.

22. John to Ben, October 13, 1827, John Latrobe Diary, MHS.

23. Ben to John, October 21, 1827, Benjamin Latrobe Diary, MHS.

24. Ben to John, January 31, 1830, Benjamin Latrobe Diary, MHS.

25. Semmes, 285.

26. Ben to John, January 31, 1827, Gamble-Latrobe Papers.

27. Semmes, 285.

28. Benjamin Latrobe Diary, May 31, 1835; November 28, 1833, MHS.

29. Benjamin Latrobe Diary, September 2, 1834, MHS.

30. Benjamin Latrobe Diary, September 6, 1833, MHS.

31. Benjamin Latrobe Diary, September 24, 1834. MHS.

32. James Dilts, *The Great Road: The Building of the Baltimore & Ohio, The Nation's First Railroad, 1828–1853* (Stanford, CA: Stanford University Press, 1993), 386–9. Dilts's study is the best of the many books on the early history of the B&O.

33. Semmes, 115.

34. The professional lineage, as measured by training and employment, moves from Latrobe to Strickland to Thomas Walter to Richard Morris Hunt to Frank Furness to Louis Sullivan to Frank Lloyd Wright. For the work of Niernsee, see Mary Ellen Hayward and Frank Shivers, eds., *The Architecture of Baltimore* (Baltimore: Johns Hopkins University Press, 2004), 124–6, 165.

Index

For the benefit of digital users, indexed terms that span two pages (e.g., 52–53) may, on occasion, appear on only one of those pages.